Schoolgirl Fictions

Schoolgirl Fictions

VALERIE WALKERDINE

VERSO

London · New York

First published by Verso 1990
© 1990 Valerie Walkerdine

Verso
US: 6 Meard Street, London W1V 3HR
USA: 29 West 35th Street, New York, NY 10001–2291

Verso is the imprint of New Left Books

British Library Cataloguing in Publication Data
Walkerdine, Valerie 1947–
    Schoolgirl fictions.
    1. Society. Role of women
    I. Title
    305.42

ISBN 0-86091-299-X
ISBN 0-86091-517-4

US Library of Congress Cataloging-in-Publication Data
Walkerdine, Valerie.
Schoolgirl fictions / Valerie Walkerdine.
        p.   cm.
ISBN 0-86091-299-X. – ISBN 0-86091-517-4 (pbk.)
1. Women–Psychology. 2. Sex role. 3. Femininity (Psychology)
        4. II geographic, etc. fh11 06-22-90. I. Title.
HQ1206.W23 1990
305.42–dc20

Typeset in Goudy by Leaper & Gard Ltd, Bristol, England
Printed and bound in Great Britain by Biddles Ltd, Guildford

For Helen, Jo, Pam, Jo and Joan and the many working-class
women who have struggled to obtain an education

Contents

Sources

'Sex, power and pedagogy' was first published in *Screen Education*, vol. 38, 1981

'Progressive pedagogy and political struggle' was first published in *Screen*, 1987

'On the regulation of speaking and silence' was first published in C. Steedman, C. Urwin and V. Walkerdine, eds, *Language, Gender and Childhood*, London, Routledge & Kegan Paul 1985

'Science and the female mind' was first published in *Psych Critique*, vol. 1, no. 1, 1985, Ablex, New Jersey

'Some day my prince will come' was first published in A. McRobbie and M. Nava, eds, *Gender and Generation*, London, Macmillan 1985

Review of Marie Cardinal (*The Words To Say It*) is unpublished (written 1985)

'Schoolgirl fictions' was given as a talk at the University of Rochester, New York State in 1985

'Breaking the Law of the Father' was written in 1984

'Femininity as performance' was published in 1989 in *Oxford Review of Education*, vol. 15, no. 3

'Behind the painted smile' is going to be published in J. Spence and P. Holland, eds, *Family Snaps: The Meaning of Domestic Photography*, London, Virago 1991

'Dreams from an ordinary childhood' was first published in E. Heron, ed., *Truth, Dare or Promise*, London, Virago 1985

'Video replay' was published in V. Burgin, J. Donald and C. Kaplan, eds, *Formations of Fantasy*, London, Methuen 1985

'Fantasy and regulation' was part of a talk, entitled 'The Mass Psychology of Thatcherism', given at the ICA, London in 1989

As to the problem of fiction, it seems to me a very important one; I am well aware that I have never written anything but fictions. I do not mean to say, however, that the truth is therefore absent. It seems to me that the possibility exists for fiction to function in truth, and for bringing it about that a true discourse engenders or 'manufactures' something that does not yet exist, that is, it fictions it. One 'fictions' history on the basis of a political reality that makes it true, one 'fictions' a politics not yet in existence on the basis of a historical truth.

(MICHEL FOUCAULT, Power/Knowledge)

As I found my own voice in analysis, droning on day after day, it gradually took the place occupied for so long by the schools. One day it was inevitable that I should cease to be a schoolgirl.

(CATHERINE CLÉMENT, The Lives and Legends of Jacques Lacan)

Preface

For many years, like many other women, I was a schoolgirl. I don't simply mean in the years of my formal schooling, but long after I had left my secondary school. And I mean more even than that at the point of leaving school I swapped one classroom for another, as a primary school teacher, or even that on entering the academy to teach I was still learning. I mean that the view I held of myself, one with which I have grappled for many years and in many of the essays in this volume, was of a struggling little girl. Though I might appear a powerful woman to the world, this did little to change the way in which I, like many other women, was infantilized, hated it and yet was terrified of the figure of the powerful woman so pejoratively set out in so many spaces, so many fictional spaces. How can it be that femininity is a fiction and yet lived as though it were real, felt deeply, as though it were a universal truth of the psyche? It is not that we are filled with roles and stereotypes of passive femininity so that we become what society has set out for us. Rather, I am suggesting that femininity and masculinity are fictions linked to fantasies deeply embedded in the social world which can take on the status of fact when inscribed in the powerful practices, like schooling, through which we are regulated.

But that is not all there is to say. It is how we live those fictional identities and their link to the materiality of the social world that interests me. Such questions are located at a place which understands the psyche as formed in and through the social. We are not simply positioned, like a butterfly being pinned to a display board. We struggle from one position to another and, indeed, to break free — but to what? The quotation at the beginning of this book from Catherine Clément suggests that there is a voice which does not belong to the father, nor to the schools of thought. It is our own voice, but what is it that we want to say, what words will take us from the position of schoolgirls to that of powerful women? Is there an authentic female voice? For me the answer lies not, as some feminists have suggested, in some kind of essential feminine voice that has been silenced, but in that which exists in the interstices of our subjugation. We can tell other stories. These stories can be very frightening because they appear to blow apart the fictions through which we have come to understand ourselves. Underneath stories of quiet little girls are murderous fantasies. These are not there because they are essential to the female body or psyche but because the stories of our subjugation do not tell the whole truth: our socialization does not work.

In this volume I try to tell those other stories, exploring the existing ones about schoolgirls and uncovering others – sometimes about girls in schools, sometimes about the fantasies of my own childhood. The book represents a journey, a process of coming into being of a woman who, at last, ceased to be a schoolgirl. I include published and unpublished articles, fragments of more 'personal' notes, together with poems and images, to convey how those fictions have formed me.

PART I

Schooling for Girls

The pieces which make up this part were written and first published between 1981 and 1985. In them I explore ways in which post-structuralist arguments may be used in relation to the education of girls and women. In these accounts I first began to take issue with some of the views about power as a possession which were current in radical educational thinking at the time. Such accounts placed teachers in authority and powerful, and pupils as powerless and oppressed. By considering the position of small boys who taunt a female nursery school teacher, I examine the problems inherent in such views. The arguments also relate to the position of 'the child' and of girls and women in child-centred educational practices. The idea of 'natural' childhood is constantly questioned in these pieces, as is the problematic nature of 'girl' and 'woman' within such practices. I suggest that arguments about girls' under-attainment often 'protest too much'. What, for example, is lurking behind the desire to prove the mathematical inferiority of girls? Although the idea of proof is central to empiricist social and behavioural science, I question not only the veridicality of claims to truth about girls but also the 'will to proof' which seems to lurk behind them. Increasingly in the arguments I use psychoanalysis to begin to explore what this might be about.

In 'On the regulation of speaking and silence' I explore the fantasy of 'woman' which is presented to us in current pedagogic strategies. In addition I argue that educational practices which celebrate 'natural language' have a real problem in dealing with the issue of children (especially girls) who are silent. It is not that such children have nothing to say, but that school does not represent, for 'pathologized' children, the safe space it is set up to be.

1

Sex, power and pedagogy

In this essay I want to address certain issues about the position of girls and women within the education system, with reference to an examination of some observations collected in two nursery schools.[1] I shall draw out certain contradictions for traditional Marxist approaches to the relations of power within educational institutions. One such view is that education, as a bourgeois institution, places teachers in a position of power from which they can oppress children, who are institutionally powerless. To somewhat overstate the case: the teacher, powerful in a bourgeois educational institution, is in a position to oppress children, whose resistance to that power, like all resistance, is understood as ultimately progressive rather than contradictory. Children's movements have tended to understand resistance in terms of 'rights' or 'liberation'. Similarly, certain feminist accounts have used the psychological concepts of 'role' and 'stereotype' to understand women and girls as unitary subjects whose economic dependence, powerlessness and physical weakness are reflected in their production as 'passive', 'weak', and 'dependent' individuals. While such accounts have been extremely important in helping to develop Marxist and feminist practices, I want to pinpoint some of the reasons why such analyses might not be as helpful as we might previously have supposed in understanding the phenomena presented here. I want to show, using examples from classroom practice, that both female teachers and small girls are not unitary subjects uniquely positioned, but are produced as a nexus of subjectivities, in relations of power which are constantly shifting, rendering them at one moment powerful and at another powerless.[2]

Additionally, I want to argue that while an understanding of resistance is clearly important, we cannot read every resistance as having revolutionary effects; sometimes resistances have 'reactionary' effects.

3

Resistance is not just struggle against the oppression of a static power (and therefore potentially revolutionary simply because it is struggle against the monolith); relations of power and resistance are continually reproduced, in continual struggle and constantly shifting.

AN EXAMPLE OF BOYS' RESISTANCE IN A NURSERY SCHOOL

The following interchange between teacher and children comes from a series of recordings made in a nursery school. The teacher, who is a woman of about thirty, is seated with a group of children aged three and four around a table. The children are making constructions from Lego; we are concerned here with the actions of three children: a three-year-old girl, Annie, and two four-year-old boys, Sean and Terry. The teacher's name is Miss Baxter.

The sequence begins when Annie takes a piece of Lego to add on to a construction she is building. Terry tries to take it away from her to use himself, and she resists. He says:

Terry: You're a stupid cunt, Annie.

The teacher tells him to stop and Sean tries to mess up another child's construction. The teacher tells him to stop. Then Sean says:

Sean: Get out of it Miss Baxter paxter.
Terry: Get out of it knickers Miss Baxter.
Sean: Get out of it Miss Baxter paxter.
Terry: Get out of it Miss Baxter the knickers paxter knickers, bum.
Sean: Knickers, shit, bum.
Miss B: Sean, that's enough, you're being silly.
Sean: Miss Baxter, knickers, show your knickers.
Terry: Miss Baxter, show your bum off.
   (they giggle)
Miss B: I think you're being very silly.
Terry: Shit Miss Baxter, shit Miss Baxter.
Sean: Miss Baxter, show your knickers your bum off.
Sean: Take all your clothes off, your bra off.
Terry: Yeah, and take your bum off, take your wee-wee off, take your clothes, your mouth off.
Sean: Take your teeth out, take your head off, take your hair off, take your bum off. Miss Baxter the paxter knickers taxter.
Miss B: Sean, go and find something else to do please.

Various people, on reading this transcript, have commented that they are surprised and shocked to find such young children not only making explicit sexual references, but having so much power over the teacher. What is this power, and how is it produced? Here, although the teacher has an institutional position, she is not uniquely a teacher, nor are the boys *just* small boys. Particular individuals are produced as subjects *differently* within a variety of discursive practices. A particular individual has the potential to be 'read' within a variety of discourses. We cannot say that the limit of the variety is determined in any direct or simple sense by the economic.[3] However, the 'materiality' of the individual does have particular effects, though those effects are not determined solely by that materiality, but also by the discourse in which it is 'read'. In this case the teacher is a woman and while that itself is crucial, it is only because of the ways in which 'woman' signifies that we can understand the specific nature of the struggle.[4] The boys' resistance to her can be understood in terms both of their assertion of their difference from her and their seizing of power through constituting her as the powerless object of sexist discourse. Although they are not physically grown men they can take the positions of men through language, and in so doing gain power which has material effects. Their power is gained by refusing to be constituted as the powerless objects in *her* discourse and recasting her as the powerless object of *theirs*. In their discourse she is constituted as 'woman as sex object', and as that object she is rendered the powerless object of their oppression. Of course, she has not in a sense ceased to be a teacher, but what is important is that she has ceased to *signify* as one: she has been made to signify as the powerless object of male sexual discourse. The boys' resistance takes the form of a seizure of power in discourse such that despite their institutional positions they achieve power in this instance.

It does not seem reasonable to assert a monolithic and ahistorical view of sexism and oppression in which the boys are either to be understood *simply* as powerless children oppressed by the control of an oppressive bourgeois educational institution or *simply* as the perpetrators of patriarchal social relations. The important word here is *simply*. For they indeed have the potential to be produced as subjects/objects in *both* discourses, but inherent in the discursive positionings are different positions of power. Individuals, constituted as subjects and objects within a particular framework, are produced by that process into relations of power. An individual can become powerful or powerless depending on the terms in which her/his subjectivity is constituted. The importance of this argument is in the way we can assert that relations of power are not invested in unitary individuals in any way which is solely or essentially derived from their material and institutional position. This should not be taken as implying that the material or economic has no importance or force.

However, the material and economic do not appear to be acting as unique and linear causes of the production of power relations in this example. The gender and the ages of the participants clearly have major effects which serve to displace other 'variables'. (The two boys are not yet capable of physically assaulting the teacher, but it may only be a matter of time.) Since the boys are both children and male, and the teacher is both teacher and female, they can enter as subjects into a variety of discourses, some of which render them powerful and some of which render them powerless. It is important to note the way in which the boys refer to the teacher and to the three-year-old girl, Annie, in the same terms. They call Annie a 'cunt'. In this way they bring the teacher down to size: she and a small girl are in discourse but the same thing – sex objects. The power of their discourse is one which renders all females typifications of the same qualities, in this case possessors of tits, bums and cunts. However, this argument must not be just a concern for theoretical distinctions. The issue I have raised would appear to have important consequences for practice. In this example we can understand the boys as both subjects in patriarchal discourse perpetrating patriarchal oppression upon their teacher and at the same time children oppressed/controlled by the authority of the teacher. Are we then to choose, as our course of action, one which wishes potentially to liberate them from their oppression[5] or are they to be suppressed as sexist perpetrators of a patriarchal order?

THE PEDAGOGIC DISCOURSE OF THE TEACHER

An important effect of this power struggle between teacher and children is the way in which the teacher interprets the children's discourse so as to lessen its oppressive effect upon her, and to justify her failure to stop them as correct. To understand this we have to be aware of the psychological and pedagogic terms in which she understands herself as teacher and the children as learners. In particular, what concerns us here is the discourse on childhood sexuality. It was not by accident that the teacher waited so long to stop the children, nor that when she did so it was with a fairly gentle rebuke which did not take issue with the content of their talk.

When I discussed the incident with her later she explained what had happened in the following way:

'The kind of expressions are quite normal for this age.... As long as they're not being too silly or bothering anybody, it's just natural and should be left ... coming out with that kind of expression is very natural.'

How does she come to 'read' the children's actions as a harmless expression of a sexuality which is normal and natural? What are the main strands characterizing childhood sexuality? To understand that question it is necessary to examine the formation of those discourses and practices which inform and constitute 'progressive education'. We can understand the formation of the practices which make up progressive education in terms of the necessity to reformulate a pedagogy which produced individuals who were controlled but not regimented. We can understand the insertion of psychoanalytic discourse as a way of appreciating those concerns which were around at the time of the formation of the new education – that is, in the second two decades of this century.

Take, for example, the following remarks made by Margaret Lowenfeld in 1935 at the end of a book on the educational importance of play:

> Play is to a child, therefore, work, thought, art and relaxation, and cannot be pressed into any single formula. It expresses a child's relation to himself and his environment, and, without adequate opportunity for play, normal and satisfactory emotional development is not possible.... Emotional satisfactions, which the mind has missed at the period to which they properly belong, do not present themselves later in the same form. The forces of destruction, aggression and hostile emotion, which form so powerful an element for good or evil in the human character, can display themselves fully in the play of childhood, and become through this expression integrated into the controlled and conscious personality. Forces unrealised in childhood remain as an inner drive, for ever seeking outlets, and lead men to express them not any longer in play, since this is regarded as an activity in childhood, but in industrial competition, anarchy and war.[6]

We can see in the end of this quotation the specific link made between the capitalist ethic, struggles and war, and the stifling of emotional expression. The rise of totalitarianism (of both Left and Right) was attributed very clearly to the failure of current education and child-rearing to produce the right kind of individuals. It was felt that over-regimentation had produced the phenomenon described at the time as 'Prussianism'.[7] Psychoanalysis understood this failure as the result of repression. In relation to this a new discursive formation was produced 'scientific pedagogy', based on a view of the production of control through self-control and self-regulation. This pedagogy monitored the form and structure of development and steered it along the right lines by provision of the right environment. Clearly, this is not the place to expand on the details of this pedagogy, but it is important here to understand the way in which it served to produce the terms and categories which provide the teacher's understanding of her experience. Central to the pedagogy was the unfolding of child development, understood as natural; and, as a central part of this, the *expression* rather than *repression* of natural childhood sexuality.[8] And of course, according to the Freudian discourse, this natural sexuality was essentially male.

The practice of the teacher here conforms to this 'scientific pedagogy'. While some activities are provided for the children, they are allowed to 'choose'. They are never coerced into doing something they do not want to do, rarely taken away from activities in which they are engaged. They are natural, normal children who should be left alone to develop at their own pace. This discursive formation, which constitutes the pedagogy and the experience of this teacher, should be seen neither as 'knowledge' in her control, with which she can consciously oppress the children, nor as a transparent 'experience' which will give the children access to knowledge which is liberating because they have produced it themselves. The knowledge is not inserted in the context of the school and set to work in the interests of the teachers to control the children. Conversely, its purpose is to produce better control through self-control and that, ironically, is what helps to produce the space in the practice for the children to be powerful. In this situation, the children have the power to define what they do within the limits of the pedagogy in that they can *choose*, and cannot be stopped in their choosing. The children recognize quickly that the uttering of the magic words 'I don't want to' quickly produces a situation in which they can control the flow of events. Thus the very discourse helps to produce the children as powerful. The space is already there for their resistance. Similarly, the discourse of the naturalness of male sexuality to be expressed, not repressed, produces and facilitates in the teacher collusion in her own oppression, since if she reads actions as normal and natural, and suppression of those actions as harmful, she is forced into a no-choice situation. She cannot but allow them to continue, and she must render harmless their power over her. The very practice which is supposed to liberate ('progressive education') produces the possibility of this discursive power in the children. There is no counter-discourse, and the children know it.

The pedagogy of 'choice' is a tool in the production of the rational ideal. Rationality, rational choice and decision-making are the ideal, the goal of the pedagogy. It assumes (following Piaget and many others) that this rational individual can be produced by leaving children alone to 'grow out of' their base animal sexuality, their aggression – that is, the non-rational. Left alone, this will be worked out and not pushed down to fester in the unconscious. Through this process children will come to act in a civilized manner. They will become agents responsible for their own actions, whose interactions are based on rationality alone, having left the irrational behind them. Thus education serves to produce them as unitary subjects making logical and rational choices.

But as we have witnessed, this rational ideal is doomed to failure from the beginning, in both its assertion of rationality and its picture of the unitary subject. What particularly concerns us here is that the very discourse aimed to set the children free from over-regulation permits any activity as a natural expression of something: something 'better out than in' It is in this sense that the children, as children, cannot be understood in the terms of 'progressive education' as produced in discourses which have oppressive effects: they simply have experiences, and experiences are transparent, the context is incidental. Leaving the children alone to their own devices means that they will reproduce those positions in those discourses with which they are familiar, and are thus not open to scrutiny and transformation. Neither the children nor the teacher can change without the production of different discourses in which to read their actions, and to produce different actions and different subjectivities. Thus we can understand the complexity of the production of the social relations in this small exchange between teacher and children. . . . The individuals in this exchange do not appear to be produced in some static and unitary reflections of social forces; neither are they given power as a simple function of their institutional position. The discursive forces which shape the pedagogy of the classroom produce a space which promotes the power of children and asserts the naturalness and harmless-ness of their actions. They show us how the teacher is rendered powerless to resist the power of the boys and how she fails to understand this as an example of their oppression of her: we can so understand it only with the superimposition of a feminist discourse. We can understand that the individuals are not produced as unitary subjects but as a nexus of contradictory subjectivities. These contradictions are produced by the way in which the 'material' of the individual provides the potential to be the subject and object of a variety of discourses which produce that indi-vidual as sometimes powerful and sometimes powerless. There is in this model no unitary rational subject of progressivism who sloughs off the irrational; neither is the individual a 'real' and essential kernel of pheno-menological Marxism, whose outer skins are just a series of roles which can be cast off to reveal the true and revolutionary self.

GIRLS AND BOYS IN THE CLASSROOM

I want to extend this analysis to examine more interactions involving small boys, but this time in play with girls in the classroom. We can apply the kind of model I have signalled above to understand the production of girls as subjects within pedagogic practices. Sex-role socialization accounts of the reproduction of girls understand them as produced as a reflection of traditional female sex roles. The economic dependence and oppression of women will produce girls whose personalities are passive and dependent, dominated not dominant. Yet as I asserted earlier, individuals are powerless or powerful depending upon which discursive practice they enter as subject. Recent work within the women's movement[9] has pointed out that the oppression of women is not unitary, and that different discursive practices have different and often contradictory histories. This means that in some practices women are relatively powerful – for example, in those practices in which they signify as mothers (for instance in custody cases). These practices are reproduced by the children in their play in the nursery classroom. This means that the girls are not always passive and dependent, just as their mothers are not, but are constantly struggling with the boys to define their play and to redefine it into discursive practices in which they can be powerful. To understand the power and resistance in the play of children, we have to understand those practices that they are re-creating in their play. These help to produce the children as re-creating the (often reactionary) discourses with which they are familiar, but also serve to constitute them as a multiplicity of contradictory positions of power and resistance.

Let us examine one small piece of play taken from the same classroom. This time, the children are playing hospitals. They have been given all the necessary equipment by a nursery nurse, and she has seen to it that the boys get the doctors' uniforms and the girls the nurses'. The nursery nurse constantly helps to maintain the power of the doctors over the nurses by asking the nurses to 'help' the doctors. One girl, Jane, changes this into a situation where she is to make cups of tea for the patients. She goes into the Wendy House and has a domestic conversation with another girl, then the following sequence ensues:

(One of the doctors arrives in the Wendy House and Jane says to him:)

    Jane: You gotta go quickly.
    Derek: Why?
    Jane: 'Cos you're going to work.
    Derek: But I'm being a doctor.
    Jane: Well, you've got to go to work, doctor, 'cos you've got to go to hospital and so do I. You don't like cabbage, do you? [he shakes his head] ... Well you haven't got cabbage then. I'm goin' to hospital. If you tidy up this room make sure and tell me.

Jane has managed to convert the play situation from one in which she is a powerless and subservient nurse to the only one in which she has power over the doctor: by controlling his domestic life, by becoming the controlling woman in the home. It is important that the other way in which she could have had power within that game – by, for example, playing a more senior doctor than Derek – is denied her by the nursery nurse's action, and it is unlikely that she would be able to take that position by herself.

In an example of play between children in another nursery school we can examine a further situation of struggle for power between girls and boys. This time the boy, Dean, is struggling for power to define and control the game. He comes to join Diane and Nancy, who are already playing mothers and daughters in the Wendy House. Diane is playing mother and controlling both the sequencing of the game and the actions of Nancy, who, like any dutiful daughter, goes along with Mother's wishes. They are playing happily until Dean intervenes. Diane tries to tell him what to do as her son, but he tries to take over her commanding position. Diane says:

> Diane: Well, I'm playing mums and dads and girls. You're not. Or my ... or my sister'll tell you off if you come in my house. She'll tell you off if you ... if you come in my house. She will 'cos because I'm making 'er bed and if you get in 'er ... in 'er bed she'll tell you off she will.
>> Let's go and get the baby, come on then, you've got to go to bed now, darling. You ain't been to bed yet, have you?
> Dean: (to Nancy) You don't like ... you don't want to play with 'er, do you?
> Nancy: Yes, she won't let me go...

Diane pushes Nancy a bit on the rocking horse and then tries to retrieve the domestic discourse:

> Diane: Darling ... I made the bed for you. Look what she's done. She's made it all dirty. All all new, I've made it all clean. Now I'll have to tidy up. Let's see my money, see if there's money. Here's your food. Meat, chicken and bacon and steak. Now d'you want the telly on? D'you want the telly on? I put it on for you. Here y'are, I put the telly on for you. You can't turn it off.
> Dean: What!
> Diane: Can you?
> Dean: I know you can't.
> Nancy: She's our mum, she's our mum, yeah she's our mum.
> Dean: (to Nancy) If you're playing with 'er I'm not gonna be your friend any more ... not ever play with you. So what you gonna do?
> Nancy: (she looks first at one and then at the other, 'turns tail' and joins Dean) I'll play with you.
> Diane: Nancy, get off that horsey and go to bed now 'cos you're being naughty.

In both these examples the struggle on behalf of the powerless child, the resistance of that child, takes the form of reading the individual as the subject/object of another discourse, just as in the Miss Baxter sequence. In both cases the girls' power is produced by their setting up the game as domestic, so that they, like their mothers, traditionally have power, though of course it is power produced through contradiction and paid for by their domestic labour: it is therefore severely limited and limiting, but not without effects. It is true that this is precisely what is asserted by sex-role stereotyping arguments, but there are several important points which, it seems to me, stereotyping arguments cannot explain. First, the girls are not always weak and dependent, but appear to be engaged in a *struggle* with the boys to read and to create the situations as ones in which they are powerful. The boys equally struggle to remove the play from the site of the domestic, in which they are likely to be subservient. It is interesting to note that in the large number of play sequences recorded in these two nurseries, there were very few in which boys played powerful fathers *when girls were present*, though they did do so when playing with other boys.

THE POSITION OF GIRLS
IN EARLY EDUCATION

Relative to boys, the academic performance of girls in the whole of the primary school is superior. Stereotyping arguments traditionally separate the domestic and the academic, arguing that girls fail in school because of their insertion into traditional feminine and non-academic roles. The academic is counterposed to the domestic. However, such a position does not appear to be able, readily, to explain why girls should actually be relatively successful in early education. I want to raise some speculations about how we might be better able to account for this phenomenon, using the notions of power and discourse outlined above.

The fact that girls can and do take up powerful positions in play seems at first sight contradictory. Girls appear to struggle to obtain power in precisely those situations which are the site of resistance for boys. The girls try to manoeuvre the situation so that it becomes domestic play and the boys try to move it to a non-domestic situation. The domestic situation is precisely a site for opposition and resistance of the power of women in the home lives of these boys. It is unlikely that either at home or in play it would be sanctioned for them to 'identify' with their mothers by taking a position of similarity – that is, acting as a sub-mother either in the home or in school – and it also seems unlikely that their fathers would take 'mothering' positions within the domestic sphere. The girls, on the other hand, can precisely so identify with the positions occupied by their mothers within domestic practices. Thus it is not surprising that the power of the domestic is a site of resistance for these boys, and one in which their resistance takes precisely that form of transforming the situation in discourse to one in which the girls and women are constructed as weak in relation to men.

However, for these young children the domestic is not the only site of apparent female power. Their school lives are controlled by female teachers. There are many ways in which the discursive position adopted by the teachers is similar to that of mothers. Indeed, the nursery school provides a context in which good mothering and good pedagogy are seen as part of the same process – of aiding child development. I would argue that the very power of women in this transitory situation, between the domestic and the academic, is precisely what permits the early success of girls. It may be the similarity between these discursive practices, both sites of female power, that allows girls to take up positions of similarity with the powerful teachers. Indeed, the girls who are considered to be the 'brightest' by the teachers do in fact operate as subjects within the powerful pedagogic discourse. Within that discourse they take the position of the knower, they become sub-teachers.[10] For example, in one of the nurseries, Nancy, considered bright by the teacher, constantly asserts that she 'knows'. She continually finishes her work before the others to shrieks of 'Done it' and 'That's where it goes 'cos I know it does'. The boys in these exchanges are, by contrast, for the most part almost totally silent. They seem to be engaged in a resistance of silence, which is of course another way of resisting the discourse. Another example, from an infant school, will show just how the 'bright' girls act as sub-teachers. This is Sally, addressing a girl whom she has been helping with her work: 'Put your book away, come on. That's good work for today . . . slow to do everything. You take a minute to do it!'

I would argue that it is the relation between the domestic and the pedagogic and the way in which women signify as mothers and teachers, taking positions of power within those practices, which provides the space for the early success of girls. This success is achieved precisely because successful school performance requires them to take up such positions in pedagogic discourses.[11] On the other hand, this is equally a site of struggle for the boys, a struggle in which they must work to re-define the situation as one in which the women and girls are powerless subjects of other discourses. It could well be this very resistance to that quasi-domestic power which explains boys' failure to do well in early education.

CONCLUDING REMARKS

I would suggest that the kind of analysis towards which I have gestured provides a potentially better alternative explanation for understanding the relation of girls and women to early education. Understanding the individuals not as occupants of fixed, institutionally determined positions of power, but as a multiplicity of subjectivities, allows us to understand that an individual's position is not uniquely determined by being 'woman', 'girl' or 'teacher'. It is important to understand the individual signifiers as subjects within any particular discursive practice. We can then understand power not as static, but produced as a constantly shifting relation.

Having said that, however, there remain certain problems of determination which do not seem to be totally resolved by this analysis. Although this essay does raise problems for arguments which advocate direct and linear cause, the economic and the material are clearly crucial to these examples. The confining of women to the quasi-domestic, while discursively powerful, remains a site of economic dependence. While this dependence does not directly produce a passive and dependent subject, it is not without effects. Similarly, the girls and women do not take up *any* position in *any* discourse. Their signification as girls and women matters. It means that the positions available to them exist *only* within certain limits. These limits are material – not in the sense that they are directly *caused* by the materiality of the female body, but certainly by the limits within which that body can signify in current discursive practices. Nor are they directly 'caused' by the economic, but it does serve to produce women as confined to the domestic. However, the contradictions, the struggles for power, the shifting relations of power, all testify to the necessity for an understanding of subjectivities, not a unique subjectivity. These contradictions also point to the necessity to rethink our strategies for action within education. They show too how resistance on the part of children is not necessarily progressive in and of itself, and that the consequences of resistance are, to say the least, contradictory.[12]

While I do not find it possible to present easy answers or immediate political strategies, I think the presentation of the complexity is important. The teachers' guilt at the possibility of oppressing children is something which may have been shared at one time or another by many of us. It no longer seems enough to believe that we are in the process of simply oppressing children. Neither can we be comforted by the thought that 'progressive education' will free children to explore their own experience, without understanding precisely how that experience is understood and how it produces the children as subjects.

Notes

1. The observations were made as part of the projects on developmental psychology and nursery education and girls and mathematics in the early years of schooling. The latter work was carried out jointly with Rosie Eynard, and further details are contained in the project report: R. Eynard and V. Walkerdine, *The Practice of Reason: Investigation into the Teaching and Learning of Mathematics*, vol. 2: *Girls and Mathematics*, University of London, Institute of Education (mimeo).

2. For example, see criticisms of the notion of the unitary subject of psychology and the assertion of the necessity for an understanding of individuals as a 'nexus of subjectivities' in Adlam, *et al.*, 'Psychology, Ideology and the Human Subject', *Ideology and Consciousness*, no. 1, 1977.

3. For example, the following (amongst others) raise the problems of 'economistic Marxism': Adlam *et al.*, 1977; M. Foucault, *Power, Truth, Strategy*, Sydney, Feral Publications 1979, and *Discipline and Punish*, Harmondsworth, Penguin 1977.

4. See, for example, the article by Fran Bennett, Rosa Heys, and Rosalind Coward in *Politics and Power*, 1980, in which they argue for an understanding of the complex and contradictory signification of 'woman' in a variety of legal and welfare practices.

5. See, for example, Shulamith Firestone, *The Dialectic of Sex*, London, Cape 1971, and Julian Hall, ed., *Children's Rights*, London, Panther 1972.

6. M. Lowenfeld, *Play in Childhood*, London, Gollancz 1935, pp. 324–5.

7. See, for example, R.J.W. Sellick, *English Primary Education and the Progressives 1914–1939*, London, Routledge & Kegan Paul 1972.

8. For example, see Denise Riley's article 'War in the Nursery', *Feminist Review*, no. 2 1979.

9. See note 4, and also, for example, Julia Brophy and Carol Smart, *Family Law and Reproduction of Sexual Inequality*, BSA Conference Aberystwyth, and certain work within the journal *m/f*, 1981.

10. See Eynard and Walkerdine.

11. Madeleine MacDonald argues that accounts of education as reproduction are problematic in relation to the contradictory nature of women's education because of the relations between the domestic and the academic: 'Sociocultural Reproduction and Women's Education', in R. Deem, ed., *Schooling for Women's Work*, 1980.

See also Carolyn Steedman's article 'The Tidy House', *Feminist Review*, no. 6, 1980, in which she talks about girls' contradictory relations of power and powerlessness in relation to the home and child-rearing and asserts the possibility of using an awareness of this to produce change.

12. Using a different theoretical framework, certain 'youth and counter-culture' studies reveal that resistance can be contradictory; for example, in relation to Paul Willis (*Learning to Labour*, 1978) 'lads' who resist school only to be confirmed in a 'macho' masculinity and the necessity of physical labour.

2

Notes about forgetting

(Written in 1981)

I go into the classroom as a teacher and I 'know' certain things. I return, several years later, this time in the incarnation of a developmental psychologist. I am surprised by what I see – that teachers put together theoretical statements which, in psychology, are totally incompatible. Why? Of course, a response, the one that was fed to me, comes easily: are they stupid, don't they know enough psychology? *How can they do it?* Yet we can ask the question: how can *I* do it? How is it that developmental psychology has caused me to forget – to forget what I knew as a teacher, to blot out as wrong the construction of the world that I had then?

To recall it is painful, for it feels like a mistake. I do not like to look at it, but I must look at it, because if I don't I will not understand how I came to that knowledge, that it was not a product of my stupidity. What Pêcheux describes as 'forgetting' is the way in which we forget the conditions of our own constitution; we take them for granted as normal, natural. Were I able to look back I could have recognized that that incompatibility exists only because I now look through the eyes of a developmental psychologist.

Through the eyes of a teacher I see the daily necessity of making sense of the behaviour of the thirty or so children in my class. The explanations I come up with are the only grounds I have on which to practise. They are conditions of practical necessity, which we ignore at our peril. What is it about modern primary school practices which produces these conditions of practical necessity? Why do I seek explanations unique to each individual? What is it that I am seeing, or rather reading off from the myriad tiny fragments of information that confront me as evidence?

These are the questions we can ask of classrooms, schools, teaching. But they are not the application of a pre-existent psychology that is already within the practices. Therefore, if we are to understand what is happening – in which psychology is already implicated – we need to stand back, not trust the obviousness of the taken-for-granted and yet remember to look at what it means to be a teacher, a pupil, a parent, a child. We look at ourselves. We have tools. The great and injurious act of forgetting which happens in institutions of teacher education means that students come, teachers come, as I once came, and forget, obliterate, imagine that they know nothing. The insertion into the new practice of psychology, or any of the other disciplines, uses that forgetting. Nevertheless, it also tells us what it is like to be a pupil again. And we can use that knowledge too. But, of course, that is to explode the boundaries between theory and practice.

3

Progressive pedagogy and

political struggle

An idealist dream, an impossible fiction or something to hope and struggle for? I would like to explore some of the problems and possibilities for and with progressivism as pedagogic mode and political strategy. I shall tend to make reference to primary school pedagogy because that's what I'm most familiar with, but I hope that these remarks will be relevant to all sections of the education system and to our own practice as teachers in higher and further education.

In 1968 I became a primary school teacher. I was swayed by the romantic promise of progressivism in education, and I linked poverty and inner-city decay with the terrible regimentation and the 'old-fashioned' repressive and silencing methods. I had read Herbert Kohl's *Thirty Six Children*[1] and John Holt's *How Children Fail,*[2] and I loved my inner-city children with a fierce passion. For under my nurturance their illiteracy would be converted into inner-city poetry. There was joy in my classroom. There were also terrible problems: how to control the children, for example. And four o'clock frequently found me sobbing quietly at my desk, behind the shut door where none of the old, strict teachers, who didn't like my ways, could see me.

Clearly, difficult as it all was, the dream of something different was at that moment very important. But since then the libertarianism upon which the progressivism of the sixties was founded has been re-examined. This libertarianism was crucial in locating the 'personal' as a central aspect of the political, and particularly to developing a whole panoply of therapeutic interventions. However, alongside a concept of liberation as personal freeing was an understanding of power which located it as a fixed possession, in this case that of the oppressive – and consequently repressive – teacher. Personal liberty became synonymous with the lifting of that repression.

18

In response to these ideas I want to offer two arguments: first, that the concepts of power and liberation are intimately connected to the radical bourgeois project, the formation of the modern state and the modern concept of democratic government. I shall argue that the forms of pedagogy necessary to the maintenance of order, the regulation of populations, demand a self-regulating individual and a notion of freedom as freedom from overt control. Yet such a notion of freedom is a sham.

Secondly, the position of women as teachers (particularly in primary schools) is vital to the notion of freeing and liberation implied in such a pedagogy. It is love which will win the day, and it is the benevolent gaze of the teacher which will secure freedom from a cruel authority (in the family as well as the school). Through the figure of the maternal teacher the harsh power of the authoritarian father will be converted into the soft benevolence of the bourgeois mother. Hence, I will argue, aspects of women's sexuality are intimately bound up with the concept of progressivism. Just as women have argued that the sexual liberation of the sixties was a celebration of masculine sexuality, so I shall argue that the liberation of children conceived in these terms did not mean the liberation of women. In some ways, it actually served to keep women firmly entrenched as vital carers. Women teachers became caught, trapped inside a concept of nurturance which held them responsible for the freeing of each little individual, and therefore for the management of an idealist dream, an impossible fiction.

Critical to my analysis is a questioning of the concept of power employed in previous formulations. I want to suggest that instead of constructing a concept of power = authoritarianism and absence of power = helpful teacher, democratic relations, such formulations deny power. (I shall return to the concept of denial used in its psychoanalytic sense.) Instead, I shall use power in the Foucauldian sense of *power/knowledge*.[3] It is in this sense that I want to raise problems for the concept of liberation as freedom from coercion, and to suggest that it is central to the concept of the bourgeois individual.

Foucault locates the transformation of governmental form, and therefore of the notion of power, as the shift from an overt sovereign power to a 'suspicious' and invisible power within those aspects of the sciences (particularly human sciences) which came to be used as the basis for what he calls technologies and apparatuses of social regulation. Basically, Foucault argues that the form of government depends not on authoritarianism but on normalization, the concept of a calculated, known population. In that sense a variety of governing practices – from medicine through law, to social welfare and schooling – began to be based on a concept of a norm, a normal individual.

In the nineteenth century science was used to calculate and produce a knowledge of the population on an unprecedented scale. The production of 'knowledges' became intimately bound up with the devising of new techniques of population management. The school was the arena for the development of one set of techniques for 'disciplining' the population. The emergence of popular and then compulsory schooling related specifically to the problems of crime and poverty, understood as characteristic of the population: criminality and pauperism.[4] Schooling was seen as one way to ensure the development of 'good habits' which would therefore alleviate these twin problems. The original strategy was to engage children in ceaseless activity, with constant surveillance to ensure these habits. Subsequently, this strategy was abandoned in the face of children's ability in rote-learning, 'to recite the Lord's Prayer for a half-penny', without actually assuming the rigid moral habits.

It was at this point that the kind of pedagogy which had been advocated in terms of overt authority began to be challenged. There were many examples of such challenges, from the work of Froebel and Pestalozzi, to Robert Owen and his school in the New Lanark Mills, to Itard and Seguin in France (whom Maria Montessori followed).[5] In their differing ways they began to advocate an education 'according to nature'.

Here 'nature' was defined in a number of ways, but most of those which are important to the inception of psychology involve a sense of 'species-being' derived from evolutionary biology. Thus, in these cases, 'education according to nature' came to mean according to the science of human nature. The critical feature here was a sense of evolution and heredity, an environment understood in quasi-biological terms. Their 'interaction' varied in different theories, but was rarely stated differently.[6]

This human nature was mapped out in the Child Study Societies which flooded the land. The calculation of the distinct qualities and characteristics of children followed many attempts to link ontogeny to phylogeny – the individual's development to that of the species – the most famous of which is Darwin's study of his infant son.[7] This classification of children proceeded in the same way as the animal/human distinction was being monitored in the Empire. The categorization of children according to the ontogenetic characteristics of their natures was similarly based on certain assumptions about the civilizing process and the place in it of 'a natural environment'.[8]

Education according to nature became the way of ensuring a natural path of development, the best kind of civilizing process.[9] Theories of instincts and animality were thus connected to the regulation of the population, many of whom (particularly the urban proletariat) displayed all too obvious signs of animal passions.[10] Degeneracy was seen as an aberration of nature.[11] The part played by the environment was made clear by the mapping of the city – the spread of typhoid, its criminal quarters, and so forth. The environment too could be watched, monitored and transformed.

I am glossing over a great deal of political struggle, but my aim is to demonstrate that the advent of naturalism – that is, the ensuring of a correct passage from animal infant to civilized adult – became understood as both 'progressive' (according to scientific principles) and effective. It would prevent the threatened rebellion *precisely because* children who were not coerced would not need to rebel – the lessons would be learned, and this time properly. Docile bodies would become a self-disciplined workforce.

What was proposed was a process – a scientific process – whereby the schoolroom could become a laboratory where development could be watched, monitored and set along the right path. There was therefore no need for lessons, no discipline of the overt kind. Power became that of the possessor of the Word, of rationality, of scientific concepts – reason's mastery over the emotions. This would ensure a stable populace and rebellion would therefore be eradicated by natural means. Interference was limited and surveillance was everywhere. The ultimate irony is that the child supposedly freed by this process to develop according to its nature was the most classified, catalogued, watched and monitored in history. Freed from coercion, the child was much more subtly regulated into normality.

These new concepts created 'the child' as the object of calculation and pedagogic practice. For example, 'language' became that standard presented in reading books created especially for the child. Using concepts derived from Etienne Balibar's examination of the French language,[12] Jacqueline Rose argues[13] that the construction of a unified nation required the production of reading material *for children*. What we now think of as 'natural language' was produced specifically as a special text stripped of the literary style of the educated aristocracy of the time. In that sense, uniformity (natural language) was created out of diversity – a wide variety of dialects, for example – and made the object of those texts used in compulsory schooling. In this way a standard – an educated standard – was produced, with the consequent pathologization of difference as deviance from that standard. (In a similar vein, Keith Hoskin[14] traces the way in which the development of silent reading transformed a system of oral recitation, and particularly facilitated the development of examinations as written work in silence, thus making the mass testing and normalization of the population possible.)

At the very moment when nature was introduced into pedagogy, the shift to covert surveillance became enshrined in a word – 'love'. 'Love' was to facilitate the development of the child in a proper supportive environment. This shift is coterminous with, and related to, another – the entry of women into elementary school teaching. The emerging human sciences, building upon previous philosophical tenets, had deemed women's bodies unfit for reason, for intellectual activity. The possession of a womb was thought to render a woman unfit for deep thought, which might tax her reproductive powers or make her less amenable to rearing children. Given the state of Empire, the concern with the race as with the species, it was considered potentially injurious to allow bourgeois women to reason.

Nevertheless, women's struggles to enter higher education were finally successful when elementary teacher training was opened to them. Frances Widdowson argues that the development of teacher training colleges went together with the concern to educate women.[15] Such a concern was not a reversal of the brain/womb polarity – precisely its opposite. Women were to be educated, in the words of the 1933 Hadow Report,[16] to 'amplify their capacities for maternal nurturance'. These capacities, while given naturally, could be enhanced so that women teachers could provide a quasi-maternal nurturance to compensate for the deprived environments of the poor. In addition, women could watch, monitor and map the child's development. Clipboard in hand, these scientific educators could survey each of their small charges, whose development was entrusted to their love.

It was always an impossible fiction. The dream of ensuring each child's pathway to reason turned the schoolroom, where pupils recited their lessons and moved up the form, into the classroom,[17] a place in which each child was considered separately. Discipline became not overt disciplining but covert watching. Regurgitated facts became acquired concepts. Knowledge became naturalized as structure or process. Teachers began to talk about 'learning *how* to learn', the surest guarantor of correct rationality. The old ways had to be outlawed to make room for natural reason. Children therefore weren't taught facts but were left alone to interact with their environment. No more would there be the horror of child labour. Classroom work was replaced by play – the *proper* medium of expression for children, the most basic and animal-like medium of unconscious fantasies and the recapitulated development of the species.[18] The classroom became the facilitating space for each individual, under the watchful and total gaze of the teacher, who was held responsible for the development of each individual. This assumed a total gaze, which could be stated, as one teacher put it, as 'knowing each child as an individual'. An impossible fiction.

THE PSYCHIC ECONOMY OF THE
PROGRESSIVE CLASSROOM

Let us imagine such a classroom. All has been transformed to make way for 'active learning', not 'passive regurgitating'. This pedagogic space is filled with groups of tables, not rows of desks. There may be no playtime, since work and play are indistinguishable, and work cards and individual assignments may have replaced textbooks. Children may choose their own timetables. Freedom is imagined. A whole fictional space is created, a fantasy-space in which the ideal nature, the most facilitating environment (rather like a greenhouse), is created in the classroom. Away from the decay of the inner city, the air in the classroom smells sweet. The teacher is no authoritarian father figure, but a bourgeois and nurturant mother. Here all can grow properly. In this greenhouse there will be no totalitarianism. It is the nursery and it nurtures, preventing the pent-up aggression leading to delinquency and war and fascism. The freedom of children is suggested by teachers who are not the oedipal father but the pre-oedipal mother, whose attachment to the children in her care, together with her total presence, ensures their psychic health.

The desire for happiness is a sentiment echoed throughout such classrooms (and deftly caught in Pat Holland's film *What are Schools For?*, where the children are allowed only happy sentiments and happy words: 'Wonderful, beautiful', coos the teacher). There is a denial of pain, of oppression (all of which seem to have been left outside the classroom door). There is also a denial of power, as though the helpful teacher didn't wield any (and indeed, we progressivists of the sixties believed we could be friends with children, be partners in learning – no power, no hierarchy, called by our first names).

The teacher is there to help, to enable, to facilitate. Only those children with a 'poor grasp of reality', those poor 'pathological' children, see her power. Because of their own authoritarian families, they react in a paranoid fashion to this nurturance – they are aggressive, they do not speak. They feel they are being watched, not nurtured.[19] Who, one might ask, has not adapted to reality? A bourgeois reality where it is impossible to see the power invested in your charitable needs, where the poor and oppressed are transformed into the pathological and inadequate.

But more than this, the happy classroom is a place where passion is transformed into the safety of reason. Here independence and autonomy are fostered through the presence of the quasi-mother. There is no severance of this mother–child dyad except to autonomy.[20] This leaves the child in a fantasy of omnipotent control over the Other – the teacher. 'His' path to rationality, displayed best in mathematics, is a path to

omnipotent mastery over a calculable universe (outside time and space –
a rationally ordered and controlled world[21]). Passion is superseded by an
'attraction to ideas', the 'love of the order and purity of mathematics'.
Such power is immensely pleasurable. But whose universe is real?

Is it the universe outside time and space where there will be no war,
no pain, no desire, no oppression?

At what cost the fantasy of liberation? I suggest that the cost is borne
by the teacher, like the mother. She is passive to the child's active, she
works to his play. She is the servant of the omnipotent child, whose
needs she must meet at all times. Carolyn Steedman[22] suggests that such
a role mirrors not the aristocratic mother but the paid servant of the aristocracy, who is always there to service the children. His majesty the baby
becomes his highness the child. The price of autonomy is woman. The
price of intellectual labour (the symbolic play of the Logos) is its Other
and opposite, work. Manual labour makes intellectual play possible. The
servicing labour of women makes the child, the natural child, possible.

The education of working-class and black children is something of a
problem, since they rarely conform to the ideal child. So too, the girl: is
she to be a knower or a potential nurturer of knowers? What price her
freedom? Although there is much to say about the education of girls and
women, let me simply state that regulation of women's sexuality,
rendering them fit only for maternal nurturance, is something which, as
scholars like Lucy Bland have demonstrated,[23] pathologizes activity and
passion. Needs replace desire. Affect replaces libido. Indeed, in progressivism girls are often held up as lacking: they seem to demonstrate either
deviant activity or a passivity which means that they must be found
lacking in reason and compensated for this lack. As I tried to show in
Chapter 1, it is masculine sexuality, to the point of violence, which is
validated by this pedagogy. It is the female teacher who is to *contain* this
irrationality and to transform it into reason, where it can do no harm – a
transformation which turns physical violence into the symbolic violence
of mastery, the law. And in each case, the woman as container soaks up
and contains the irrationality which she best understands.

The extent of validation of violence among boys is shocking in classrooms today, and the downplaying of this aggression in reasoned argument is itself an interesting transformation of power. Here it is the
knower who can win and apparently topple the power of the teacher,
through argument. Disciplining becomes knowing.

Although some have suggested that progressivism frees working-class
children from harsh authoritarianism, I would suggest precisely the opposite. Progressivism makes the product of oppression, powerlessness, invisible. It is rendered invisible because within the naturalized discourse it is
rendered 'unnatural', 'abnormal', 'pathological' – a state to be

corrected, because it threatens the psychic health of the social body. It is therefore very important to reassert the centrality of oppression and its transformation into a pathology in terms of a political analysis of the present social order. For example, what working-class mothers say to their children is either counted as nothing (it doesn't count as natural language in the deprivation literature) or romanticized and fetishized as the working-class culture of *Nippers* reading books, bingo and chips, the colourful banter of cockney market-traders. Even in the 'equal but different' model of working-class language displayed (differently) in the work of William Labov and Harold Rosen, for example,[24] the historical *production* of the 'natural' is completely elided. As Jacqueline Rose argues in *The Case of Peter Pan*, 'there is no natural language, especially for children'. Yet within the progressivists' nurturant welfare state, with its inadequate families aided by our latter-day charity, bourgeois culture is taken as nature.

Meanwhile, meanings are struggled over in the classroom. 'The Child' is created as a sign, to be read and calibrated within the pedagogic discourses regulating the classroom. The child is defined and mapped in its relations of similarity and difference with other signs: activity, experience, play rather than passivity, recitation, work, and so forth. Through the regulation of this pedagogy children become subjected in the classroom.[25] The classroom, then, is a site of struggle, not of an unproblematic fitting of these categories on to children but of a constantly erupting pathology, like the unconscious, breaking the smooth surface of the pedagogic discourse.

Many studies, of which the most famous is ORACLE,[26] have claimed that progressivism has never been tried in Britain, that most British classrooms are not child-centred, despite the orthodoxy. We are faced with children working, following the rules, trying to find out what to do – this despite the fact that there are taken to be no rules, only the pure joy of discovery. It often seems that the teachers produce the very categories that children are taken to be discovering. Children are bewildered because they don't know the rules, use strategies which aren't supposed to exist. Teachers turn out to be more traditional than expected and feel guilty because the future and 'freedom of our children for ever' is laid at their door. They are the guardians of an impossible dream, reason's dream of democratic harmony.

Notes

1. Herbert Kohl, *Thirty Six Children*, Harmondsworth, Penguin 1971.
2. John Holt, *How Children Fail*, Harmondsworth, Pelican 1969.

3. Michel Foucault uses the couple *power/knowledge* to express the positive effectivity of knowledge of populations in the possibility of government. For a general treatment see Gordon, ed., *Power/Knowledge*, Brighton, Harvester. For a specific treatment in relation to primary school pedagogy, see Valerie Walkerdine: 'Developmental Psychology and the Child-Centred Pedagogy', in Henriques *et al.*, *Changing the Subject: Psychology, Social Regulation and Subjectivity*, London, Methuen 1984.

4. See Karen Jones and Kevin Williamson, 'The Birth of the Schoolroom', *Ideology and Consciousness*, no. 6, 1979.

5. See Walkerdine; and Carolyn Steedman, 'Prisonhouses', *Feminist Review*, no. 18, 1985, for more details. While the former were attempts in the eighteenth and nineteenth centuries, Montessori followed up by applying the techniques used to train and test the humanity of 'wild boy of Aveyron' to the education of 'idiots' and the poor of the Italian city slums in 1910–20.

6. A rare difference was the work of the Soviet psychologist Lev Vygotsky, working in the 1920s and 1930s. Although he did not deviate from a 'developmental' model, he made a concerted effort to situate that development within the social and not just phylogeny.

7. Charles Darwin, 'A Biographical Sketch of an Infant' (1840), *Mind*, no. 7.

8. The take-up of 'Social Darwinism' had widespread effects, and the emerging anthropology sought to map the animal/human distinction on to nature in different environments in the 'discovered' lands of the Empire. Here was a ready test of the 'civilizing process'.

9. Because it worked *with* nature and not against it, it became a pedagogy of development. Thus the regulation of the population could become self-regulation of a natural system, operating according to universal laws of development. See, for example, Nikolas Rose, *Social Regulation and the Psychology of the Individual*, London, Routledge & Kegan Paul 1985; and Denise Riley, *War in the Nursery*, London, Virago 1983.

10. The feared uprising of the urban proletariat was associated with the violence of 'animal' or 'pre-human' emotions.

11. Nikolas Rose.

12. Renée Balibar and D. Laporte, *Le français national*, Paris, Hachette.

13. Jacqueline Rose, *The Case of Peter Pan or the Impossibility of Children's Fiction*, London, Macmillan 1985.

14. Keith Hoskin, *Cobwebs to Catch Flies: Writing (and) the Child* (unpublished manuscript), University of Warwick, Department of Education 1985.

15. Frances Widdowson, *Going up to the Next Class: Women in Elementary Teacher Training*, London, WRRC/Hutchinson 1983.

16. Consultative Committee of the Board of Education, *Infant and Nursery Schools* (Hadow Report), London, HMSO/1933.

17. David Hamilton, *On Simultaneous Instruction and the Early Evolution of Class Teaching*, University of Glasgow, Department of Education 1981.

18. Ideas about play spanned work from child psychologists (Klein) to work on animal ethology demonstrating that young animals played, making it therefore natural.

19. This idea is further elaborated in Chapter 5 of this book.

20. In this discourse, separation from the Mother/Other is not to anywhere or to a relation to the father/phallic/paternal space but to an autonomy conceived as 'individuation'.

21. This is further developed in Valerie Walkerdine, *The Mastery of Reason*, London, Routledge 1988.

22. Carolyn Steedman, 'The Mother Made Conscious', *History Workshop Journal*, 1985.

23. Lucy Bland, 'Guardians of the Race or Vampires upon the Nation's Health? Female Sexuality and its Regulation in Early Twentieth Century Britain', in E. Whitelegg *et al.*, *The Changing Experience of Women*, Oxford, Martin Robertson 1986.

24. William Labov, 'The Logic of Non-Standard English', in Ashar Cashdan, ed., *Language in Education*, Open University/Routledge & Kegan Paul 1972. For Harold Rosen's critique of Bernstein, see his *Language and Class*, Bristol, Falling Wall Press 1972, and *The*

Language and Class Workshop series.

25. For further elaboration see Valerie Walkerdine, *The Mastery of Reason*.

26. ORACLE, Observational Research and Classroom Learning Evaluation, was written up as a series of books, for example, Maurice Galton, Brian Simon and Paul Croll, *Inside the Primary Classroom*, London, Routledge & Kegan Paul 1983.

4

Extract from field notes written in

primary school staffroom

(Lunch time, 1982)

The staffroom is full of women eating cottage cheese or grapefruit.

Each of them knows about diet and eating and sexuality. They are willing and happy to talk about these, caught inside what they are: the unique combination of worker and woman, dependent and independent, free and trapped.

5

On the regulation of speaking and

silence: subjectivity, class and

gender in contemporary schooling

> [We argue that] the structure of the social system and the structure of
> the family shape communication and language and that language shapes
> thought and cognitive styles of problem-solving. In the deprived family
> context this means that the nature of the control system which relates
> parent to child, restricts the number and kind of alternatives for action
> and thought that are opened to the child; such construction precludes a
> tendency for the child to reflect, to consider and choose among
> alternatives for speech and action.
> (R.D. HESS AND V. SHIPMAN, 1965, p. 869)

The family and the primary school are sites for the regulation and
production of the modern conception of the individual. In this essay I
want to explore, in a preliminary way, some aspects of current practices,
concentrating on how the power to speak and conflict have been
regulated and understood. In particular I shall be concerned with the
idea of the rational, independent, autonomous child as a quasi-natural
phenomenon who progresses through a universalized developmental
sequence towards the possibility of rational argument. This 'normal
development' is taken to be facilitated by a sequence of cognitive
development on the one hand and language development on the other,
both being viewed as depending on the presence of the mother. I shall
explore the connection between the family and the school, examining
these as sites in which individuals are understood as being actively
produced. In particular I shall focus on some contemporary effects of
historical shifts from overt regulation of the population to apparatuses of
covert regulation which depend upon the production of self-regulating,
rational individuals. Such accounts of normal development seek to
describe all children and all families. But since normalization hinges on
the detection of the pathology, the targets of intervention continue to be

the poor, the working class, and ethnic minorities. In such practices, the position of women as mothers and teachers is central and strategic.

As I shall show, psychoanalysis is doubly implicated here. On the one hand aspects of psychoanalysis have been crucial in the regulation of sexuality, passion and the irrational. More recently, normalized accounts focusing on the mother's role have made women the object of the production of a maternal nurturance, understood as the guarantor of the rational subject. However, I shall seek to go further than a simple deconstruction of the productive power of modern apparatuses. Intertwined in modern practices are the workings of desire, which suggest a complex subjective investment in what I shall call 'subject-positions'. These positions, given in the relations of the practices themselves, are not unitary but multiple and often contradictory, so that the constitution of subjectivity is not all of one piece, without seams and ruptures.

This means that we can examine those very practices and ruptures as sites of production of subject-positions and of either potential coherence or fragmentation. Utilizing some insights from a reworking of certain concepts adapted from Lacanian psychoanalysis and Freud's analysis of mechanisms of defence,[1] I shall suggest how it might be possible to rework existing explanations in order to examine the production of class and gender relations within and between existing practices. In doing so, I hope to illustrate how relations of power and desire interpenetrate the complex workings of apparatuses for the production of subject-positions, and how those positions, in their contradiction and multiplicity, are lived. I shall suggest that the modern conception of the rational, contained in logocentric discourses, sets up as its opposite an irrational. This is invested in and understood as the province of women, who must contain it at the same time as being responsible for its removal in their children. A crucial consequence of this analysis is a reworking of conflict and its relation to language. The achievement of rationality becomes, in part at least, understood as the transformation of conflict into rational argument by means of universalized capacities for language and reason.

SPEAKING AND SILENCE:
THE TRANSFORMATION
OF CONFLICT INTO DISCOURSE

Classic studies within feminism examining silence have concentrated on 'finding a voice'. Here, feminism was understood as providing both a place and power to speak. In this context, silence has been understood as both repression and resistance.[2] A refusal to speak was taken as a psychic repression, or a suppression of the articulation of forbidden discourse.

'Speaking out', in this sense, is seen as the articulation of a difference in contrast to its repression, which is seen as a deviance, illness or absence. However, the issue of silence and speaking is not a simple matter of presence or absence, a suppression versus an enabling. Rather, what is important is not simply whether one is or is not allowed to speak, since speaking is always about saying something. In this sense what can be spoken, how and in what circumstances, is important. It not only tells us about its obverse, what is left out, but also directs attention to how particular forms of language, supporting particular notions of truth, come to be produced. This provides a framework for examining how speaking and silence, and the production of language itself, become objects of regulation.

I shall begin by drawing on Michel Foucault's classic study, *Discipline and Punish*.[3] Here he charts the emergence in the nineteenth century of modern techniques of population surveillance, showing how the development of apparatuses and technologies of regulation were crucially dependent upon the newly emergent 'sciences of the social'. The regulation of conflict (of crime, pauperism, deviance as pathologized) is central to such sciences and technologies. Here I can do no more than signal some displacements which followed from this. However, it is particularly important that from the outset a regulation of conflict and rebellion was aimed at the poor, at a population newly contained in towns and cities.[4] At first such regulation involved overt surveillance and attempts to inculcate 'good habits', but in the problems associated with such overt practices covert self-regulation became favoured. That children who were so obviously watched and monitored might still rebel, for example, remained a continuing problem. In transformations relating to pedagogy, love became the basis of techniques designed to avoid problems associated with overt surveillance. Now the aim was to produce citizens who would accept the moral order by choice and free will rather than either by coercion or through overt acceptance and covert resistance. But this investment of love in the child occurred in conjunction with other transformations which, as I shall show, are particularly important to understanding the regulation of speaking and silence. For example, the emphasis on caring nurturance located in women was also central to the medicalization of their sexuality.[5] The latter itself involved a regulation of passion and, in the process, a displacement of irrationality. The heralding of the rational, the production of the bourgeois citizen capable of reasoned argument, was itself made possible through new knowledge and practices, producing the irrational through an opposition. Reclaiming irrationality – speaking out – then, cannot be simply a release from repression, nor a new freedom, the power to speak, but must be understood in terms of the relations of its own production.

The natural was produced in those practices which proclaimed its possibility. It is centrally important to deconstruct the claims to truth of that natural reason and language. Thus, there is no liberation of a repressed voice so much as a new natural language which was made to speak itself, whose absence became a pathology. It is particularly evident in the regulation of those practices surrounding the family and school. Here the production depends upon the positioning of women as mothers and teachers, who provide the 'facilitating environment'. Women become guardians of the irrational: their love becomes nurturance. They ensure the production of individuals who are self-regulating through the powers of rationality. Not swayed by irrational forces and free from conflict, they are to become the free agents of bourgeois democracy who will, by choice, accept their place in the new order and will not rebel. As I shall show, the regulation of conflict becomes centrally its displacement on to rational argument, crucial to which has been the production of theory and practices centring on a naturalized sequence of child development. Through this means the child becomes the target of interventions destined either to facilitate the 'natural' emergence of rationality or to understand its absence as (ab)normal, pathological, therefore to be corrected by a variety of medical, educational and welfare agencies. Central here is the idea of an autonomous agent, who attributes feelings to him- or herself and does not feel an excess of passion or conflict. Such an agent is a citizen who, as in the humanist dream, sees all relations as personal relations, in which power, struggle, conflict and desire are displaced and dissipated.

My aim is to begin to explore how the practices operating in schooling, and in the family, position the participants. They aim at producing an autonomous and rational individual, who is class- and gender-neutral, while at the same time ensuring that these categories assume a built-in deviance, a problem to be dealt with and corrected. In contrast to a view which aims at the liberation of individuals from repressive forces, I shall go on to indicate how the regulative features of practices themselves, in providing multiple sites for the creation of subject positions, also create a complex machinery of desire.

THE SUBJECTS OF SCHOOLING

The school, as one of the modern apparatuses of social regulation, not only defines what shall be taught, what knowledge is, but also defines and regulates both what 'a child' is and how learning and teaching are to be considered. It does so by a whole ensemble of apparatuses, from the architecture of the school to the individualized work cards. Here I am concentrating on modern primary school practices which relate specifically to the development of the child-centred pedagogy.[6] These practices depend centrally upon a conception of learning and development as individually paced, counterposing this to any instruction of the class as a whole. Knowledge is defined in terms of experience and activity: in the words of the Plowden Report, 'concepts to be acquired, not facts to be stored'. In general terms, the pedagogy is individualized and conceptions of the child and of knowledge both depend upon a naturalization of a conceptual apparatus of structure. Knowledge, understood as concepts, is acquired and produced through the development of an active learner who develops 'at his own pace', by actively incorporating experience. This itself is defined in relation to an environment which is taken to consist of a world of objects. The teacher does not actively teach – indeed, *must* not teach – but must passively become part of the facilitating environment which observes and monitors the sequence of natural development.[7] In this way, the very pedagogy itself produces the possibility of individualization.

These taken-for-granted assumptions have a complex history involving the production of a range of systems of categorization which on the one hand are claimed to be universal, yet at the same time produce differences and effects on class and gender lines. Central to claims to universality are certain truths located in the body. At least since Descartes, reason has been located in the body. The Cogito and the rational individual (of property, wage-labour, etc.) form the centrepiece of a variety of interlocking practices. But the body in question is not any body. Women's bodies became understood as incapacitated for reason. Hystericized and medicalized, they were capacitated for reproduction of the species, not the production of knowledge. Women's bodies were both the place where the production of reasoning beings as children was assured, and yet also a constant source of danger. For example, educating women, inasmuch as it might adversely affect their reproductive capacities, was discouraged as endangering the future of the species.[8] Women had therefore to become both the producer of reason through child-rearing, and its opposite. Passive, receptive and nurturant femininity became the obverse of reasoning or masculinity, itself made possible through active exploration. However, a constant threat was the intrusion of the irrational. Medicalization of women's bodies became a surveillance of passion, of an active sexuality. As Catherine Hall points out (1979), it was bourgeois women, confined at home as guardians of the moral order, who ensured the safety of the reproduction of children, whose path towards rational adulthood was assured by their presence, a presence at once cold and hygienic. All active desires of women were thereby transformed into a cool, calculating and passive nurturance. At the same time the pathologization of passion, activity, on the part of the women regulated their fitness for motherhood.

From this century many examples could be given of how women's sexuality and their fitness for maternal nurturance become the object of interlocking apparatuses and technologies. An obvious one is in the decision-making process which may operate in child custody cases. Here my concern is with those interventions which first relate the promotion of natural reasoning to language, and secondly link mothering to the production of both.[9] In each case what is vital is that the links hinge on various notions of 'deprivation', and position the mother in relation to the child in very specific ways. Correlatively, this argument was linked to assumptions about the management of conflict in relation to socialization practices in home and family.

In primary schooling we can uncover a remarkable congruity in the positioning of the teacher and assumptions about the mother who must provide the 'facilitating environment' for the production of rationality. The teacher was to become a passive observer, watching the unfolding of development. Like that of mothers, teachers' passivity is vital to the possibility of children's activity. Teacher training for primary schools has developed in relation to the amplification of women's capacities for maternal nurturance.[10] Women, who had previously been excluded from education on the grounds that it would endanger their reproductive capacities, were now allowed to train as teachers, producing an effect whereby women could safely be educated in so far as this made possible the staffing of the caring professions. This effect is still present, as even a minimal examination of current statistics on women's entry to higher education and employment will show.[11] But if passive, nurturant femininity was necessary to produce active learners, in this respect, the education of girls as 'children' represents something of a problem. Modern conceptions of child development understand children as active, inquiring, discovering. Yet that activity also defines an active masculinity of which passive femininity is the obverse. The Plowden Report, for example, consistently transposes 'child' into 'boy'.[12] By definition, active childhood and passive femininity exist at the intersection of competing discourses. For girls, therefore, their position as children must remain shaky and partial, continually played across by their position as feminine. Conversely, for boys masculinity and childhood work to prohibit passivity. And in both cases passion and irrationality are constantly displaced.

But it is in the understanding of silence and the management of conflict that these contradictions are particularly apparent, and the issues of class are to be foregrounded. If the normal child is self-regulating, any overt conflict, a failure of reason, will be displaced on to pathology. Yet the pathologies are different for different discourses; for example those regulating the normal child (male) and normal femininity.[13] What is crucial, therefore, is both the truth of the normal and the pathologization of its obverse.

Both the family and the school are sites of an array of practices which aim for the covert regulation of the population. These practices depend upon the revelation of conflict, of power relations, of aggression, but also upon their dissipation. This dissipation is the responsibility of women who, in humanist developments of psychoanalysis and child development, nurture, free and aid autonomy. There is no overt policing and monitoring, but a covert regulation through which passion is transposed into feelings, the irrational into the rational, power into interpersonal relations, and conflict into aggression. But this move towards self-regulation depends not only upon an active learner who develops through action on objects but also upon the medium of argument, language, which itself emerges naturally through a sequence of development. Speaking and silence therefore become normalized as the facilitation of a universal linguistic system. Silence is pathologized as absence, for although language is natural it develops only if facilitated by a family (or more particularly a mother) who interacts, extends, elaborates the utterances of the child. Silence is a pathology if the school and family simultaneously permit and celebrate the possibility of speech.

TALK ABOUT IT: THE INCITEMENT TO DISCOURSE

This emphasis on language did not immediately fit easily within the child-centred discourse. The pedagogy of experience and natural development eschews all texts. It is founded upon 'doing'. The action upon and interaction with the world was, in the post-Plowden climate of the late 1960s and the 1970s, an object world. Denied as a social space in its own right, the classroom was an 'environment' where a number of children might experience together. In this respect, at first talking was subsumed to 'doing'. It was only following the impact of structural linguistics on studies of children in the 1960s and 1970s that an emphasis on language became implicated within the child-centred pedagogy. For this talk had to be dissociated from the passive regurgitation of the 'old' system of overt regulation and passive remembering. Talk became an aspect of freedom, of the facilitation of language, which unfolded almost of its own accord in the right conditions. Language development as a naturalized system was thus added on as an extension of child-centredness, an addition to the production of rationality. Studies of the failure of urban education in the American ghettoes became studies of the environmental facilitation of natural language. While mothers were implicated, teachers everywhere began to be taught how to talk to children. They learnt to extend and expand utterances. Language was categorized into functions and its presence checked and monitored. In such practices, although texts as textbooks had been the object of ridicule, they began to re-enter the scene. But they were not the same texts. Nothing could enter below the baseline of an unsullied natural experience. Thus texts had to build upon natural language and 'tell it like it is'. Children could create their own texts in their own words, and those texts which were produced were to be explication of the everyday experience and language of, particularly, inner-city children. They were taken to represent reality, not to intervene, and therefore went alongside a view of facilitation which apparently existed outside any regulation.[14] Like natural reason, natural language was allowed, permitted, desperately facilitated. It is therefore very difficult to understand such practices as regulative. Regulation had gone underground.

In such a climate of enablement an absence of language and of reason can be nothing but a pathology, and its cause must lie in the environment itself, the centre of which was the mother.

THE FAMILY AS CAUSAL

The mother and child are both caught in the play of practices for ensuring the possibility of self-regulated, rational and autonomous subjects. Women, I suggest, in the necessity to ensure a stable, nurturant and facilitating environment, are the price paid for autonomy, its hidden and dispensable cost. Some feminist accounts of women's psychology have taken up this point, wanting to extend autonomy to women. But if we understand independence and autonomy as something denied to women, then, like the work on silence and repression, we tend to assume a model of liberation from oppression and repression in which women can be set free to take their place as fully fledged individuals. Indeed, some accounts of women's psychology present this as a kind of rebirth, like a butterfly emerging from a chrysalis. But might we not emerge as individuals only to be further implicated in the patriarchal and logocentric tradition which proposes the bourgeois individual as guarantor of the new order? Here I want to take a rather different approach, examining first how woman and child have been coupled in the production of the autonomous child in the practices of home and school.

If individuality depends on the presence of naturalized language and reasoning, its absence is pathologized. After all, if development is natural, its absence is a very fundamental absence in that which permits or facilitates the very centre of human development. From here, it is not just the absence of language which is pathologized. The normal woman is invested with a nurturance which is naturally given by the workings of her reproductive system; this amounts to a capacity for facilitating and enabling the natural development of children. Far from being passionate, this love is Platonic. Passion and activity are pathologized. It follows that resistance to rationality in the form of any expression of conflict becomes an excess, a pathology, the cause of which is the mother. In this process the failure of overt regulation, the obvious resistance manifested in crime, poverty or threatened anti-establishment uprising, is removed from social relations to become established as an aspect of the psyche.

The declared failure of overt practices of regulation gradually forced another, and more covert, tactic. This has involved a further double shift particularly significant in the regulation of women, as the infant's relationship with the mother – or, more particularly, the bourgeois mother, confined in the home – is understood as the basis of conflictual behaviour. Between the two world wars, Melanie Klein posited an innate tendency to aggression to account for conflict, observable as a struggle between love and hate, which was fuelled by primitive desires or instincts, directed towards the mother. Liberal practices designed to facilitate the letting out of aggression through play, in play therapy, child-rearing and in schooling, relate to this approach. But this emphasis was followed by another shift as post-Kleinian psychoanalysis focused more on maternal nurturance and the actual bodily presence of the mother as against destructive fantasies. These moves marked the location of the mother firmly in the home, to be responsible for the ensuring of self-regulation through nurturance. That is, self-regulation was made possible through the toleration of the presence and absence of the mother, understood as the child's overcoming frustration.

Conflict has thus first been located causally within the family, laid at the door of the mother, and finally shifted to an experience of frustration. In all this, as in all subsequent humanist developments within psychology, the relational dynamics, the regulation of practices themselves, become 'feelings' which are experienced as attributes which individuals must learn to recognize – for example, frustration as their own irrationality, their own feelings. And additionally, as rationality is separated from irrationality, fantasy becomes secondary to an 'adjustment to reality', the pinnacle of logocentrism. Power and desire are therefore both crucially absent from this framework.

RATIONALITY AS A REGULATIVE DEVICE

In the shift from overt to covert regulation, then, a capacity for language has been linked to natural reason, and conflict has been individualized, reduced to feelings or a mastery of frustration. The production of self-regulating individuals now depends crucially on how conflict is managed between parents and children. At the centre of explanation of maternal deprivation in relation to pedagogy lies the absence of 'reasoned argument' as a control device in working-class mothers. Regulative devices of other kinds, such as threats or smacks, are simply taken to be pathological. If reasoning is natural, then the problem becomes mothers who do not foster it. Classic studies such as that of Hess and Shipman[15] utilize the early work of Basil Bernstein to legitimate their claims. It is important that both Hess and Shipman and Bernstein point to evidence of the presence of language (that is, that working-class children 'have' language), but for different purposes. Hess and Shipman, unlike Bernstein, treat purpose as synonymous with presence. They fail to recognize what comes over again and again in their own research and other studies of this kind: that differences in regulative devices have to be understood in relation to distinct practices. In one very telling piece of evidence presented by Hess and Shipman, mothers were asked to say how they would prepare their young children for school. I reproduce it below:

> 'Suppose your child were starting school tomorrow for the first time. What would you tell him? How would you prepare him for school?' One mother, who was person-oriented and used elaborated verbal codes, replies as follows:
> 'First of all, I would remind her that she was going to school to learn, that her teacher would take my place, and that she would be expected to follow instructions. Also that her time was to be spent mostly in the classroom with other children and that any questions or problems that she might have she could consult her teacher for assistance.' 'Anything else?'
> 'No, anything else would probably be confusing for her at her particular age.'

They then go on to discuss the potential value of the mother's contribution to the child:

> In terms of promoting educability, what did this mother do in her response? First, she was informative; she presented the school situation as comparable to one already familiar to the child; second, she offered reassurance and support to help the child deal with anxiety; third, she described the school situation as one that involves a personal relationship between the child and the teacher; and fourth, she presented the classroom situation as one in which the child was to learn.

They then go on to exemplify the opposite position by reference to a second mother:

> A second mother responded as follows to this question: 'Well, John, it's time to go to school now. You must know how to behave. The first day at school you should be a good boy and do just what the teacher tells you to do.'

And they comment:

> In contrast to the first mother, what did this mother do? First, she defined the role of the child as passive and compliant; second, the central issues she presented were those dealing with authority and the institution, rather than with learning; third, the relationship and the roles she portrayed were sketched out in terms of status and role expectancies rather than in personal terms; and fourth, her message was general, restricted and vague, lacking in information about how to deal with the problems of school except passive compliance.[16]

The oppositions are clearly set up here by Hess and Shipman. In their terms the first mother personalizes the relationships, suggesting security and warmth. The second mother reveals to her child an overt system of regulation. This is identified as harmful. This process is well illustrated by Turner's[17] summary of social class differences in disciplinary techniques produced in the mid-1960s.[18] Where everywhere middle-class parents are identified as more 'permissive' in relation to children's transgressions and disobedience, they also 'provide more warmth and are more likely to use reasoning, isolation, show of disappointment or guilt-arousing appeals in disciplining the child.' Working-class parents, on the other hand, 'are more likely to use ridicule, shouting or physical punishment in disciplining the child, and to be generally more restrictive.'[19] Permissiveness in child-rearing is thus associated with an absence of coercion, an absence of overt regulation which is seen as punitive and harmful. As in the child-centred pedagogy, freedom is taken to be this absence, in which reasoning prevails. But what this identification of absence as deviance conceals is the movement towards covert regulation of conflict, which everywhere aims at its displacement on to self-regulation through reasoning and 'internalized reactions to transgression'.[20]

The practices of regulation pinpointed in the extracts set out each of the danger spots of the production of the autonomous individual: the presence of the mother, her facilitation of natural language, the personalization of emotion and its displacement from overt conflict on to rational argument. Thus working-class mothers are themselves pathologized and responsible for the pathology in their children by going out to work; regulating their children through overt displays of positional power, there is little personalization and an absence of expansion of language and reason as a regulative device. These absences and the presence of the 'wrong' attributes provide evidence necessary for the intervention of medical, welfare and educational agencies to correct the pathology in a variety of ways.

John and Elizabeth Newson, in their study of seven-year-olds in Nottingham,[21] make clear some of the conditions necessary to the covert regulation of conflict and the production of autonomy. Although they demonstrate the illusory nature of choice, by pointing both to the fact that some conflict between parents and children is necessary and to the 'engineering' of willingness by covert means, they are trapped within a permissive discourse. This understands power only as overt regulation and therefore psychically harmful:

> Some conflict between parent and child is almost inevitable: it arises because parents require children to do things, and this interferes with the child's autonomy as a person, with wishes and feelings of his own. In disciplinary conflicts, by definition, we have a situation where certain individuals exercise their rights as people of superior status (in age, power and presumed wisdom) to determine what younger and less experienced people, of inferior status, may or may not do. If the child complies willingly of course (even if his willingness has been engineered by offering him the illusion of choice) his self-esteem can be kept intact: but whenever he is forced into an unwilling compliance by the threat of sanctions, whether these be pain inflicted or approval withdrawn, he will inevitably suffer in some degree feelings of powerlessness and humiliation.[22]

They make it clear that autonomy relates to the regulation of conflict. Feelings are attributed to the child and parental power or authority is understood to be bad. Overt regulation, in the form of threats, compliance and sanctions, produces 'feelings' of powerlessness and humiliation. These are clearly to be avoided. It is an 'illusion of choice' which seems the key here to what they recommend. The child must experience him[sic]self as in control, as the author of his intentions, of free will, independence – autonomy. Thus any practice which might inhibit that illusion is frowned upon.

But the problem with reducing powerlessness to a 'feeling' is that it becomes a property of the person. The child is therefore not helpless or powerless before the practices and authority relations which position him: s/he feels powerless. Such feelings can be overcome by means of an 'illusion of choice'. The child will thus experience 'himself' as empowered, free, in control. S/he will not therefore recognize the regulative chains of the practices in which s/he is positioned and is able, and moreover willing, to accept 'his' lot, adapt to reality, deal with frustration: in short, become a self-regulating, democratic citizen. But in so far as 'he' 'experiences frustration', 'feels powerless', and so forth, these feelings are pathological. What is more, we can locate both a cause – failure of maternal nurturance of the correct kind – and a remedy – some process of re-presenting that nurturance, some therapeutic practice. Powerlessness can hardly be recognised as an effect of regulation in those practices in which power itself is denied.

But from a different position power and powerlessness can be understood as aspects of the regulation of practices themselves, and not as unitary or simple possession.[23] If we examine in more detail what working-class mothers are taken to do, it becomes evident that to some extent they expose the fraudulence of choice. In so doing, these mothers constantly present their children with power and regulation. They may persist in telling their children that 'they cannot have everything they want'. They remind them that for a variety of tangible reasons, they do not have the choice, a central component of the bourgeois order which is continually held out to them as a possibility. So working-class mothers, in making it clear that children cannot 'just ask and get', that money is scarce, their time is limited, etc., shatter the illusion. But such shattering is difficult to live if dreams of fulfilment – of constant presence, constant happiness – are proffered as reality. Difficult to live, too, if other practices depend for their operation on that choice.

Thus the pathologization of overt regulation produces a truth which locates effects of poverty and oppression in the psyches and family relations of the poor and oppressed. The rational individual who is self-regulating and imbued with feelings, who has adapted to reality, exists in a personalized world untrammelled by power and desire. Yet it is not sufficient simply to point to such effects. This itself encourages a voluntarism which assumes that change can follow from subjects' recognizing and choosing to stand outside the conditions of their own regulation. Because modern social apparatuses both define and delimit normality, they also operate through the regulation of desire. Hence the workings of subjectivity enter into the production of the illusion of choice and fulfilment. But this subjectivity is not unitary. It is multiple and contradictory. Here, I suggest, it is precisely in the failure of the processes aimed at producing rational individuals, those aspects which are pathologized, that we might find a starting point in understanding multiple and contradictory subjectivity. For this enterprise I suggest that we might utilize certain concepts from Freudian psychoanalysis, but in a rather different way.

In the following section I shall sketch out some possible aspects of an analytic framework which uses both aspects of psychoanalysis and ideas developed from post-structuralism. I shall then go on to illustrate this through some examples from my own research. My aim here is less to provide a fully-fledged analysis than to point to a direction in which work might proceed.

PSYCHOANALYSIS, POWER AND DESIRE

Along with other work in the tradition of post-structuralism,[24] I have implicated psychoanalysis in the production of norms crucial to modern apparatuses of social regulation. Here, however, I shall be drawing on aspects of psychoanalysis which exist outside the framework of normative models and social welfare agencies, a body of work which, in principle at least, does not maintain an absolute distinction between the normal and pathological. Nevertheless, since psychoanalysis is implicated in those apparatuses of regulation as well as particular practices of child-rearing and schooling, it helps to create the very subject-positions I wish to deconstruct. Here I want to draw attention to two features of the regulation of practices and the constitution of subject-positions within them which are integral to my framework, discussed more fully elsewhere.[25] First, following Foucault, power is implicated in the power/knowledge relations investigated in the creation and regulation of practices. Here, power is not a single possession of an individual, nor is it located in a unitary, static sense. Rather, power is shifting and fragmentary, relating to positionings given in the apparatuses of regulation themselves. Thus adults – mothers, for example – do not possess power by virtue of simply being in authority as in the Newsons' account. Nor can power be eradicated by personal harmony. Power exists in the apparatuses of regulation.

From this it follows that women have power only in so far as they are positioned as mothers in relation to certain practices concerning the regulation of children. In this sense, although the effects of the regulation of a child are to be understood as real, they are not to be caused in any simple sense by the mother but by the very regulation and constitution of mothering in modern practices of child-rearing. From this perspective, we might thus examine a child's experience of regulation not as an essential effect of the mother, but as an effectivity produced in practices of mothering. However, there is every reason to suppose a child may understand or experience a mother as the source of power and not its effect. Secondly, as I have argued, the practices which produce subject-positions are of necessity multiple, and those positions themselves are often diverse and contradictory. From here we can understand the mother–child relation as only one of a diversity of sites in which positions are created. This means that we can examine what happens at the intersection of practices. Obvious examples of such intersections discussed already would be the relation of the position of ideal rational and active 'child' on the one hand and passive, nurturant femininity on the other. From here we may ask: what is the effectivity of such positionings for the lives of particular girls and women? Similarly, what is the relationship between child-rearing practices stressing that 'you cannot have what you want' and a pedagogy based on an illusion of choice for working-class children? In each practice an acceptable response in one will be the target of negative evaluation in the other. What I am suggesting is that the very contradictory nature of such positionings produces effects likely to result in anxiety states. It is to examine these effects that I wish to invoke certain insights from psychoanalysis.

I want to begin by making reference to a paper by Cathy Urwin[26] in which she reworked certain concepts taken from Lacanian psychoanalysis utilizing insights from post-structuralism. This enabled her to include and interrelate the concepts of power and desire in the workings of regulatory practices. Using an examination of recent studies in child language development, Urwin presents a reworking of Lacan's mirror stage to encompass a post-structuralist engagement with regulatory practices. This reworking emphasizes the mirror in Lacan's account as a metaphor for the illusion of perfect control. She exemplifies how discursive relations enter into the imaginary activity of the mirror by suggesting that the production of meaning through ritualized communication procedures positions the mother as the one who, to the infant, is apparently the source of power. This is achieved as she offers the infant an illusion of perfect control, by enabling it to control her within particular practices through the use of idiosyncratic but meaningful activity. None the less her participation is governed by her own positioning within discursive practices. Later the infant must negotiate separation and attempt to deal with the painful consequences of giving up its illusory control, itself produced through the entry into discursive relations. This is achieved through the introduction of a third term and processes of identification, enabling the infant to take the place of Other within the regulation of practices. Urwin argues that the crucial relation of power and desire may be understood through the infant's taking, in a ritualistic way, the position of that Other, switching both position and power, moving from dependent to dominant and vice versa.

As in Lacan's account, Freud's analysis of narcissism is taken as central. The affirmation contained in the mirror provides the infant with a narcissistic sense of omnipotence. The Other and regulation confirm the infant's fragile sense of self. However, the infant's relations with others can also be experienced as extremely persecuting. That is, relations and positions which do not permit the power/desire relations, giving the

infant narcissistic control, may be experienced as destructive and annihilating. Urwin remarks:

> It is not simply a question of distorted feedback from a strange adult who fails
> to understand the baby's messages.... Rather, like the mirror in Lacan's
> account, which is as controlling as it is controllable, here the illusion of
> control has its counterpart in the illusion of total subjugation. (It is for this
> reason that narcissism and paranoia are juxtaposed in Lacan's reading of
> Freud.)[27]

Separation from the mother in this account is understood in terms of the
uptake of positions within practices themselves. It is therefore no simple
move away from dependence on the mother's presence (as in the work of
Bowlby, for example). The effect of the illusion of control is to provide a
sense of affirmation and power which has real effects within the practices
in which it is inscribed. This means that separation becomes understood
in terms of relations within and between practices.[28] That is, the move
from something is always a move to something else, and the move from
one practice regulated in one way to another differentially regulated
provides for the infant a sense of power or powerlessness, affirmation or
persecution. Moreover since, as in Lacan's approach, identification with
the Other is to be the object she most desires, it follows that the experience of annihilation or persecution will relate to the experience of lack of
continuity or resources in being the object of the Other's desire within
the new practice. Either the subject will experience this as the necessity
for her/him to change (and therefore risk loss of total control or positive
identities) or the Other will have to change, so that the subject becomes
the object of desire. But the projects for wished-for transformation in
each case are shaky and highly likely to produce forms of anxiety, overt
conflict or other modes of defence.

I want to argue that the production of narcissism and paranoia relates
to the effectivity of identification with the Other who apparently regulates a practice. This is not a unitary quality of the person, as I have
already stressed. Subjects are created as and in positions, not alone, but
in practices and specific relational dynamics. In Urwin's as in Lacan's
accounts, the Other of identification is not reducible to the nurturant
mother. There are many Others who exist in practices, affording the
possibility for multiple and contradictory subject-positions. It is this
multiplicity which produces the totality of shifting relations of power and
powerlessness which is subjectivity. Hence the very apparatuses of
regulation and the practices provide the possibility of the multiplicity of
subjectivity and the experience of incoherence or fragmentation as it
exists across practices.

It is by means of such an account that it might be possible to explore the effects upon, for example, working-class children and girls on entering into new practices. However, further conceptual tools are necessary. A valuable psychoanalytic concept, first put forward by Freud, suggests itself. This is the defence mechanism of splitting.[29] Freud initially developed the concept of the splitting of the ego. The basis of this splitting is a disavowal of castration. That is, the subject denies in consciousness the reality of castration – that females do not possess a penis. This produces neurotic and phobic symptoms. What we have here is a denial of difference: its effects are precisely those of desire. To invest the woman with a penis in fantasy (most particularly in fetishism) is a denial that she does not possess it. Thus fantasy and reality exist side by side, so that Freud was led to describe the ego as split. The effects of this denial are ultimately a delusional reality.

Lacan uses this paper as central to his concept of a fundamental splitting of the subject and the delusional reality created in the fantasies of ideology, of the Imaginary. In this analysis, castration is a marker of a power difference. I am therefore suggesting that we might understand the effects of such a denial in terms of the effectivity of the positioning of a subject within a diversity of practices.

In conjunction with Urwin's analysis, it might be possible, first, to examine the effects of the transposition from one practice to another, and possible experience of persecution produced by this shift in relations. Different practices may produce different effects. In this case, the differences which concern me are those of class and gender. However, the shift from one practice to another, the effectivity of castration as a marker of power, relates centrally to the breaking of the mother–child dyad and the move from one set of discursive practices to another. This is in contrast to a simple move from dependence to independence, as I have stressed. That is, any shift is a move both out of and into another set of discursive relations and therefore involves a complex of positionings.

THE PRODUCTION OF PERSECUTION

As I have shown, present practices assume a universal class-and-gender-neutral 'child', who, in development, passes from one 'environment' or 'context' to another through the utilization and facilitation of cognitive and linguistic capacities. Basic to these practices is a reduction of difference to an add-on effect. There is also a denial of power and desire, the latter being reduced to the meeting of needs which hinge on the presence/absence of the mother. I am arguing for specific effects of a move from one practice to another in a discourse which does not recognize the effects of that transition. That is, current practices operate on a system of disavowals and denials, of castration, for example – girls can be like boys – or of class – mental labour is achieved through 'doing' or manual activity. This reduces the traumatic effects of the experience of difference to a lack or failure in the subject or the mother. In consequence, through operating on the basis of denials, the very practices themselves help to create and read back the effects as pathology. Given extreme feelings of persecution, the stages of transition will relate to attempts to deal with the loss of identification. Such effects may be open hostility, conflict, neurotic withdrawal as silence (and therefore accepting the regulation while covertly being hostile) and, later, apparent quiescence which none the less involves a disavowal. For example, our education system in its most liberal form treats girls 'as if' they were boys. Equal opportunities and much work on sex-role stereotyping deny difference in a most punitive and harmful way. Operating in these practices is a partial and shaky denial of castration. The 'clever girl' is positioned as though she could and can possess the phallus, while she has to negotiate other practices in which her femininity is what is validated.[30]

In this sense the 'delusional reality' consequent upon psychic defences is produced in those very practices which deny differences by failing to engage with the contradiction and pain produced through the act of splitting – of being positioned like a boy and like a girl and having to remain 'sane'. A denial of the reality of difference means that the girl must bear the burden of her anxiety herself. It is literally not spoken. She is told that she can be successful, yet the painful recognition that is actually likely to result from the fear of loss of one or the other (her femininity, her success, or both) is a failure to be either, producing neurotic anxiety, depression or worse. At best we might hope for the disavowal of the career girl. For in fact it is virtually impossible, in our times at least, for the girl to maintain positive identifications in both dimensions, both of which are necessary to the maintenance of her sense of coherence or identity. Yet the deleterious effects of non-acknowledged contradictions depend upon a circulation of denials – of difference, power and desire – within the very practices which regulate and position subjects. In a sense, then, rather than perpetuating the denial operating in the spurious circulation of needs, fulfilment and happiness, a recognition of struggle, conflict, difficulty and pain might actually serve to aid such girls.

At each intersection of practices, each site of difference, there is a boundary to be negotiated. As new identifications are created, so too is the potential for loss, annihilation and disavowal. Indeed, we might argue that within our present system of schooling, the success of working-class children and girls depends upon the effectivity of disavowal and therefore upon intense and persecutory pain experienced by such children. They have been chosen to succeed, yet the very possibility of their success depends upon a splitting – the negotiation of an impossible array of identifications in which they, becoming what the school wants, can no longer be what their family wants, and vice versa. They feel desperate that they can exist in neither, that everything is lost in terrible and painful isolation, that nobody understands, neither at home nor school. We might predict a terrifying experience consequent upon effects of simultaneous desire for identification and fear of total loss and annihilation.

In a recent series of interviews which I conducted with male and female academics, many women experienced such anxiety. Central features of such effects are silence, lack of confidence, the suppression of anger and hostility, contributing to the apparent docility of the person who believes that if they open their mouth they will 'say the wrong thing', and be thrown out of paradise – the longed-for resolution of the bourgeois dream. Sennett and Cobb[31] discuss similar effects with respect to class. In describing the experience of male manual workers and those with working-class backgrounds who became white-collar workers, they provide powerful evidence in support of the thesis I have set out. Indeed, they use the term 'splitting' although their reference point is the work of Laing on the politics of schizophrenia.[32] In describing the pain of becoming bourgeois, Sennett and Cobb point to the central experiences: of passivity, of the fear of letting go of work, the necessity to learn a new set of rules, yet constantly fearing forcible exclusions from the desired location; thus an enforced docility and passivity. They point to the apparatus of bourgeois individualism, of autonomy, choice, of 'being somebody', counterposing this with ways in which working-class people get through or make sense of their lives. These relate particularly to the idea of 'self-sacrifice', the displacement of one's own desires on to the fulfilment of and through others, and argue that 'splitting', the putting up of boundaries, is a necessary condition of survival for most people in 'getting from day to day'. It is therefore not insane, but the basis of sanity. As they put it, 'Society imposes the necessity for defensiveness.'[33]

What is highly significant in their analysis is the way in which they demonstrate the practical necessity of boundarization within particular practices. This is a very different reading from one which would understand such coping strategies as pathological, the product of an unstable family, inadequate nurturance, and so on. But my analysis would go further to suggest that not only are the effects of such practices deeply persecuting and deleterious, but their pathologization renders these effects as experiences of abnormality. It also suggests that a denial of

power in the creation of individuals does not serve to remove such effects
(and here, the humanist concept of the happy factory mirrors the happy
school and the happy family) but rather serves to strengthen their effectivity through the pathologizing of those who do not display the qualities
appropriate to natural, normal and healthy adjustment. But since such
defences might provide strategies for survival within existing practices,
they provide important gains as well as losses. They have positive effectivity.

Here I suggest that Urwin's modifications to Lacan's account provide
important insights in relation to the crossing of boundaries and to the
potential for the constitution of subjectivity in schooling. Important to
this analysis of power and desire is the positioning of the subject within
practices. Identification with a powerful Other within the practice and
the crossing of boundaries between practices is therefore central.
However, since Freud's splitting related primarily to castration it must
locate as formative the practices in which the relations of the family are
played out. In that sense, then, a variety of potentially conflictual and
contradictory identifications is possible, relating to the others in the
family constellation – parents, siblings, other caretakers, suggesting
multiple sites for identification splitting. From the present perspective
what is important is that while the Other of identification is apparently
the source of power, experienced as a possession, in practice the power is
an effect of the positioning of the Other within a particular practice. This
power is therefore constantly mobile and shifting and cannot be understood outside power/knowledge relations and therefore apparatuses of
regulation. This allows the coherence of fantasy, fact and fiction, and
goes beyond Lacan's structuralist appropriation of the imaginary and
symbolic. Possession is a fiction, which is lived as fact through the
veridicality of the practices themselves.

I would suggest that it is precisely the circulation of terms and positions and practices which allows the slippage from one position to
another. That is, while the insertion of the subject into a variety of
practices in which the phallus is, differentially, invested may have
different effectivities, it may well be that it is the relations within and
between them which is one of the conditions for psychic life. A girl who
is positioned as clever in school while also the subject of masculine desire
in another practice is still relating to the phallus. However, one practice
assures her that she can be it, while another ensures its possession only
through her being the object of sexual desire, and therefore the assumption of femininity. In each case we may assume that actual men and boys
are involved, yet a myriad of other places sediment the position. The girl
may want to have a relationship with a boy as one source of affirmation[34]
but there are many others, circulating in a variety of practices and

cultural forms. Similarly and conversely, we do not have to assume (as some feminist arguments for single-sex schools have done) that the absence of male teachers for girls is equivalent to the removal of the phallus, since in schooling the inscription of the phallus is in the very academy itself.

A BID FOR POWER

In stressing the productive potential of the power/knowledge relations of schooling and the multiplicity of positions for children to enter, the issue is now the relationship between those positions and the effectivity of their content. As I have argued, practices aim to produce learners who are active, discovering, autonomous and capable of rational argument. This does not mean that they will be effective, but it does mean that difference becomes pathologized. In attempting to understand how particular children live the effects of those multiple positionings, a first step is to explore the effectivity of different solutions. In this way we might examine the issues of conflict and silence. That is, how might a girl's docility in school produce both losses and gains? She might be denied the status of 'active learner' and yet at the same time be enabled to maintain another site of power, for example by taking the position of the Mother. Yet she must experience pain and anxiety if the contradiction between those positions is not recognized and understood as an effect of the pathologizing process. What, too, if that pathology operates in relation to different and contradictory assumptions of the normal? How then are these resultant splittings lived?

In this respect it is important to recognize that if rational argument is taken to be the pinnacle of intellectual achievement, itself produced through an active and inquiring learner, certain behaviours are not only experienced within the workings of the pedagogy, but they are validated. Let us follow this through with respect to conflict. We have seen that through the transformation of overt to covert self-regulation, conflict is displaced on to personal feelings and rational argument. Although some frustration is inevitable, it must be allowed to be personalized and rationalized. Thus, the school provides a facilitating and nurturant environment in which an illusion of choice and control is presented to children. In this pedagogy conflict is expected, choice is essential and some aggression inevitable. It is presented and understood as children's reactions to frustration, which must become rational argument. Hence displays of conflict are tolerated if they are understood as relating to frustration and activity. Naughtiness in young children, for example, is to be expected, validated and associated with masculinity. Furthermore, conflict is positively sought after and validated if it is understood as rational argument, the guarantor of 'brilliance' or 'real learning'.[35]

Conflict is therefore permitted only if it follows specific paths, otherwise conflict is pathologized. In this case the crucial distinction is between 'rational argument' and 'antisocial behaviour' (associated with delinquency). I want to give some examples of how this might work for particular children, beginning by examining a brief extract from a recording made in a fourth-year secondary mathematics lesson. The girl in question, Charlotte, displays open conflict in her attacking of the teacher's 'claim to know', yet it is precisely this move which, while it threatens his power, leads him in an interview afterwards to evaluate her as 'brilliant'.

> In a lesson on braille, the teacher begins by asking how many combinations of dots they can find, given that they can use any combination of up to six dots. Charlotte volunteers an answer, as does a boy, but the latter's answer depends on leaving one block blank with no dots on it. The teacher agrees with this and is immediately challenged by Charlotte: 'You said count the dots.' The teacher replies ... 'I think it's just as good maths if you count this one or you don't as long as it is made clear what you're doing.' But she persists, 'we were talking about dots.' He says, 'I'm quite happy for you to take that attitude. I'm not arguing with you.'[36]

Girls like Charlotte who challenge in this way are 'active' – they act like boys – they are 'real children', have 'real understanding'. They come across as supremely confident. I suggest that their confidence lies in their claim to the phallus. That is, Charlotte resists the teacher, but her resistance is simultaneously a bid for his power, an identification with him and the powerful Other within her practice. But not just Charlotte's desire is involved. The teacher's judgement of her is also to place her as the object of his gaze, as an example of the kind of pupil he desires to produce. She is the object, then, of his desire, the 'Other of her Other' in the classroom. He says of her:

> '[She is] the one with the keenest brain in the sense of ideas. And she's the great problem-solver. ... She's a tremendous abstract thinker, she's great at the kind of maths that, perhaps, we don't recognize enough.'

No wonder, then, that there is simultaneously for both the teacher and Charlotte a narcissistic bid for position and a threat of annihilation which both must face. The teacher has to deal with her bid to oust him, which is presented in his response as a fear of losing control of the class. He 'will not argue with her'. Charlotte also takes a risk – she could be laughed out of court. Yet something allows her to make that bid which would keep others totally and definitively silent. While they are silent they will never be able to stake out their claim to brilliance, which must exist as a secret fantasy desired as much as they fear its loss. I would suggest that what gives Charlotte the confidence to take the risk is that she has been affirmed in such a position in other practices, especially in the bourgeois practices of her family and their similarity with the practices of the school.

Nevertheless, it may be important that the fear of power, of taking the position of the Other through narcissistic identification, carries this threat of annihilating or being annihilated. In this sense the investment in the Other as a source or site of safety might make such a risk too difficult to bear. Passivity and silence never bring that threat to the surface. The good girl never has to face an overt attack on the Other. Given the pejorative as well as positive evaluations of 'good' and 'hard-working' within the practices,[37] such a girl will never be positioned as 'brilliant' like Charlotte. However, in certain academic practices the relatively privatized act of writing allows the display of such bids for power without the necessity of facing the threat of annihilation within the social relations themselves. Yet this has particular effects. It produces attainment which is correct and therefore validated, but denied at the same time – the right answer produced in the 'wrong' way, by hard work and not brilliance.

Good performance combined with docility and helpfulness presents a striking picture not unlike that expected of primary school teachers, who must possess capacities of nurturance to be 'amplified', yet must reach the standard of attainment necessary for teacher training. Conversely, girls who are 'nice, kind and helpful' are most suited to facilitating nurturance. It is perhaps important, then, that many young girls do not understand high attainment and femininity as antithetical. Girls who 'possess' both characteristics are highly validated. Yet in a recent study an overwhelming number of girls of all ages gave descriptions of their ideal girls which included the terms 'nice, kind and helpful'.[38] Moreover, many girls expressly mentioned 'naughtiness' and 'horridness' as pejorative categories. They strove to be 'good', not to require 'telling off'. Not to need 'telling off' seems to indicate a different discourse from that of 'being cross' and the personalization of feelings. These girls respond to the power invested in the positioning of the teacher as necessitating either an active suppression and/or its conversion into helpfulness. Here, then, is no reaction to frustration, no rational argument, but a painful suppression of conflict which appears in the girls' accounts in two ways. First, it is displaced on to boys who are 'horrid', 'naughty', 'annoying' 'bullies', and 'bad'; secondly, it is the object of masochistic self-mutilation.[39] Some girls whom I interviewed expressed such intense self-hatred that they could attribute to themselves no good qualities at all. It seems to me that a ceaseless array of ensnaring positions circulate here. For example, a girl who is desperate to suppress her 'horridness' can never become 'brilliant': she is constantly caught, not simply as a puppet at the mercy of different positionings, but by the grip of her refractory desires fixed in those practices themselves. Girls who gain power through becoming like the teacher[40] cannot possibly challenge the rules for which they are responsible as guardian. Such a move would bring that threat of powerlessness or annihilation, a threat to the desired position.

Three six-year-old girls from the above study present some idea of a range of positions.

Janie, a working-class six-year-old, at the top of her class, was almost totally silent both at school and at home. She was well behaved and polite and reserved her unacceptable comments for whispering. During one home recording she spent an hour and a half in silent work activity, not uttering a single word.

Janie's silence helps legitimate a position of good behaviour, which, since she says nothing, means she can say nothing wrong. If you cannot be clever, at least there are rewards for being 'nice, kind and helpful', and no pejorative evaluations of horridness. Horridness is hidden, subverted. Let me give two further examples of six-year-old girls.

Emily is a poor girl. She is classically passive and helpless. She cries on entering the classroom, refusing to leave her mother. The teacher comforts her. Whenever she tries to do work she gives up, asks for help, or, more often, sucks a thumb, has a pain and is let off further work. All her negative feelings are apparently displaced into hysterical symptoms such as bodily aches and pains. She is rarely, if ever, overtly naughty. Yet she is also comforted, cuddled, looked after. The teacher frequently worries about her and so comforts her and never forces her to do any work.

Eleana is also extremely passive and very poor. She appears unable to follow simple instructions and the teacher has difficulty in getting her to do anything. She appears as a classic victim and has two categories for the children in her class – those who 'tell on' her (girls) and those who 'tell her off' (boys). She is thus positioned as the passive recipient of a brutal authority. Here is no personalized 'being cross'. However, Eleana commits secret and silent acts of destruction: she breaks the heads off dolls.

This, then, is no natural passivity. Where Emily receives the teacher's nurturance, Eleana's passivity is desperate, erupting secretly into active destruction. While these girls seem precluded from engaging actively with rational argument, on the other hand, in the interviews with academics to which I referred earlier, it was quite common, especially in

those women and men who came from upper-middle-class families, to
describe their facility with rational argument as a sham. They could win
over anybody, yet they saw it as too easy in its effect. Secretly, they felt
'hollow': that they were not really clever, that it was simply an elaborate
theatre. Yet since this cleverness was associated with 'hard work', itself a
feature of working-class life (as opposed to symbolic activity viewed as
'play'[41]), they found it extremely difficult to do and had often made
working-class students at university the target of their abuse. The
following two interviews with male academics from different class backgrounds reveal different strategies and experiences of the negotiation of
boundaries. The first, a memory of working-class school days, reveals the
difficulty of negotiation of boundaries and the problems of 'being made
visible' as itself a threat and source of terror:

> 'It goes back to the instance I described in primary school, made to stand in
> front of the class and do up my shoe laces, stand up in front of the class and
> do up my tie and secondly, the ... this school was, as I would not put it, in
> class terms, completely removed from the kind of experience I'd had in what
> had been a very localized primary school and so I didn't want to be drawn to
> attention in front of these people about whom I felt very edgy ... in case I
> couldn't keep up that standard.'

Another male academic, with a middle-class background, also discusses
the negotiation of boundaries. But his resistance is active and engages
directly with the bid for power and simultaneous annihilation of the
teacher:

> 'Being an intellectual was an act of fucking defiance by the time I was fifteen
> or sixteen.... I remember things like ... I remember realizing that a very
> good strategy for throwing people – the authorities, fixing them, tricking
> them, was to just mix boundaries.... I remember going into a physics lesson
> one day with a copy of Joyce's *Ulysses*.... I realized that by being an in-
> tellectual you could even gain the support of the anti-school people, because
> the teacher came in and he said, "What are you doing bringing this filth into
> the classroom?", and I said, "I got it from the school library."'

In this example, there is a deliberate play on the boundaries, open
conflict, yet it is intellectually powerful. Here is intellectuality, rational
argument. Yet there is also considerable anger. Unsurprisingly, in these
interviews there was also a huge array of anxieties about the public
display of rational argument and the private expression of irrationality
and emotionality. One may then ask, polemically: where is women's
denied anger? It seems to be located in 'man'. And where is men's
denied irrationality? It seems to have been invested in 'woman'. The
Logos itself, then, must be deconstructed.

WOMAN, GUARDIAN AND CONTAINER
OF THE IRRATIONAL

Using the kind of analysis I have set out here, we can understand the
Logos, and the pedagogic production of 'rational argument' itself, as a
historically specific phenomenon. The investment of reason in the sexed
body, as the foundation of modern Western scientific rationality, not
only locates self-control in rational argument, but also places it at the
centre of an omnipotent fantasy of control over the workings of the
universe. Mastery and control of the 'real' are centrally located in claims
to truth and therefore to possess knowledge. In this sense mastery,
control and bourgeois masculinity are conjoined in that uncertain pursuit
of truth. Yet this very uncertainty provides the conditions for an ever-
elusive and therefore incessantly sought-after masculinity. Rationality
and rational argument become, in relation to their centrality in particular
academic and public practices, aspects of individuality to be attained and
regulated. In this sense such aspects of masculinity are not possessions of
biological males. Females may cross over to the side of masculinity, in so
far as they are permitted entry into those practices. Similarly, since it is
bourgeois individuality, possessed of rationality, which is taken as the key
to normality, the working class can in principle become 'bourgeois
individuals' by dint of those liberal practices which provide that possibility. However, such individuality and autonomy are produced at a
price. Playful rationality is made possible through work, the hidden work
of servicing, manual labour and nurturance. Here, the ultimate irony is
to be found in the position of the middle-class male, whose powerful
position is guaranteed by the trap of reasoned argument.

But if the truth of individuality can be deconstructed, we can then
also simultaneously deconstruct its Others, those opposites which render
it possible. Here I have tried to show how women, endowed with a
natural capacity for nurturance, become the safe place where rationality
is assured. Our current pedagogy and child-rearing practices which
celebrate the Logos are made possible by the facticity of the nurturant
mother, the helpful teacher. Yet this capacity for nurturance occludes
women's sexuality. This is the point of fear, for it contains the irrational
which permits rationality, constantly threatening to erupt through its
surface. It may be important, therefore, to explore the possibility that the
production of autonomy, of rational argument and the Logos itself,
rather than breaking the mother–child dyad, actually depends upon the
maintenance of a fantasy of omnipotence, of control over the Other. The
practices pointed to by the Newsons, Turner, and others discussed earlier
make it clear that autonomy depends on an 'illusion of choice', which is
simultaneously an illusion of control. It is therefore vital to recognize that

the truth-effects of that positioning of women actually make possible the fantasy of complementarity in which mothering assumes that needs can actually be met, that rationality is not ruptured by the constant play of the irrational on its surface. This fiction of fulfilment, of nurturance, of the bourgeois individual, is at the expense of the positioning of woman as the mother, who contains, soaks up, allows, facilitates the rationality of the child. She is therefore, in being the guardian, the safeguard for the production of the autonomous and rational knower; also its opposite.

In this the fraudulence of the Logos is that it holds masculinity not in an assurance of control but in a desperate terror of its loss. It is important, then, that we, as women, should not also be caught in an attempt to master the Logos, to take it as our guarantee and arbiter of truth, and of the possibility of change and transformation. As I have tried to indicate, its very production and reproduction depend upon a denial of desire and a displacement of the irrational on to women. However, the history of the Logos, and of scientific rationality, builds upon an even longer history, that of religion. In displacing religion, science sought to remove the soul. The Logos provided a mastery over – the regulation of – natural forces, rather than a supreme Other, God, whose power controlled the universe. The soul was that which existed beyond the materiality of the body, its excess. The displacement of the soul became also the displacement of the outside, represented to some extent by women's-power-with-nature, rather than the control over nature.[42] Women, the site of the terror, had to become imbued only with a passive receptivity which facilitated rationality in others.

In this respect Lacan's examination of female mysticism and paranoia[43] is relevant here. It hinges particularly on the notion of the soul and of a fantasy of a good and perfect Other, God, who holds the power to liberate, to allow the subject to endure the chains of subjugation in order to be freed on death. The soul thus represents an excess, that which resists subjugation, is 'let out', only to make possible the docility required for the enduring of servitude. The passive, docile subject endures subjugation by means of this excess. It is displaced and stifles the possibility of rising up against the oppressor. This subjugation is endured by the splitting of rationality from its excess. In paranoia, a 'delusional reality' exists alongside that which resists subjugation. Passivity and docility might permit the subjugation in relation to an oppressive order, which allows it to be endured in the hope of release into the gaze of the good and perfect Other. Since helpful, kind, nurturant femininity assumes a giving, a containing, then it also suggests the necessity of containing rage and desire – the desire for a place where one day the soul will be free, where the girl (the worker, too) can bask in the light of the all-loving and accepting gaze – to have made it on to the side of the empowered.

The fantasy of the all-loving, all-giving Other, then, is created in the very practices which reward that docility: good behaviour, good performance. But if the Supreme Other is a fraud, the docile child, worker, is set up. Set up to want, to desire the excess of that *jouissance* which is here and yet constantly out of reach, and permits the most punitive and harmful self-mutilation.

BY NO MEANS CONCLUDED

Bourgeois democracy operates in relation to a nexus of practices which aim at the production of a self-regulatory citizen, who has integrated love and hate, and for whom no fantasy perfect good or evil Other exists. The displacement of religion into science displaces that perfect Other, God, that safe place in the sky, on to an 'adjustment to reality', to the existing social order. The human sciences, having first been concerned with 'docile bodies', felt the resistance inherent in an enforced docility. Self-regulation, the apparent freedom of activity, permitted that rational subject endowed with free will and free choice. The self-regulating citizen depends upon the facilitating nurturance, caring and servicing, of femininity. I have explored the possibility of an alternative analysis which might understand the effect of such a history in the production of subjects. Subjectivity as multiple, produced in contradictory and shifting positions, through power and desire, has specific and harmful effects upon those whose lack of fit is rendered pathological. In examining the creation of normalization I have sought to deconstruct an absolute distinction between the normal and the pathological and the truth of a rational and universal subject. If practices and positions are historically specific, not timeless truths, we can deconstruct the power of their obviousness.

The Logos seeks knowledge through rational argument, split from the irrational. Yet other discourses, other practices, are possible which do not recognize this splitting, or reduce it to feelings. Although it is that side associated with the 'feminine' and the 'mad', such conditions remain essentialized only so long as we assume a complementarity and an absolute distinction rather than seeing these as sites of splitting and disavowal. However, in so far as those practices exist, they produce the effectivity of those knowledges and positions. There may be other knowledges, other truths, which resist a reduction to a simple and logical coherence. As long as we fail to engage with those, we are prohibited from examining the effectivity of our positionings and workings for transformation. Change is not a matter simply of deconstruction. A new reading permits the possibility of struggle to work for transformation of that sociality, those practices, and of the subject-positions produced within them. An ahistorical account of human subjectivity fails to engage with the very spatial and temporal specificity of truths and practices. There can be no truth which stands outside the condition of its production. In this pursuit, analysis of these conditions and exploration of our own historicity are inextricably intertwined.

There is, in this account, no lone individual, no single point of causality, but subjects created in multiple causality, shifting, at relay points of dynamic intersection. We can take apart the facts of complementarity, of male and female, rational and irrational, active and passive, mental and manual, which form the sites and possibility of our subjugation and of our resistance. We might then adopt a double strategy: one which recognizes and examines the effects of normative models, whilst producing the possibility of other accounts and other sites for identification. Current accounts of the family and schooling which deny power and desire in a humanistic conception of nurturance serve to help keep us locked inside a powerful fiction of autonomy and possibility, which is not to be countered by a total pessimism but rather by a working with and through an exploration of both our own formation in all its historical specificity and the formation of other possibilities of practice, as well as locations from which to struggle within existing ones. Thus, a working within those apparatuses of our present means not only our attempts at deconstruction but the possibilities for explorations which do not seek a knowledge which claims itself as true for all people, places, times.

NOTES

1. See Lacan (1977); Freud (1951).
2. See, for example, psychoanalytic studies, particularly approaches to Freud's 'Dora' case (Moi, 1981; Rose, 1978).
3. Michel Foucault (1977).
4. Walkerdine (1984); Foucault (1979); Jones and Williamson (1979).
5. I have argued elsewhere (Walkerdine, 1984) that the displacement of passion in favour of a medicalized hygienic, dispassionate nurturance in mothers is an important aspect of the regulation of female sexuality. Passion (particularly in the family) was considered quite unhealthy. Weeks (1981) and Foucault (1979) point to the preponderance of incestuous practices in the working-class families at the time. For further detail about the moral regulation of female sexuality as its hygienization and medicalization, see Bland (1981).
6. Walkerdine (1984) discusses in some detail the emergence of such a pedagogy and its strategic relation to developmental psychology. I shall not rehearse that argument or that history here.
7. See, for example, Walkerdine (1983).
8. Sayers (1982); Le Doeff (1981/2); Dyehouse (1977).

9. There is a large body of work on this debate. See, for example, articles in Williams (1970), Labov's (1970) famous 'The Logic of Non-standard English' and debates in Basil Bernstein's (1975) work.

10. Davin (1978); Widdowson (1983); Steedman (1982); Dyehouse (1977).

11. See discussion in Walkerdine (1984).

12. Walden and Walkerdine (1983).

13. In particular, activity and passivity represent normality in one and pathology in the other. See, for example, the classic study from psychiatric practice, Broverman *et al.* (1970).

14. Examples of such curriculum interventions would be Leila Berg's 'Nipper' reading books, which were to show the reality of urban working-class life, and Halliday's 'Breakthrough to Literacy', in which there were no reading books. Children made their own texts with word and sentence makers.

15. See quotation at the beginning of this chapter.

16. Hess and Shipman (1965), p. 173.

17. Turner (1973).

18. Becker (1964).

19. Quoted in Turner (1973), p. 136.

20. Ibid.

21. Newson and Newson (1976).

22. Ibid., pp. 331–2.

23. Foucault (1979); Chapter 1 of this book.

24. Foucault (1979); Donzelot (1979).

25. I have argued elsewhere that high attainment in girls, combined with passivity, is important to the maintenance of the 'caring professions' in which the women are good enough to go on to tertiary education, but not good enough to be 'brilliant' as in the ranks of the 'real understanders'. See Walkerdine (1983).

26. Urwin (1984).

27. Ibid., p. 301.

28. Ibid.

29. Freud (1951).

30. In Walden and Walkerdine (1985) we discuss such positionings with respect to a study of girls and boys in the fourth year of primary school and the first and fourth years of secondary school. It is important that such positionings are conscious and can be specified by the pupils, but the child who actually manages to exist positively at the nexus of contradictory positionings is rare.

31. Sennett and Cobb (1977).

32. See also Denise Riley (1983), who criticizes Laing's view of the family. Importantly, of course, Laing was also making use of the psychoanalytic concept of splitting, but accuses the family, particularly the mother, in the foundation of its oppression.

33. Sennett and Cobb (1977), pp. 304–5.

34. See Wendy Hollway (1984) for examples of this.

35. Walden and Walkerdine (1983); Chapter 6 of this book.

36. Walden and Walkerdine (1983).

37. Walkerdine (1983).

38. Ibid.

39. Recently, following an examination of girls' comics in which slavery, and the silent acceptance of oppression in order to secure the longed-for happy ending, are the norm, I began to ask people about their fantasies. Fantasies of mutilation amongst women and working-class men abound; of crippled orphans, sickly children, cancer, and anorexia, as though only mutilation ensured the possibility of keeping one's place through self-control and docility produced in the most dangerous and punitive of forms.

40. See Chapter 1 of this book.

41. Play as a pedagogic device as opposed to work is worthy of examination in its own right. I have argued elsewhere that its utilization is both gender- and class-specific (Walkerdine, 1983).

42. Easlea (1980).
43. Lacan (1983).

References

Becker, W.C. (1964) 'Consequences of Different Kinds of Parental Discipline', in M.L. Hoffman and L.W. Hoffman, eds, *Review of Child Development Research*, New York, Russell Sage.

Bernstein, B. (1975) *Class, Codes and Control*, vol. 3. London, Routledge & Kegan Paul.

Bland, L. (1981) 'The Domain of the Sexual: A Response'. *Screen Education*, no. 39.

Broverman, I. *et al.* (1970) 'Sex-role Stereotypes and Clinical Adjustments of Mental Health'. *Journal of Consulting and Clinical Psychology*, no. 34, pp. 1–7.

Davin, A. (1978) 'Imperialism and Motherhood'. *History Workshop Journal*, vol. 5, pp. 9–65.

Donzelot, J. (1979) *The Policing of Families*. London, Hutchinson.

Dyehouse, C. (1977) 'Social Darwinistic Ideas and the Development of Women's Education in England, 1800–1920'. *History of Education*, vol. 3, no. 1.

Easlea, B. (1980) *Witch Hunting, Magic and the New Philosophy*. Hassocks, Sussex, Harvester.

Foucault, M. (1977) *Discipline and Punish*. London, Allen Lane.

Foucault, M. (1979) *The History of Sexuality*. London, Allen Lane.

Foucault, M. (1980) *Power/Knowledge: Selected Interviews and Other Writings 1972–1977*, Colin Gordon. Hassocks, Sussex, Harvester.

Freud, S. (1951) 'The Splitting of the Ego in the Process of Defence', *Standard Edition of the Complete Psychological Works of Sigmund Freud*, vol. 23, London, Hogarth Press (first published 1940).

Hall, C. (1979) 'The Early Formation of Victorian Domestic Ideology', in S. Burman (ed.), *Fit Work for Women*. London, Croom Helm, pp. 15–32.

Hess, R.D. and Shipman, V. (1965) 'Early Experience and the Socialisation of Cognitive Modes in Children', *Child Development*, vol. 36, no. 3, pp. 869–86.

Hollway, W. (1984) 'Gender Identity in Adult Social Relations', in Henriques *et al.*, eds, *Changing the Subject*.

Jones, K. and Williamson, K. (1979) 'The Birth of the Schoolroom', *Ideology and Consciousness*, no. 6.

Labov, W. (1970) 'The Logic of Non-standard English', in F. Williams, ed., *Language and Poverty*. Chicago, Markham.

Lacan, J. (1977) *Ecrits: A Selection*. London, Tavistock.

Lacan, J. (1983) 'God and the *jouissance* of Woman', in J. Mitchell and J. Rose, eds, *Feminine Sexuality: Jacques Lacan and the Ecole Freudienne*. London, Macmillan.

Le Doeff, M. (1981/2) 'Pierre Roussel's Chiasmus', *Screen Education*, vol. 34, pp. 37–50.

Moi, T. (1981) 'Representation of Patriarchy: Sexuality and Epistemology in Freud's Dora', *Feminist Review*, no. 4.

Newson, J. and Newson, E. (1976) *Seven Years Old in an Urban Community*. Harmondsworth, Penguin.

Riley, D. (1983) *War in the Nursery*. London, Virago.

Rose, J. (1978) 'Dora – Fragment of an Analysis'. *m/f*, no. 2.

Sayers, J. (1982) *Biological Politics*. London, Methuen.

Sennett, R. and Cobb, R. (1977) *Hidden Injuries of Class*, Cambridge, Cambridge University Press.

Steedman, C. (1982) *The Tidy House: Little Girls Writing*. London, Virago.

Turner, G.J. (1973) 'Social Class and Children's Language of Control at Age 5 and 7', in B. Bernstein, ed., *Class, Codes and Control*, vol. 2. London, Routledge & Kegan Paul.

Urwin, C. (1984) 'Power Relations and the Emergence of Language', in Henriques *et al.*, eds, *Changing the Subject: Psychology, Social Regulation and Subjectivity*. London, Methuen.

Walden, R. and Walkerdine, V. (1983) 'A for Effort, E for Ability: The Case of Girls and Maths', *Primary Education Review*, Summer.

Walden, R. and Walkerdine, V. (1985a) *Girls and Mathematics: From Primary to Secondary Schooling*. Bedford Way Papers, 24. London, Heinemann.

Walkerdine, V. (1983) 'Girls and Mathematics: Reflections on Theories of Cognitive Development', paper given at the ISSBD Conference, Munich.

Walkerdine, V. (1984) 'Development Psychology and the Child-centred Pedagogy: The Insertion of Piaget's Theory into Primary School Practice', in Henriques *et al.*, eds, *Changing the Subject*.

Weeks, J. (1981) *Sex, Politics and Society*. Harlow, Essex, Longman.

Widdowson, F. (1983) *Going Up to the Next Class: Women in Elementary Teacher-Training*. London, WRRP.

Williams, F, ed. (1970) *Language and Poverty*. Chicago, Markham.

6

Science and the female mind:

the burden of proof

Since its inception, psychology has continuously produced evidence attempting to prove certain facts about gender and sexuality. Many women have been caught up in this spiralling whirlwind, trying to disprove the proofs, countering evidence with other evidence, showing that 'we can do it too'. But what is it about, this relentless will to truth, this push to prove? To cite the example that I shall dwell upon, why does there appear to be an increasing necessity to prove the mathematical inferiority of girls?

Instead of defensiveness, I want to prove the offensive, to turn the tables on this proof. Again and again, the proof is designed to provide positive demonstration that boys possess certain capacities – 'it' – while, with equal certainty, girls have a lack, an absence, to be filled with glowing 'equal opportunities' or early remediation. I would suggest that lurking behind the very positivity of this proof is not a certainty but a fear, a fear of loss of power. Why else should proof be pursued with such unrelenting zeal?

If we, as women, enter that game, we are continually caught in the circuit of claim and counter-claim. We are necessarily on the defensive. This is precisely why it is necessary to turn the tables on proof, to begin to show it up for what it is. Our strong case rests not on our defence but on undermining the very claims upon which the 'truth' about women is founded. We must examine what elaborate fears and desires construct such fantasies and fictions, and read them back as fact.

I shall examine such questions with reference to the issue of girls' performance in mathematics. It is my contention that, constantly and continually, girls have to be proved to fail or to be inferior at mathematics, despite the extreme ambiguity of the evidence. In spite of many obvious successes (Walden and Walkerdine, 1983), girls' performance is constantly demonstrated to be different from, other than that of boys. Its very difference, and the constitution of that difference as in some way a deficiency, surfaces time after time. My contention is that this proof of the existence of thē Other, girls' performance as difference, is a constant reassertion that 'woman' exists in her difference from and therefore deficiency in contrast to those rational powers of the mind that are a constituent of 'man'. Female equivalence, or an absence of difference, therefore presents a constant threat to sexual difference and to the existence of 'man' as supreme and omnipotent mathematician, the architect of 'reason's dream', created in the image of God, 'the divine mathematician'.*

But if 'man' is itself an elaborate fiction, a fantasy of total control, what is being controlled, what loss guarded against? Although mathematical reason is often presented as the ultimate certainty, we might see it rather as an elaborate construction, a discourse itself constructed out of fear, a power built on the terror of powerlessness. If 'woman' is subservient in this fantasy, then any failure to find difference threatens the very possibility or existence of that power. Thus it might be said that proof itself is vital to the maintenance of that power. The stories have to be constantly retold (Bhabha, 1984), the truths produced afresh.

It is in this respect that evidence plays a vital part in the construction of a 'truth' about mathematical performance. Modern psychological knowledge is founded upon the demonstration of truth according to the production of evidence, backed by certain kinds of truth-tests or guarantees (statistical sources, for example) and certain methodological criteria that define how and within what limits acceptable evidence may be produced. Thus psychology produces knowledges which have powerful and real effects upon the practices that depend on them. For example, modern methods of teaching mathematics depend largely upon the possibility of observing, monitoring, and developing 'mathematical thinking'. Therefore pedagogic practices themselves depend upon the production of similar evidence in the very production of 'pedagogic facts' in the classroom.

---

*In this analysis, my use of the terms 'man' and 'woman' refers to a whole body of work which does not equate the signifiers 'man' and 'woman' with actual men and women. It is precisely this difference which allows the possibility of 'man' and 'woman' as fictions, invested with fantasy. The relations, for example, between actual men and 'man' is the object of a vast amount of work within post-structuralism and cultural appropriations of Lacanian psychoanalysis. For psychologists interested in gender, however, it is crucial because psychology claims to be talking about 'the real' of sex and gender. This means that proof becomes what we can know of the real. This kind of analysis, however, aims to deconstruct the claims of such positivism. For further work in this area see, for example, Elizabeth Cowie (1978).

The most developed analysis of the modern production of scientific truth and the effects of that truth on modern forms of government is to be found in the work of Michel Foucault. I shall rely on his analysis of power/knowledge (Foucault, 1977; Henriques *et al.*, 1984) to examine the relationship between, on the one hand, fantasy and fiction, and on the other, the production of proof as fact which is utilized within educational practices for the administration of actual children, thereby having powerful effects. This analysis of the relation of knowledge and power differs from that in which science is contrasted with ideology, or in which power is taken to be a possession such that schooling reproduces relations of production by virtue of the institutional power of teachers. Such formulations tend to rely on power as in imposition through the overt and hidden curriculum. Rather, it is necessary to understand the school as a place in which certain truths have constantly to be proved. It is therefore a site of production in its own right.

My argument is that the school is a place in which the fantasy becomes inscribed in fact, a truth which is to be proved. In developing this analysis, I shall seek to do two things. The first is to examine how the power/knowledge relations are set up to prove the mathematical inferiority of girls. The second is to explore how such relations are lived in the classroom, so that power becomes inscribed in the mastery of mathematical discourse and in the articulation of rational argument. I shall tentatively suggest that the fantasies inscribed in that power are played out with respect to sexual difference by means of a different psychic organization in relation to authority and the demonstration of conflict.

SOME CURRENT EVIDENCE ABOUT GIRLS

In her evidence to the Cockcroft Committee of Inquiry into the Teaching of Mathematics (1982), Hilary Shuard cites historical evidence about the mathematical education of girls. She quotes from the 1912 Report on the Teaching of Mathematics the evidence of a headmistress who states:

> A teacher of girls is, perhaps, too easily satisfied when her pupils are working steadily and conscientiously along the lines which she has laid down for them: a boy is almost certain to go off at a tangent.... Routine does him less harm, because he is less susceptible to its influence. Probably one of the weaknesses of girls is that they will submit to so much dullness without resentment.... Many girls who are, apparently, good workers are mentally lazy; they reproduce, but they do not produce.

We could, of course, pass such a statement off as mere history, asserting that things have changed. However, not only is it common to hear such statements made by current teachers, in almost identical terms, but also Hilary Shuard herself says, 'The evidence cited later in this appendix shows that some of the reasons given for the girls' need of mathematics in the 1912 report are now advanced as reasons for their failure to perform better at the subject' (p. 275). Shuard is clearly in support of these approaches. In an article in *The Times Educational Supplement* she refers to some of the arguments. The article is accompanied by a photograph of junior school girls at work with the following caption: 'Most girls are conscientious and hard-working like these two from ... junior school.' In the body of the article, Shuard reviews some of the evidence that demonstrates not only that girls are well behaved and hard-working in the classroom, but also that they perform better on those aspects of mathematics which are taken to require low-level rule-following, so that we can invoke such factors as these to account for the phenomenon of girls' 'failure' in mathematics.

How does it come about that attributes which on one level might be considered good qualities – industriousness and diligence – are understood as causal of girls' apparent failure in mathematics, and how are such accounts presented as scientific evidence?

HOW TO READ THE DATA

The issues that will form the central focus of this examination are the way in which certain observations made about girls in relation both to their classroom performance and to results on mathematical tests are presented as 'hard evidence'. For example, when confronted with the evidence that girls are, indeed, well behaved, diligent, and so forth, it is hard to discount such data, especially when they accord so nicely with, so to speak, the 'evidence of our own eyes'. Similarly, when Hilary Shuard states that 'The items on which girls did significantly better were easier, with an average success rate of 64%, as against an average success rate of 49% for the items on which boys did significantly better' (Committee of Inquiry into the Teaching of Mathematics, 1982, p. 277), it seems difficult to treat this as anything other than scientific fact. The figures refer to an analysis carried out by Shuard of sex differences in performance on a mathematics survey given to over 2,000 ten-year-olds in England and Wales (Ward, 1978). Shuard goes on to say that girls performed better than boys on 11 out of 91 items, while boys performed significantly better than girls on 14 items. This means that, in fact, on 66 out of 91 items there were no statistically significant sex differences. Since those items on which girls did better were 'easy', Shuard concludes in *The*

Times Educational Supplement article that girls are good only at those aspects of mathematics which are low level. Girls' 'low-level skills' are taken to be produced by rule-following, rote-learning, and improper conceptualization. We can then go on to understand their performance as not really good at all. The same slippage occurs in a review by Geoffrey Howson (1982) of Walden and Walkerdine's *Girls and Mathematics: The Early Years* (1982). In this review, Howson berates us for our interpretation of the Assessment and Performance Unit's data on the sex differences in performance taken from their 1978 survey of mathematical attainment. Suffice it to point out here that the debate centres on matters of 'hard fact', cohering particularly around the issue of the interpretation of statistically significant differences as 'real', taken to means 'of practical consequence'.

Central to Howson's criticism is his statement concerning our 'misinterpretation of hard facts'. Facts are hard, incontrovertible, the rock on which this kind of empirical psychology is founded. Yet it is precisely the very historicity of such facts, the specific conditions for the production of evidence, which I shall now explore.

That body of theory which is used to explain performance in mathematics in the primary school is based on ideas derived from theories of cognitive development. This means that successful mathematics performance is taken to be produced by the attainment of concepts of particular *stages* of logical thought, etc. In this view of learning, *real understanding* (based on concepts) is to be contrasted with *rule-following* or *rote-memorization*, which is stressed by old theories and practices of maths teaching and yields success without the solid foundation of real understanding. (An easy example is the contrast between understanding multiplication as a cumulative addition and only being able to chant one's tables.)

It is therefore axiomatic to the view of mathematics learning dominant in primary schools that proper success is produced on the basis of real understanding. Success is judged in terms of the mastery of concepts in a mode of practice designed to promote and produce 'real understanding' – learning through activity, not chanting tables, etc. Success at mathematics is taken to be an indication of success at reasoning. Mathematics is seen as *development* of the reasoned and logical mind. This is where the important issue of girls' success comes in. Those explanations that allow girls' success at all say that it is based on rule-following and rote-learning, not on proper understanding. Hence they negate that success at the moment they announce it: girls 'just' follow rules – they are good compared with 'naughty' boys who can 'break set' (make conceptual leaps). Girls are good at computation, which is known to be low level. Everything that heralds the success also testifies to it as failure, as something that amounts to nothing.

This explanation is totally *internal* to the theory about the production of reason and rationality. Girls may be able to do mathematics, but good performance is not to be equated with proper reasoning. It is this which is taken into account in relation to later 'failure' where abstract reasoning is required. On the other hand, boys tend to produce evidence of what is counted as 'reason', even though their attainment may itself be relatively poor. This differentiation between classroom performance, its posited cause, and therefore the problem of 'the real', returns again and again. Throughout the age-range, girls' good performance is downplayed while boys' often relatively poor attainment is taken as evidence of real understanding such that any counter-evidence (poor attainment, poor attention, and so forth) is explained as peripheral to the real (Walden and Walkerdine, 1983). It is interesting that in the case of girls (as in all judgements about attainment), attainment itself is not seen as a reliable indicator. In this view, right attainment can, in principle, be produced for wrong reasons. It becomes important, therefore, to establish as permissible only that attainment taken as premised on 'real understanding'. Only this attainment, then, is *real*. The rest, although apparently real, is actually false.

Counting girls' performance as evidence is not distinct from the issue of what it is taken to be evidence of. We have not only to debate about the data but also to engage with why this distinction is made at all, what it means, and what its effects are in terms of practical consequences for girls' education. Classically (within philosophy, for example), the truth of such statements has been the subject of epistemological critiques. But what the latter do is treat truth as though it were a timeless matter, separating the conditions of the production of truth from that truth itself. Rather than discuss the merits and demerits of epistemology, we need to examine how the *truth* about girls comes to be understood in these terms at all. The question is not 'Are the arguments true?' but 'How is this truth constituted, how is it possible, and what effects does it have?' Arguments derived from Foucault can help us begin to deconstruct this truth about girls. Only if we understand its historical production and its effectivity can we begin to go beyond it. I will argue that we can chart the historical antecedents of the position that females do not possess a capacity for reason and so document how and why the arguments in support of that position have such force now, and how we might challenge them.

REASON AND GENDER

My argument, in a nutshell, is that ideas about reason and reasoning cannot be understood historically outside considerations about gender. Since the Enlightenment, if not before, reason, or the Cogito, has been deeply embroiled with attempts to control nature. The rationality of the Cogito was taken to be a kind of rebirth of the rational self, in this case without the intervention of a woman. The rational self was in this sense a profoundly masculine one from which the woman was excluded, her powers not only inferior but also subservient. The 'thinking' subject was male; the female provided the biological prop both to procreation and to servicing the possibility of 'man'.

Perhaps the best-known example of such a philosophy is in the work of Rousseau, who described a 'reasoning woman' as a monster. While Emile's education was a discovery, Sophie's was a lesson in the art of pleasing and being subservient to men. The female 'monster' threatened to wrest control from the man, rather than support its very existence. The reasoning and educated woman as monster may be a very old idea, but it lives on in the many attempts to demonstrate the incompatability of femininity and scientific endeavour. What is of particular concern to us here is the transformation of a philosophical doctrine into the object of a science in which reason became a capacity invested within the body, and later mind, of the man, from which the female was, by definition, excluded.

The development of science from the seventeenth century was intimately connected to the control of nature by man. From the nineteenth century, particularly with the work of Darwin, the human was also accorded the status of natural (rather than God-given). 'Human nature' therefore became the object of a scientific inquiry that, from its inception, was deeply patriarchal. It legitimated doctrines that existed previously within philosophy, and with the transformation of this doctrine into a science, the female body and mind both became objects of the scientific gaze. In this way it began to be possible to make 'true' statements about female nature, no longer an object of debate but resolvable by resort to evidence. Yet 'female nature' does not pre-exist the development of those doctrines, bodies of knowledge, and scientific practices that produced it as its object. In this sense, the truth of scientific statements is not discovered; it is produced.

Moreover, we can monitor the effects of such 'facts' on the fate of particular girls and women. For example, the legitimation of their exclusion and of practices of discrimination could now be based on fact: the *proven* inferiority of girls and women. It was quite common in the nineteenth century to exclude women from higher education and the

professions on the grounds that they were swayed by their emotions and
not, therefore, invested with the capacity to make rational judgements. It is
by arguments such as this that the sexed body (the seat of 'nature')
becomes the site for the production and explanation of mind. Since the
very differentiation between men's and women's bodies is central to this
approach, there is no way reason can ever be gender-neutral.

This shows how we get today's common sense about 'women's minds'
being the opposite of hard sciences and mathematics. Often social
psychologists are content simply to state that these are the views that
women and men, girls and boys have about femininity and masculinity,
perhaps as a function of socioeconomic factors, etc. But unless we
change the way in which such ideas are internal to, and productive of,
the means by which we understand reason, we are left with only attitude
change or economic change as the difference which will make the difference.

Helen Weinreich Haste (1979) reproduces nicely for us the 'common
sense' which accrues from such discourses. She asked science students
and schoolchildren to rate science and scientists on the dimensions of
hard/soft, masculine/feminine, etc. These bipolar constructs, of course,
are already given in the 'common sense' of which I have spoken. It is not
surprising, therefore, that science came out as 'hard, intellect-based,
complex and masculine'. However, what is also important is that there
was no 'feminine discipline' cluster – the arts were not seen as feminine
either (cf. Parker and Pollock, 1981).

Although such work as Weinreich Haste's gives us important information, we need to understand how such views came to be held. Otherwise
we are again left with a quasi-scientific judgement that such views, are
'incorrect', and therefore attitude change is needed to modify them.
Such a position plays down the way in which these are sets of attitudes
about women produced in a manner that is related to central conceptions about science and rationality.

Woman as the object of nineteenth-century science was gentle, not
profound, the holder of the moral order, mothering. The picture painted
was of the weak and fainting women of the Victorian middle classes
whose minds, like butterflies, were unable to concentrate, moving from a
little embroidery to a little this, a little that – gentle accomplishments,
but no profundity. It certainly matters that individual women may not
have fitted this stereotype, but it is equally important that no woman
would be able to stand outside the power of that scientific truth. Women
could resist that power – they could dare to be different. But the
necessity to struggle and the form that struggle took was completely
bound up with determining that truth. And because the account was
located in women's bodies, it immediately placed them as naturally

external to a capacity for reason. It is important not to see this as a distortion or a simple mistake, but as a productive force which had effects.

Developing from this poor, frail, moral woman whose failure to reason was produced through incapacity rather than oppression, we come to the arguments which see it as dangerous for women to reason – physiologically dangerous and endangering the future of the species by engaging in the strain produced by an act so unnatural for women's bodies. By the twentieth century, we see such a view encapsulated, for example, in Felter's 1906 article in *Educational Review*, where he argued that for girls at puberty to use up energy in intellectual work would endanger the development of their reproductive organs, producing the possibility of infertility and thus endangering the species.

Weakness and sensibility are the dominant and distinctive qualities of women.... No doubt this organization was necessary in the sex to which nature was to entrust the repository of the human species.... The latter would have perished a thousand times, had it been reduced to the tardy and uncertain help of cold reason. (p. 50)

What a burden, therefore, girls and women had to bear; not only were they harming themselves but they were now also endangering the species. Such moral imperatives would render opposition difficult for girls, and it is not surprising that those who opposed were understood as 'hard', 'masculine' women of dubious sexuality, the target of pejorative evaluations and general scorn.

The regulation of sexuality therefore became central to such concerns; femininity itself became the target and object of a variety of scientific theories and medico-legal practices (Foucault, 1979; Weeks, 1979; Bland, 1981). The rearing of children in the privacy of the home became a norm, from which deviations could be plotted as abnormality. This relates specifically to the rise of the bourgeoisie in which the woman becomes 'mother', looking after children, replacing the employed nanny of upper-class homes. Within that deviation, issues of class are foregrounded, not as causal but rather in the displays of abnormal, nonnurturant, passionate and active sexuality amongst working-class women. At the same time, teaching became a profession open to bourgeois women, requiring 'natural capacities for nurturance' to facilitate child development. The rise in bourgeois women's education and in teacher training go hand in hand (Dyehouse, 1977; Widdowson, 1983).

It is also possible to demonstrate why particular struggles on the part of women took the form they did. If these practices excluded women from various public domains by confining them to the domestic sphere, then clearly resistance by certain groups of women would be concerned with gaining entry into the barred fields of education, the academy, and politics. Indeed, women's struggles in education related specifically to being allowed to enter the public domain. Changes in educational practices at the time made the written examination the arbiter of success and entry into higher education. Ability was then taken to be established by examination performance. This allowed the possibility of entry into the academy on the basis of merit rather than birth, and was particularly important to the emergent bourgeoisie.

Bourgeois women's resistance, therefore, took the form of being allowed to enter examinations – to prove themselves equal to men. Cambridge local examinations were opened to girls in 1863, but many problems remained. Women had still to prove themselves equal to men – that is, as rational. They had to fight on the same terms and could not change them. Their examination failure would only further the cause of their incapacity, as is still the case. Girls entering these exams had to struggle against enormous odds. Not only were they putting their 'maternal femininity' at risk, but often mathematics teaching in the schools was totally inadequate.

Making exam entry the focus of the debate also had consequences that are still significant today. Since this competition could only ever be open to a small percentage of girls, the focus became the recruitment of girls into higher education and the professions. Then as now, the focus on failure was concentrated almost exclusively on failure to obtain high-grade passes in O level exams and to enter for the university entrance A level exams. Through science, the majority of girls in the nineteenth century were positioned fairly and squarely as mothers, and through science their effectiveness in that job was monitored.

So, discussions about failure have focused on a minority of girls. Of course, it is not surprising that later science 'discovered' the 'female intellect'. Thus women, taken also to possess the capacity to reason, were allowed to enter the competition, if they had *enough* ability. But this means that the terms of the debate are never changed: it is still up to women to prove themselves equal to men. I have tried to show why we should not unquestioningly accept these terms but should question their very foundation. We are not duty-bound to accept existing truth conditions. I would argue that showing the truth about girls to be a production in which there are no *simple* matters of fact is a central and strategic part of our struggle.

If those successes for which girls have struggled are refused as data, then it continues to be possible to explain, as a fault within women themselves, the relatively small number of women in the professions (except the caring professions, to which women are 'naturally' suited). 'Brilliant' women are few indeed in number, but women's painstaking attention to detail, and their 'capacity for hard work', make them excellent material for the support of a 'brilliant academic' role. For the rational self of the Cogito, like the reasoning child, cognitive development, 'proper conceptualization' and rationality are attained naturally; no work is involved. In modern lower-school practices, work is downplayed in favour of play. When girls work hard, therefore, there is something wrong. Women's labour (domestic and otherwise) makes intellectual inquiry, as play, relatively easy; it shoulders all the work that makes such creativity possible.

CARING AND THE CARING PROFESSIONS: THE OTHER OF REASON

Within both the development of women's education and the rise of child-centred education, there are important shifts in the definition of pedagogy which I have charted elsewhere (Walkerdine, 1984a, b). For the present purposes, however, let us dwell on the concept of 'the child' (gender unspecified) who is taken to develop within a 'facilitating environment'. The two terms form a couple: a *child* developing in an *environment*. Further analysis suggests that the mother and the teacher both become part of the environment. They are defined by the very qualities that are opposite to those of 'the child', who is active, inquiring and whose activity leads to 'real understanding'. The teacher and the mother, by contrast, are necessary not to instruct but to watch, observe, monitor, and facilitate development. They are defined as 'passive' in relation to the child's 'active'. They are nurturant, facilitating, sensitive and supportive, and they know when to intervene but not to interfere.

I have argued elsewhere that this opposition of the passive teacher to the active child is necessary to support the possibility of the illusion of autonomy and control upon which the children-centred pedagogy is founded (see Chapter 3 of this book). In this sense, then, the 'capacity for nurturance' grounded in a naturalized femininity, the object of the scientific gaze, becomes the basis for woman's fitness for the facilitation of knowing and the reproduction of the knower, which is the support for, and yet opposite of, the production of knowledge. The production of knowledge is thereby separated from its reproduction and split along a sexual division which renders production and reproduction the natural capacities of the respective sexes.

The facilitating and nurturant Other is necessary, in both domestic and pedagogic practices, to the possibility of a naturalized sequence of development that is facilitated in the child. Certain things follow from this. For instance, 'the child' as signifier within the circulation of meanings in developmental psychology, family, and pedagogic practices sits uncomfortably upon actual little girls. For if 'woman' is Other to rationality, its support and facilitation, how is 'girl' lived: as 'child' or potential 'woman'? There are certain contradictions in these positions which are lived out in the very practices for the production of mathematical attainment.

Let us explore two aspects of this. First, girls' attainment, relative to boys', is itself not in any simple sense the problem. Rather, the pointed cause invests the attainment with value as reproduction (rote-learning, rule-following) and not production (real understanding). It follows, therefore, that this attainment, while the object of much agonizing about the poor performance of girls, is precisely that combination which is required for the entry of girls into the 'caring professions', in this case specifically the profession of teaching young children. Recruitment to elementary teacher training requires advanced qualifications, but usually a lower standard (poorer pass marks, for example) than that required for university entrance.

Second, the production of reasoning requires an investment of desire in knowing, as in the phrase 'attracted to ideas', for example. Although I shall not develop this argument here, I have suggested (in Chapter 5) that rational argument requires the transformation of conflict into discourse, such that the nurturant Other facilitates an illusion of autonomy or control, rendering invisible the *power* of parenting and teaching. In addition, mathematical reasoning presumes mastery of a discourse in which the universe is knowable and manipulable according to particular mathematical algorithms. This, along with the production of 'hard facts', is usually understood as the very basis of certainty. Conversely, however, we might understand it as the fear, the necessity of proof against the terror of its Other – that is, loss of certainty, control, and attempted control of loss. We might understand it as the impossibility of the object of desire, 'woman', and elaborate fantasies to control consequent desire and avoid dependency or powerlessness.

Such sentiments may be glimpsed in the work of Piaget, one of the founding fathers of the scientization of natural reason. He stated, in an early (1920) paper, 'The love of beautiful bodies elevates itself to the love of beautiful souls and from there to the very idea of beauty' (Piaget, 1977). The love of beautiful bodies – passion – was to be left behind in childhood sexuality. The move from pre-logical thought consists in the move towards logic and away from clouding emotion and sexuality. Although Piaget's work is classically considered as gender-neutral, it is most significant that it is founded on the very same premiss as the move towards natural rationality that excludes femininity. In this respect, then, it can be argued that the effects of such assumed gender-neutrality are not neutral as far as sexuality, and therefore the dichotomy male/female, are concerned. The regulation of female sexuality and its medicalization in the nineteenth century pathologize passion in favour of nurturance. Passion and desire become problematic, for example, in the subsequent psychoanalytic work of the British School following Winnicott and Bowlby, in which attachment, bonding and nurturance replace passion and desire.

CURRENT EDUCATIONAL PRACTICES

In modern elementary schooling, the 'nature of the child' is the bedrock upon which all educational practice is founded. It is the monitoring, observing, and facilitating of that sequence of development to which practice is devoted. The dichotomy between rote-learning and real understanding, activity and passivity, which I have already noted with respect to the performance of girls and boys and teachers and children, appears also with respect to the shift from the old 'traditional' pedagogy to the modern 'child-centred' practices.

In such practices, teaching as the transmission of facts was understood as regimenting and stifling discipline, to be replaced by a classroom in which, based on the facts of the New Psychology, everyone was to learn at their own pace (Walkerdine, 1984a). In consequence, into the new pedagogy was built the shadow of its Other, the old pedagogy – chalk and talk, the fearful and dangerous spectre of authoritarianism. Thus any evidence of rote-learning was taken to be not only success for the wrong reasons but a danger sign, itself threatening the moral order, a pathology to be remedied. It is the location of this feared and frightening Other that it is important to understand with respect to those classifications, particularly where they relate to girls' performance. Yet, as I argued above, the contradictions in the practice set girls up to achieve the very thing which is simultaneously desired and feared – passivity. It is feared in children, and yet it is the very quality desired in care-givers.

With this in mind, I want to explore briefly some aspects of the production and regulation of girls' attainment. Here, I will dwell specific-ally on the distinction between the desired and feared qualities, to show the double-bind of positions for girls and to suggest some possibilities for the continuity of girls' particular classroom style in the face of pedagogic practices designed to render its opposite the norm for all children.

The question remains, of course, what precisely is it that produces these current truths? I have tried to demonstrate that current claims themselves rest upon a constant 'will to truth' (Foucault, 1977, 1979) which, while investing certainty in 'man', constantly seeks to find its Other and opposite in 'woman'. This truth is constantly reproven within classrooms in which the very apparatuses differentiate between success and its posited causes. This has profound material effects upon the life chances of girls.

In the following pages, I shall do no more than exemplify how we might approach the issue of the production of femininity and masculinity with respect to schooling in general and mathematics in particular. I want to point to the relationship between the effectivity of positions of child, girl, boy, teacher, and how they circulate as signifiers within the discourses of the child-centred pedagogy. However, their effectivity on actual children is neither fixed nor singular. Particular girls, for example, become subjected within the practices in so far as they provide evidence that itself is then read within the discourse which positions them, for example, as 'hard-working' and 'not brilliant'. Such positions have real and material effects on the life chances of these girls. However, this is not coterminous with the psychic economy into which the girls are inserted.

It is necessary to make reference to certain relations. It is suggested above that within current school mathematics practices, certain fantasies, fears and desires invest 'man' with omnipotent control of a calculable universe, which at the same time covers a desperate fear of the desire of the Other, 'woman'. 'Woman' becomes the repository of all the dangers displaced from the child, itself 'father' to the man. As we have seen, the necessity to prove the mathematical inferiority of girls is motivated not by a certainty but by a terror of loss. In all these respects, I have wanted to suggest a story in which these very fantasies, fears, desires become the forces that produce the actual effectivity of the construction of fact, of the current discursive practices in which these fantasies are played out and in actual positions in such practices which, since they can be proved to exist, literally have power over the lives of girls and boys, as in Foucault's power/knowledge couple.

What might it mean to examine how these positions are lived? It is my contention (following Henriques et al., 1984) that the signifier 'woman' does not describe or represent a unitary signified. Rather, any woman exists at the nexus of contradictory discourses, practices, and therefore positions. In this case, we could take the signifiers 'child', 'teacher' and 'girl', or the dichotomies 'active'/'passive', 'rote-learning'/'real understanding', as examples. We can ask how the contradictory positions created within these practices are lived and how these effect the production of subjectivity – for example fears, desires and fantasies (cf. Chapter 5). In the interest of illuminating these practices and this production, it will be necessary to make brief reference to the necessity and possibility of reworking certain concepts from Freudian psychoanalysis.

The first and most important thing to state is that there are no unitary categories 'boys' and 'girls'. If actual boys and girls are created at the intersection of multiple positionings, they are inscribed as masculine and feminine. It follows, therefore, that girls can display 'real understanding' or boys 'nurturance'. What matters is what the effects of these positions are. Walden and Walkerdine (1983) have explored the way in which some girls do indeed appear to display that combination of qualities that makes them both the 'ideal girl' and the 'ideal child'. This, however, is rare. Here, therefore, I shall concentrate on the designation 'rote-learning' and its related signifiers 'rule-following', 'hard work', and 'passivity'.

At first sight it seems curious that such qualities could be displayed inside a pedagogy designed not only specifically to produce their opposite but also to avoid their appearance at all costs. It is important that in this respect the pathologization of these qualities, linked to the fear of totalitarianism and authoritarianism, has related to certain developments in post-Freudian psychoanalysis, notably the work of Klein. However, much as their appearance is dreaded, it is also needed. Such ascriptions are frequently correlated with 'helpfulness', in which helpful children become an important part of the maintenance of calm, order, and the smooth regulation of the classroom. It is common for female teachers to fear such qualities as much as they want them. In a recent study (Walden and Walkerdine, 1983), many female teachers openly despised the very qualities of helpfulness and careful, neat work which at the same time they constantly demanded from their pupils, often holding up the work books of such girls as examples, or reprimanding the boys for not behaving like the 'responsible' girls. Yet they would simultaneously present such characteristics in girls as a problem. Furthermore, it was common for female teachers to dislike intensely the girls who displayed them. They would describe them as 'boring', 'wet', and 'wishy-washy'. Such girls had no 'spark', 'fire', or 'brilliance'. Yet it is such girls who had become these teachers. When describing themselves as children or making reference to girls who reminded them of themselves, it was precisely such qualities that they discussed. They made reference to their own 'passivity', 'lack of confidence', and 'getting trampled on'. They found it easier to find desirable qualities in boys, the Other of their desire. This suggests that their own identification with the girls in their class was extremely problematic, and also that this helped to produce an elaborate splitting such that the desirable qualities of children were seen as displayed in boys and yet disavowed in girls, and in themselves as teachers. Not surprisingly, then, it is the qualities relating to femininity as nurturance which were posited consciously and obviously as desirable in both teachers and girls alike.

In the classroom discourse, there appears to be an *overt* message concerning activity, exploration, openness, and so forth, derived from the child-centred pedagogy. However, Walden's (unpublished) work in primary classrooms suggests that the discourse of good behaviour, neatness and rule-following exists *covertly* alongside the overt message. It would have to be covert because it is the exact opposite of what is supposed to take place. Moreover, all those aspects – good behaviour, neatness and rule-following – are taken to be harmful to psychological and moral development. Thus they act as a fear- and guilt-inducing opposite. It is not surprising that teachers cannot afford to acknowledge the presence of such qualities in the classroom or, if they do, to pathologize their appearance in girls, while failing to recognize that they are demanding the very qualities they simultaneously disparage. This possibility allows us to explore how girls come to desire in themselves qualities that appear opposite to those of 'the child' whom the pedagogy is set up to produce. Clearly, further investigation would have to engage with the classroom production of such contradictions, examining both the overt pedagogy and its covert shadow.

It is common in some psychoanalytic discourses, for example, to counterpose 'fantasy' to 'reality', yet it is this division that appears most questionable. After all, if some girls respond to the covert regulation of the classroom, we cannot say that such behaviour is pathological with respect to the real. It is precisely that certain aspects of the regulation of the practices are themselves suppressed. Simultaneously, the 'reality' of the child-centred pedagogy seems to be the object of an elaborate fantasy. It appears that here in the practices there circulates a vast and complex network of meanings, in which the play of desire, of teachers for children, of children for each other, envy, jealousy, rivalry, and so forth are continually created and re-created. It is necessary not to counterpose fantasy to reality, but to demonstrate how fantasies themselves are lived, played out, and worked through in their inscriptions in the veridicality of discourses and practices.

NICE, KIND, AND HELPFUL

In our work with girls, throughout all age-groups, 'nice' and 'kind' and 'helpful' were the three commonest signifiers posited as the most desirable characteristics for girls to possess. Nice, kind, and helpful girls are like the teacher. Within this discourse, anger and conflict are displaced. Central to the child-centred pedagogy is the displacement of conflict into rational argument. Authoritarian teaching as the recognition of facts, where power is overt, is replaced by covert power in which the overthrow of the Other is by means of mastery of a rational discourse. Power is apparently invested in equality, in which the teacher, like the child, can be 'won over' by an argument. The pedagogy aims to produce such 'rational powers of the mind'. However, girls who are nice, kind, and helpful are guardians of the moral order, keepers of the rules. In Chapter 1, I made reference to the sub-teacher position adopted by some young girls, where helpfulness was closely linked to taking the position of the teacher – that is, helping other children complete their work and disciplining them. A girl so positioned could hardly break rules for which she is responsible as guardian. Yet 'breaking rules' is read as a precursor of 'breaking set', the very basis of rational argument.

Conflict itself within the pedagogy is *overtly* produced as positive if it becomes rational argument. However, covertly, the rules of the class-room are to be kept and many girls are set to keep them. That such girls strive to avoid being 'told off' is therefore hardly surprising. It suggests that two different readings of authority circulate and pupils are set up to read these differently, according to their investment of desire and the fantasied qualities of the Other. Some girls' readings are not patho-logical. They are produced in the actuality of the covert regulation of the classroom. They are lived out through their desires, as much as those of the boys. Thus the fact that some boys experience authority as something to be mastered, while some girls experience it as brutal and to be avoided at all costs, becomes more understandable. Girls who strive to avoid 'being told off' also maintain a position as moral guardian. It is a powerful position, but it means that the very act of overthrowing the Other in rational argument is likely to produce a terror of loss of position. Similarly, overthrowing a brutal authority risks an outpouring of aggres-sion, the terrifying fear of destruction or being destroyed. It would seem, therefore, that it would be very difficult indeed for such girls to produce the very behaviour (rational argument) that would win them the acco-lade of 'real understanding'. For example, attack and defence are read as part of an academic game in which the conflict involved is downplayed and displaced. But if the authority provides a site of protection from the threat of destruction or being destroyed, rational argument may appear as overwhelming conflict, a game in which the stakes are much too high to enter (see Chapter 5). There is therefore a specific range of inter-actions and behaviours that are recognized as real understanding. They consist of a certain kind of articulateness in which the rules of the mathe-matical discourse are challenged in such a way that there is often an explicit threat to the teacher.

Other forms of challenge to the teacher's authority come from breaking the rules. By and large, boys do both, but with different consequences. The challenge to the teacher that comes from an attack on the discourse itself is understood by the teacher as 'clever'. When it is displayed by girls, it poses more of a problem. In one first-year secondary class, for example, the top girl was considered brilliant and hard-working by the teacher but 'boring' by the other girls. The next girl, Emma, displayed those characteristics considered positive when displayed in boys. According to the (male) teacher, she is 'interested in ideas and abstract problems', 'a great problem-solver, natural talent'. She is 'constantly trying out ideas'; this makes her 'lazy, selfish'. She constantly challenges the teacher's authority within the discourse – that is, she challenges the mathematical rules with which he operates. Yet this very kind of behaviour puts her in a double-bind that is not present for the boys. Boys are often understood as 'lazy', for example, but this is seen as a rather charming feature. Of the girls in the class, many picked Emma as the very person they were glad they were not. They were afraid of being like her and noted a lack of femininity, saying of her, 'She's skinny'.

Consider also here two assessments of boys and girls made by two elementary school teachers talking about the children in their class: 'Boys are more creative, divergent, tangential. They see more opportunities to explore. Girls are harder working but worry more' and 'Boys do tend to make an intellectual leap towards the end of the third year [of the junior school, i.e., age ten]. Perhaps girls are more accurate up to that point.'

THE DISAVOWAL OF WORK

As we saw in Chapter 5, it is quite common for middle-class men to talk about challenging the teacher's authority as a form of resistance which they knew was better than the anti-school position adopted by many working-class boys. These boys are brilliant – their nonconformity is the mark of their cleverness. They do not drop out; they get places in universities: 'Being an intellectual was an act of fucking defiance by the time I was fifteen or sixteen' and 'I remember things like ... I remember realizing that a very good strategy for throwing the authorities – foxing them, tricking them – was to just mix boundaries.... I remember going into a physics lesson one day with a copy of Joyce's *Ulysses*.... I realized that by being an intellectual you could even gain the support of the anti-school people, because the teacher came in and said, "What are you doing bringing this filth into the classroom?" and I said, "I got it from the school library".'

In addition, such men disparage hard work. An Oxford ex-public school boy said on the subject of finals, 'I went to see my tutor one day and he said, "How much work are you doing?" I said, "Well, you know, seven or eight hours a day". "Do you want to get a First!" I said, "No." He said, "Four or five hours is quite enough". And it was true.'

The child-centred pedagogy disavows 'work'. Hard work is both a danger sign and becomes converted into pleasurable activity, play. Playing is taken to be what children do naturally. Yet if we pursue further the hidden and subverted Others, the categories of opposition, work appears as just such a category. Domestic and manual labour are opposites to intellectual labour – the symbolic play of the Logos. Yet domestic and manual labour are taken to indicate a lack, something missing. Of course, intellectual activity, in whatever location, is quite impossible without the other kinds of labour that provide a servicing function. The passive and facilitating labour of the elementary school teacher is one such example.

In the domestic labour of the home, in modern approaches to child-rearing as in teaching, women are supposed to observe and monitor, cater for the freedom and playfulness of the children. Their own labours that allow this to happen are totally subsumed under the fact that play is facilitated in children and therefore proper and not deviant development is assured. The labour of women teachers of young children relates directly to the concerns mentioned earlier in relation to the history of women's education. That is, women can be educated enough to join the caring professions – to reproduce the knowers – yet not enough to know.

Many current practices base their discrimination against girls on the 'hard facts' of science, where proof positive is what is taken to be the factual basis of those practices which, for example, require higher pass marks of girls than boys on transfer from primary to secondary schooling on the grounds that girls' early good performance is surpassed by boys' later spurt. However, it is common to enter girls at the age of sixteen for less prestigious public examinations than boys on the grounds that girls' lack of confidence is better suited to their success in such exams. Even though the girls outperform the boys in class, it is the boys who are entered for the more prestigious exams. As one teacher put it to me, if he had a boy and girl in his class who had the same level of attainment, but the boy was 'lazy' and the girl 'hard-working', he would enter the boy and not the girl for the more prestigious exam. His rationale was that if the boy could produce such attainment without apparent effort, what would he produce if he tried! On the other hand, the girl must be working to the 'limit of her capacity'. Her attainment therefore counted for so much less than his!

It is overwhelmingly the case that those women who enter school teaching (particularly at the elementary level) were girls who did well at school, but whose success is attributed to hard work, diligence and not brilliance. Recently, when discussing some fieldwork on six-year-old girls with the female staff of the school in which the work had been carried out, I talked about one of the girls, Jenny, doing well at six, who was quiet, diligent, confident, but hard-working. I said that she reminded me of myself (I had been called a 'plodder' at school). To a woman they all said that they had been thinking the same thing about themselves! And indeed this is accurate – they would have been recruited into teaching from the ranks of the hard workers. The same phenomenon that we witnessed in the classroom was intimately bound up with themselves, with how they came to be what they are, with their own insecurities about not being 'good enough' (supportive, facilitative, or nurturant), and with continued effort at self-effacement.

As much as masculinity is invested in mastery of the Logos, of the Cogito, and therefore of control of the universe of rational discourse, femininity is inscribed in its Other. Masculine desire might relate, in Lacan's terms, to being the object of the mother's desire, but femininity must traverse a complex path of shifting relations. The little girl's desire, in being the Other, the object of the male fantasy of omnipotence, invests her with a fantasy of protection, of safety from conflict for ever. Lacan's (1983) account of female paranoia is very instructive in this respect. If masculinity, mastery, and rational argument is winning, what would the little girl gain or stand to lose if she could overthrow the master? Where would her protector be? Whose desire would shine its light on her face, waiting for the returned gaze? Mastery of the universe, of rational discourse, might contain a terror of loss of control, of certainty; yet, equally, its opposite and Other, femininity, might relate to another terror, a loss of any object of desire. These fantasies, circulating in their complementarity, might act powerfully to produce and reproduce such positions. In this view, therefore, complex fears and desires are invested in the continuity of these positions as much as their transformation. Offering girls, as is often suggested, Lego and boys dolls, can hardly match the whirlpool of such desire. Yet the deconstruction of the fiction and an exploration of the fantasy upon which our current facticity is based might allow us to begin to search afresh for the conditions of possibility for our transformation.

REFERENCES

Bhabha, H. (1984) 'The Other Question: The Stereotype and Colonial Discourse'. Screen, no. 24, 18–36.
Bland, L. (1981) 'The Domain of the Sexual: A Response'. Screen Education, no. 39, 56–68.
Committee of Inquiry into the Teaching of Mathematics (1982) Mathematics Counts (The

Cockroft Report). London: Her Majesty's Stationery Office.
Cowie, E. (1978) 'Woman as Sign', m/f, no. 1, 49–64.
Dyehouse, C. (1977) 'Social Darwinistic Ideas and the Development of Women's Education in England, 1800–1920'. History of Education, no. 3, 41–58.
Felter, G. (1906) Educational Review, no. 31, 26–35.
Foucault, M. (1977) Discipline and Punish. Harmondsworth, Penguin.
Foucault, M. (1979) The History of Sexuality, vol. 1. Harmondsworth, Penguin.
Henriques, J., Hollway, W., Urwin, C., Venn, C. and Walkerdine, V. (1984) Changing the Subject. New York, Methuen.
Howson, G. (1982) Review of Walden and Walkerdine's 'Girls and Mathematics: The Early Years' Education, no. 159, 16–18.
Lacan, J. (1983) 'God and the jouissance of Woman', in J. Mitchell and J. Rose (eds), Feminine Sexuality: Jacques Lacan and the École Freudienne. London, Macmillan.
Parker, R., and Pollock, G. (1981) Old Mistresses. London, Routledge & Kegan Paul.
Piaget, J. (1977) 'Psychoanalysis and its Relation with Child Psychology, in H.E. Gruber and J.J. Vonèche, (eds), The Essential Piaget. London, Wildwood.
Walden, R. Girls' Achievement at Mathematics: How a Myth is Made. Doctoral Dissertation, University of London.
Walden, R. and Walkerdine, V. (1982) Girls and Mathematics: The Early Years. London, Heinemann.
Walden R. and Walkerdine, V. (1983) Girls and Mathematics: From Primary to Secondary Schooling. London, Heinemann.
Walkerdine, V. (1984a) 'Developmental Psychology and the Child-centred Pedagogy', in J. Henriques et al., eds, Changing the Subject.
Walkerdine, V. (1984b) 'It's Only Natural: Rethinking Child-centred Pedagogy', in A.M. Wolpe and J. Donald, eds, Is There Anyone Here from Education? London, Pluto.
Walkerdine, V. 'Deconstructing Identity: Reconstructing Subjectivity', in K. Gergen and J. Shotter, eds, Social Constructionism in Psychology.
Ward, M. (1978) Mathematics and the Ten Year Old Child. London, Methuen.
Weeks, J. (1979) Sex, Politics and Society. London, Longman.
Weinreich Haste, H. (1979) 'What Sex is Science?' in O. Hartnett, G. Boden and M. Fuller, eds, Sex Role Stereotyping. London, Tavistock.
Widdowson, F. (1983) Going Up to the Next Class: Women and elementary teacher training. London, Hutchinson/WRRC.

7

Notes written after an interview for a

job

(Used in an in-service course with primary teachers, 1985)

The taxi drops me in front of this building – a model of post-war educational expansion, all glass intercut with purple boarding. Immediately I am reminded of the new grammar school I went to in 1958. As I walk up the steps I shudder. I had been in this town for three years and yet never entered here. The entrance hall buzzes with the conversation of women, mostly young and with local accents. Children's work is displayed, tacked to the corrugated card in the foyer. I begin to feel sick as I mount the stairs. At the end of the day I turn down a responsible job, nauseated by the emotions that are welling inside me and yet realizing how much those emotions, the conflicts and contradictions, are those of women – women trying to progress in education, and higher education particularly. It is some aspects of those desires and contradictions that I wish to discuss by raising these examples.

For many years after I entered higher education at postgraduate level, I was dogged by a feeling of failure, a lack which had to be kept hidden. People would often ask me in all innocence where I did my first degree. After all, it is not common to undertake a PhD in developmental psychology without a secure academic background. Sometimes I would lie. At other times, half in pride, half in terror, I would reply that I didn't have a first degree. My impression was that many people were shocked, but some – mainly, I noticed, the men – were charmed. I became for them the epitome of the clever working-class girl from the North – a teacher who made it! They would offer me patronage – a patronage which, in my feelings of inadequacy and isolation, I would want to accept and yet feel disgust at being set up as the object of this romantic vision – like the sexual fantasy of the slave, the orphan, the waif and stray who becomes the protégée of the prince, the nobleman in the protection of the court. Rags to riches. They wanted to be the protector and I wanted to bask in their protection. It provided an entry into a bourgeois world and an academic elite, so unlike the protection of, and dependency on, my mother. She, in my fantasy, was going to trap me, tie my hands to the sink; while they would liberate me to the possibility of my entry into education. I am sure that many of us have experienced this patronage and are ashamed of our past. But I want to suggest that such a desire, and its contradictions, are central to our understanding of certain issues relevant to the education of women.

Let me pursue this story a little further. When I walk into the foyer of the Institute of Education I feel none of that nausea. It is not a 'training college'. There are no eighteen-year-olds to remind me of my past. It is a vast and prestigious building in the centre of a sophisticated and cosmopolitan city. The shame I feel is the shame of the lure of these things and the terrible disdain for the provincial, the feminine. Here I can feel that I am an academic. Many times in the past I have said, in times of distress, that people would 'find out that I am only a teacher'. These were usually times of acute intellectual insecurity. Somebody would find out that, after all, I am stupid.

'Being a primary school teacher is not second-rate', shouted one of my friends as I was wallowing in envy and self-pity. 'But it is!' I replied. And here we come to the arguments about the status and importance of the caring professions, the minefield of the 'status' arguments about mothering. 'Caring for children is a central job, which should be accorded more status.' I wish I felt it were that simple. Indeed, being a primary school teacher is second-rate. It is the province of women. It is a way out for working-class girls (out of what and into what?). When I left school I wanted to get out, to go to London, to leave home. I wanted to be a teacher because I was afraid. I went to Goldsmiths' because my teacher told me that it was the best training college in the country. It was also in London. To leave home for London when everyone in my family had always been local, got married and had children. To get out, yes. But to arrive at Goldsmiths' and discover that some people were doing degrees and that they looked down on those doing teacher training! Second-rate, when I had been told it was the best! I bought a London University scarf, but it was a pretence. There is no doubt that my later entry into higher education was mixed with these aspirations. They are about gender and about class. I did envy, and I did want.

PART II

Fictioning Femininity

The essays and other pieces in this part were written between 1984 and 1989. They include some previously unpublished pieces as well as published work. All deal more explicitly with psychoanalysis and the fictional representations of girls and women. It is clear that all these pieces were profoundly influenced by my going into analysis and the insights into my own history which followed from that. In the later pieces I begin to challenge the feminist assumption that our phantasies are encompassed only by being the object of the male gaze. I suggest that there is 'more than meets the eye', that there is 'something else' hidden beneath the surface representations – something which has to be defended from exposure, something which the surface smile, the returned look, covers over. This is very frightening because it appears to transgress the cosy fictional spaces set up for women to enter. Socialization does not work, the roles do not fit, yet how painful and difficult it is to bring to the surface that which was never absent but had to be so carefully hidden from view!

This work was also influenced by my beginning to make art work after a gap of over twenty years. Why did I stop that activity which at school I loved more than anything else? To be a good girl, to be a teacher? Certainly in my mind women artists were associated with a deviant sexuality for which I longed (wild hair, paint-spattered clothes, untidy appearance) but I was terrified of revealing my longing to the world. What, then, lurked beneath the careful nurturance of the primary school teacher? What had to be defended against in producing this fiction?

8

Some day my prince will come:

young girls and the preparation for

adolescent sexuality

INTRODUCTION

My first inspiration for the title of this chapter came from a fragment of childhood memory told to me by a friend, now adult. It was of her grandmother, seated at the piano, surrounded by her family, playing her favourite song, 'Some day my prince will come ...'. Judging from the rendering of the song, it acted as a catalyst for an outpouring of un-fulfilled desire and it is clear that, old as she was, her prince had not yet arrived. That an old woman can still harbour desire for romantic fulfil-ment encapsulates the theme which I want to explore: the way in which girls are prepared for entry into heterosexual practices and, in particular, for romantic love. Here I intend to explore this theme by examining some aspects of the ideological preparation for adolescent sexuality in children's fiction, particularly girls' comics. I shall use this examination as a vehicle for discussing the relation between the psychic production of feminine desire and cultural forms and practices.

It will be my argument that young girls of primary school age are presented with, and inserted into, ideological and discursive positions by practices which locate them in meaning and in regimes of truth. In the insertion of young girls into positions which serve to produce and reproduce femininity, the organization of psychic life embodied in the dynamics of the family is centrally and strategically important. In psycho-analytic studies of the preparation for feminine sexuality, the strategic dynamics relate to the shifting for the girl of desire from the mother to the father (or, more particularly, the symbolic form of the phallus in Lacanian theory, as I will explore later). I want to show that cultural products for girls, by exploring those dynamics in symbolic form, may be of strategic importance in presenting psychic conflicts lived out in fantasy

87

situations, and also in presenting resolutions and potential resolutions to these conflicts. They may also serve to prepare the ground for the insertion of the little girl into romantic heterosexuality. In his discussion of feminine sexuality, Freud said: 'The constitution [of the little girl] will not adapt itself to its function [heterosexual femininity] without a struggle' (Freud, 1933, p. 117).

I want to explore some of the cultural practices which locate the girl in that struggle. Contrary to some classic approaches to feminine role models, I shall not argue that young girls passively adopt a female role model, but rather that their adoption of femininity is at best shaky and partial: the result of a struggle in which heterosexuality is achieved as a solution to a set of conflicts and contradictions in familial and other social relations. That the girl appears willingly to accept the position to which she is classically fitted does not, I would argue, tell us something basic about the nature of the female body, nor the female mind, but rather tells us of the power of those practices through which a particular resolution to the struggle is produced. Girls' comics, because they engage with the production of girls' conscious and unconscious desires, prepare for and proffer a 'happy-ever-after' situation in which the finding of the prince (the knight in shining armour, 'Mr Right') comes to seem like a solution to a set of overwhelming desires and problems.

CURRENT APPROACHES TO SEXISM IN LITERATURE

The issue of 'sexist bias' and stereotyping in literature for children has long been an important issue in feminist analyses of educational practices (see, for example, Lobban, 1975; Dixon, 1977). While these approaches have been of critical importance in raising the issue of content, they have tended to minimize the importance of the text itself as productive of meanings. Such approaches rely on a view that sexist literature presents stereotyped images which offer a biased and distorted picture of reality. For example, by showing women always at the kitchen sink they do not reveal that many women engage in paid labour outside the home. Gill Pinkerton (1982), in an article on producing non-sexist materials for the primary school classroom, aimed to

> extend children's thinking beyond stereotyping, both through in-depth discussion and by providing a range of material – stories, pictures, films, people – which presents broader images of what girls and boys, men and women are really like.

The objective here, then, is to get the children to see that other views and images are possible, and therefore to bring about a change in thinking and action.

Now, all this may seem fine, since indeed it forms the basis of the taken-for-granted approach to sexism in literature in school. However, I think there are at least two difficulties with this position. First, it assumes that by presenting a 'wider range of experience', children's views of themselves and of possible courses of action will change; secondly, that unproblematic transformation will come about through the adoption of non-stereotyped activities. Such an approach assumes a passive learner, or rather a rationalist one, who will change as a result of receiving the correct information about how things *really* are. It assumes that when the little girl sees the veil of distortion lifted from her eyes, she too will want to engage in those activities from which she has been precluded by virtue of her gender. There are two important points in response to this position. The first deals with the central importance of cultural practices in *producing* forms of thought and positions for women; the second deals with the inscription in those positions of desire – that is, how we come to want what we want. Recent work in the field of cultural practices has stressed the importance of the way in which texts, such as books, films, advertisements and so forth, operate in terms of systems of signification. Thus the text has to be actively read in order to engage with the way in which images and other signs, verbal and non-verbal, are constructed.

In this sense, then, we can say that texts do not simply distort or bias a reality that exists only outside the pages of books – in the 'real world' – but rather that those practices *are* real, and in their construction of meanings create places for identification, construct subject-positions in the text itself. So we need not point to some untainted reality outside the text, but should examine instead how those practices within the text itself have relational effects that define who and where we are. They are not just images, which are distasteful, to be tossed away and replaced by more politically acceptable ones. I suggest that we have to engage with the production of ourselves as subjects in and through our insertion into such cultural practices, of which children's literature forms a part. The content of such literature is not just grafted on to a cognate and waiting subject, who can be so easily changed. Rather, the positions and relations created in the text both relate to existing social and psychic struggle and provide a fantasy vehicle which inserts the reader into the text.

FANTASY IN CHILDREN'S LITERATURE: THE CASE OF GIRLS' COMICS

Girls' comics are a very powerful form indeed. They implicitly offer guidance as to how young girls may prepare themselves to be good enough to 'win' the glittering prizes: the man, the home, the adventure, and so forth. They do this, but they do it at a level which the alternative images or role models for girls simply cannot reach: they work on desire. In her analysis of the adolescent magazine *Jackie*, Angela McRobbie (1982) discusses the codes through which adolescent femininity is constructed and therefore may be read. The positions that magazine offers relate to heterosexual practices about 'getting and keeping a man', and while pre-teen comics do not do this in any overt sense, they engage with the construction of femininity in such a way as to prepare young girls for the fate that awaits them. How, then, are young girls prepared? The textual devices turn around stories which are based in most cases on classic fairy tales. They end with happy-ever-after solutions, mostly around the insertion of the girl into an ideal family. Meanwhile, in getting there, the girls in these stories are apparently hapless victims of circumstance, scorned, despised and hard done by. The resolution in the family is, I will argue, the oedipal resolution played out. The happy family is produced through the traumas associated with the loss and abandonment of the mother in favour of the oedipal love of the father. And, as we know, the father simply precedes the prince. The hetero-sexual practices of *Jackie*, then, offer a solution, a way out of the misery of the femininity struggled over in the pages of these comics.

The comics I have chosen are two of the most popular amongst junior school girls: *Bunty* and *Tracy*. For the most part, the stories develop themes of family relationships. To do so, they use particular kinds of narrative device. I shall not attempt a comprehensive examination of these devices – particularly the use of strip cartoons, the style of drawing, and so on but will concentrate particularly on those devices which allow certain very distressing issues to be the focus of the stories. Often these stories contain a catalogue of dreadful events which befall their heroines. How can comics full of frightful stories sell so well and be so gripping? Why are the heroines of these stories more often than not helpless victims? I shall attempt to answer these questions by outlining the themes of the stories, mentioning some remarks made by Freud which relate to similar content which emerged in his clinical work. There are eighteen strip stories in these two comics. They are nearly all about girls who are *victims*: of cruelty and circumstance. Eleven are about girls who do not have, or do not live with, their parents. Indeed, the circumstances are so fantastic that they would, on the surface, appear to bear very little relation to the lives of their young readers. I say *on the surface* because it is precisely the organization of *fantasy* (rather than the realist approach of anti-sexist literature) which is so important in understanding the relation of such literature to the psychic organization of desire. After all, fantasy is the tool *par excellence* of psychoanalysis.

FANTASY AND FICTION

Freud, in his early work (1909, pp. 237–41), discussed the importance of fantasy[1] in the production of the material which was the subject matter of the analysis itself. He posited various structures and mechanisms through which, in his terms, reality was 'mediated' by fantasy, such that the material of everyday life was not lived in any simple sense through mechanisms of perception. In particular he argued that it was quite common for children to fantasize about alternative parentage: 'Chance occurrences ... arouse the child's envy, which finds expression in a phantasy in which both his parents are of better birth' (p. 239). Such fantasies have certain effects upon the lived relations of the family themselves, but are also devices which allow certain difficulties to be dealt with. What is the effect of fantasy, and how does it operate? I want to explore this in two ways. First, I shall examine the content of the two girls' comics in question, then I shall go on to relate this to other cultural practices in which fantasies are produced, particularly in this case fantasies connected with romantic heterosexual love.

It is my contention that the very 'unreality' of the stories presented in these comics is one basis of their strength rather than weakness. That is, they engage precisely with the kinds of issues mentioned by Freud. They allow engagement with difficult emotions and less than perfect circumstances by devices which permit the young readers to identify with the heroine in the text. Thus they encourage the working out and potential resolution of certain conflicts.

The market for these magazines is working-class pre-pubescent girls. The stories themselves therefore relate to fantasies about family, sexuality and class. In several ways the stories construct heroines who are the target of wrong-doing and whose fight against private injustice is private endurance, which always triumphs in the end. By contrast, boys' comics deal with public bravery and public fights against injustice which are rewarded openly. Now, as I have said above, it has classically been the position, in relation to issues of sex and class in children's literature, to regard such material as biased, bad and unreal and therefore to be countered with an appropriate realism. But the alternative realism is based on politics of rationalism, of rational transformation, change through the imposition of the 'right line', the undistorted picture of reality. 'Reality' is not in this simple sense hidden or distorted. What we have to examine is the materiality of the fantasies created in these comics, in terms of what is spoken, what is understood, and how it is resolved.

Readers are constructed in the text, readers construct readings of the text – a complex interplay which does not recognize a simple split between a pre-given psychological subject who reads and a text in which meaning is produced (Henriques *et al.*, 1984). Realist approaches to reading, which prevail in the radical work on children's fiction, treat readers as pre-existing classed, gendered and racial subjects who are formed through certain material relations of production, who have a 'lived reality', a material base, which stories help or hinder. It is in this sense that we can understand the movement towards more 'real' texts which 'reflect the reality' of (predominantly) working-class life. What, then, are these children, faced with what is represented as their 'reality', to do with such realist texts? What if the readers do not 'recognize themselves' and their lives in the stories, or what if they do not *want* to recognize? And what about desires to have and to be something and somebody different? Classic fairy tales are quite fantastic: they do not bear any resemblance to the lives of ordinary children. Yet they act powerfully to engage with important themes about 'what might be'. In other words, I am arguing that they engage with the very themes, issues, problems, fantasies (of escape, of difference) which the realist, 'telling it like it is' stories do not engage with at all.

The comic stories do. Certainly they present miserable circumstances, difficult lives, but they do so in such a way as to provide solutions and escapes, ways out, in fantasy and in practice, by the proffering of what and who one might be. The stories romanticize poverty and portray a way of dealing with it which is almost masochistic – it is desirable precisely because it can be suffered virtuously and moved beyond. Poverty is presented as the result of tragic circumstances; so too are families who are wicked, oppressive – the result of some dreadful accident of fate. The major narrative device which renders these difficult circumstances palatable is precisely that they *are* fantastic. That is, they are removed from the everyday in various ways: a different historical period or geographical location, and the overwhelming use of 'surrogate' parents and siblings. In the majority of stories, the children do not live with their biological parents or siblings but are removed by various tragic circumstances to surrogate families who are cruel to them. It is my contention that it is these devices which help make possible the engagement with difficult material. That is, identification is possible at the level of fantasy – where an identification with a 'reality' presented as mirroring the life of the readers may well be rejected as 'not like me' or indeed 'too close for comfort'. The argument is, then, that the distance, the difference, renders these stories *more*, not less effective, and such effectiveness is not to be easily countered by a simple realism.

The realist text and approach to change using stereotypes concentrates on *images*. Images can be good or bad, true or false. The concept of fantasy being put forward here is one which presents not a rational or passive appropriation of an *image*, but an active engagement with, and construction of, the imaginary fulfilment of a wish. It is in this sense that fiction is not a mere set of images, but an ensemble of textual devices for engaging the reader in the fantasy. Because the fantasies created in the text play upon wishes already present in the lives of young children, the resolutions offered will relate to their own wishes or desires. In this conception of change, there is no simple response to a positive image but a complex psychic organization. So the reader who engages in this fiction lives a 'real' life which is at the same time organized in relation to fantasy. To understand children's fiction in this way gives quite a different view of the presentation of fiction and its effect on, and relation to, the lives of young girls.

Let us now examine in greater detail the content of *Bunty* and *Tracy*, for their thematic organization. Apart from the *eleven* stories about girls who do not have, or do not live with, their parents, the other *seven* are as follows:

1. A girl who is helpful and does good and kindly deeds for others except when she puts on a glove puppet, at which point her character completely changes and she becomes vicious, angry and evil. Of course, as soon as she takes off the glove puppet, she has no recollection of her evil deeds.
2. A girl who is perfect at school: clever, beautiful, helpful, sensible; but whose cleverness and good deeds make her the object of envy, and therefore unpopular and unhappy.
3. A girl who lives with her mother, who has been made redundant. The girl is saved from having to sell a precious camera by her ingenuity in using it to make money by taking and selling photographs. These turn out to be related to good and kindly deeds for others.
4. A girl whose mother is a teacher, who has chosen to teach in a 'rough' comprehensive and is constantly trying to reform the children. Her daughter, by her ingenuity and good deeds, helps her mother to manage the school (of course without her mother's knowledge).
5. A girl who was a Victorian serving girl but has been frozen for one hundred years in a block of ice (!) and is found by a family with a daughter of the same age who passes her off as a cousin.
6. A girl gymnast from an Eastern bloc country who is helped to escape by a British girl gymnast.

7. A horse who develops the theme of jealousy: another horse is jealous of her but the heroine's horse helps the other unselfishly despite the other's jealousy.

Even where the girls are presented in an ordinary family setting, the stories tend to centre on the resolution of certain problems – often to do with internal family relations. For here, too, the girls are often in receipt of gross injustices. They are constantly misunderstood and misjudged, but the theme that is played out again and again is that despite everything, the girls engage in selfless acts of helpfulness and courage in the service of others. These can be illustrated by the résumés of the 'story so far' given at the top of each picture-strip. In the story 'Joni the Jinx', the caption reads as follows:

> When orphan Joni Jackson was adopted by Kate and Robert Stewart, she looked forward to the kind of happy family she had always dreamed of. But things didn't quite work out as planned.

In this story the adoptive parents are keen to do their best, but they argue over how to present themselves properly to the social worker, and tensions between the husband and wife are brought to the fore. In each case, Joni, helpful and thoughtful as she is, takes this to be *her* fault in the sense that it is her presence which has caused these tensions to surface.

In another story, 'Cherry and the Chimps', an orphaned girl is found living with chimps in Africa by a wicked couple, who use her as a slave to serve them and to run their chimp circus act. She is constantly abused. The misery and unhappiness are resolved only by the reappearance of her real parents, who were thought to have been killed in a plane crash.

In 'She'll Stay a Slave', the heroine, Jenny, is an orphan, a slave to her cruel cousin, but she is predictably very clever and helpful, despite the fact that her wicked cousin is always exploiting her, trying to spoil her success, and so on. The caption is as follows:

> Jenny Moss lived with her Aunt Mary and Uncle John. Her cousin Paula treated her like a slave and Jenny put up with it as she mistakenly believed that Paula had saved her life after an accident. Jenny was one of three girls being considered for a scholarship to Redpark College – but Paula tried to spoil Jenny's chances of winning as she did not want to lose her 'slave'.

These tales of cruelty go on and on. They range from a girl who is made to act as a robot in a circus act by wicked relatives and suffers pain and humiliation in silence because she believes her relatives are paying for hospital treatment for her sick brother, to a girl who is forced to act as a ventriloquist's dummy because the real ventriloquist, her grandfather, is ill. Then there is the tale of Victorian orphan sisters who go from disaster to cruel disaster: at the end of one episode one sister suddenly goes blind!

I want to examine certain themes which appear constantly throughout the comic stories. The first theme is that of the production of girls as *victims*. I have already noted the large number of girls in these stories who are victims of circumstance and of cruelty. Let us examine how these aspects of the stories function in the circulation of meanings and the presentation of key signifiers at the level of fantasy. The themes present cruelty and harsh personal circumstances as potentially exciting because they are the subject of adventures. Equally important is the resolution: the way of dealing with the violence, cruelty and harsh circumstances. The theme which is present in these and all other stories in the two comics is selfless helpfulness. In the 'victim' stories the heroines carry on doing good deeds and accepting their fate in the most selfless manner. Indeed, the manner in which they do so is starkly contrasted by the villains of the stories, who may be other children or older relatives. These are shown as nasty, vicious and jealous: they wreak vengeance on the 'good' and selfless girls, who respond to their torture only by continued helpfulness, despite everything.

What seems to me important about this is that if cruelty is seen as exciting and works at the level of fantasy to romanticize difficult practical and emotional circumstances, this suggests a passive, not an active, response to the violence (which in psychoanalysis would relate to the displacement of angry and hostile feelings on to others). It also provides the conditions for resolution: selflessness, even though it brings pain and suffering, brings its own rewards (knowledge of good deeds and right-eousness). If the heroines are displayed as passive victims of circum-stance, all bad and difficult actions and emotions are invested in others. The heroines suffer in silence: they display virtues of patience and forbearance and are rewarded for silence, for selflessness, for helpfulness. Any thought for the self, any wanting, longing, desire or anger is in this way produced within the texts as bad. This provides for the readers a value-system in which certain kinds of emotion are not acceptable, and a set of practices in which their suppression is rewarded by the provision of the longed-for happy family, the perfect bourgeois setting. So, bad and difficult circumstances are to be celebrated and triumphed over by the psychic organization of emotions and the selfless production of good deeds. Through the narrative device of the inadequate or 'bad' family structure which is also the result of circumstance, not choice, the girls are shown as being able to bring about by their own actions the conditions for the restoration of the *desired* family structure.

The idealized family is the bourgeois and respectable nuclear family, located in a desirable house with money and possessions. Class and gender relations are therefore dealt with by the idealization of a certain kind of family, but also by the relations *within* the family, notably between mother and father, and between siblings. Importantly, these are always sisters: relationships with brothers are never explored. Paternal and maternal relations tend to be displaced on to adoptive parents, aunts and uncles, grandparents or simply evil couples, who, through various circumstances, have taken possession of the girl in question. Sibling rivalry and jealousy is a theme well explored, but it is always located in the anti-heroine or parent substitutes: the heroine rises above it. Critically, then, certain material circumstances are presented as lived and worked through in various ways which lead to the presentation of the bourgeois individual, feminine and actively passive. So, while such self-less identities are not likely to be achieved by the readers, what I am suggesting is the possibility of the psychic *effect* of the resolution of conflict in which all features to do with anger and jealousy are displaced as bad.

This effectively means that girls are presented with heroines who never get angry. Their victory is in their very passivity and helpfulness. Selflessness is contrasted with selfishness, anger, greed and jealousy. So, for example, anger signifies as wholly negative, and is therefore never used in any positive way: it is never justified, nor is rebellion ever sanctioned. This leads to the suppression of certain qualities as bad and therefore not to be displayed, or to be acknowledged at peril.[2]

It is in this way that girls become 'victims' − for example, angry and hostile feelings are projected on to the Other and are suppressed in the self − passivity is thus *actively* produced as the result of an internal struggle. The overwhelming characteristic of the 'good' heroines is their selflessness. They do countless good deeds by helping others. Thus selflessness becomes a virtue and doing anything for oneself is, by implication, bad and selfish. Girls can therefore move mountains (metaphorically, of course!) as long as they do it *for others*. This means that many acts are possible, but doing anything for one's own benefit is not. Girls in these comics are encouraged in a view of self which exists only *for* and through others. Such girls will always fail: how can they possibly be selfless enough? Another significant and perhaps surprising feature of the stories is the positive manner in which academic achievement is treated. Heroines are usually clever, and often at mathematics, the area in which girls are commonly supposed to fail (Walden and Walkerdine, 1982). Achievement brings parental pride. Academic achievement is thus acceptable; it is for others, for one's family or for the school. In the comics it is actually 'taken for granted' that girls are clever: it is certainly not presented as antithetical to femininity, as some of the stereotyping arguments would suggest.

I argued in Chapter 1 that it is precisely the slippage afforded in the term 'good girl' which allows girls to be good and helpful and like their mothers at home, and good and helpful and clever in the classroom. This fits with the studies which reveal that, relative to boys, girls' performance is extremely good in primary school.

In one story the girl who is top of her class also looks the best in the school because she takes pride in her school uniform. When a friend says to her: 'How do you manage to look so smart in our grotty school uniform? Mine hangs like an old potato sack!', our heroine replies: 'Well, you can improve it a bit by ironing and by taking in a stitch here and there....' This signifying chain from neatness and helpfulness to academic attainment is really important in that there are no pejorative connotations attached to academic performance at this stage at all. However, there is a marked split between arts and sciences. Although heroines are often represented as good at maths and sciences, these are dull subjects: it is the arts which hold the romance and the excitement. In the story 'I Want to Dance', the heroine has won a scholarship to a prestigious boarding school in some science fiction setting in the future. Here the girls are called by numbers and not names, are made to study even when asleep, and music is forbidden: indeed, the heroine destroys a precious tape recorder for fear of being expelled. We have, therefore, another example of textual splitting: romance and excitement are the order of the day. While it is taken for granted that girls are good at maths and sciences, it is in the arts that the key to romance lies. Thus attainment in the arts is posed as a positive and desirable goal. It is the investment of desire in the arts and the absence of desire from the sciences (I *want* to dance) which is crucial in the formation of semiotic chains. Arts are not posed, therefore, as potentially antithetical to other desirable outcomes, as is the case in *Jackie*, where there is no place for any notion of educational achievement.

THE PREPARATION FOR THE PRINCE

The themes which appear in the comics act as powerful signifiers keying into struggles which are central to the production of femininity and female sexuality. Although there is little overtly sexual about the significations here, girls may be *prepared* in certain important ways for current adolescent heterosexual practices which appear to offer a way out, a resolution to their victimization. That is, although heterosexuality is not an overt *issue*, the other features of femininity are so produced in the pages of the comics as to render 'getting a man' the 'natural' solution.

These 'regimes of meaning' are as follows. Girls are victims of cruelty, but they rise above their circumstances by servicing and being sensitive to *others* – selflessness. The girl who services is like the beautiful girl whose rewards for her good deeds is to be taken out of her misery: she is freed by the prince. The semiotic chain slides into romance as the solution, with the prince as saviour. It is here that girls are produced as victims ready to be saved, prefiguring the heterosexual practices of *Jackie*. Cruelty and victimization are the key features, but it is precisely those features which are salient in the production of women as passively sexual. Victimization and martyrdom in Christian myth – for example Lacan's reference to the ecstasy of St Theresa – carry similar significations, in this case women giving themselves for and to Christ. In her article 'Sexual Violence and Sexuality' (1982) Rosalind Coward also analyses represent- ations of female sexuality which suggest that women are the passive victims of violence. She gives examples of photographs of women in poses of passivity connoting sexual pleasure. In one of these the 'victim' appears dead. Coward's gloss to these photographs reads: 'The represent- ation of female sexual pleasure, submission and the ultimate passivity, death' (p. 19). She states:

> This leads on to the question of the code of submission, which is similarly problematic. This is the dominant code by which female sexual pleasure is represented as simultaneously languid and turbulent, the combination of orgasm and passionate death. The explicit association with death which is frequently seen is extremely disturbing: women are shown in passionate submission, their posture evoking at best romantic deaths, at worst sexual murders. This, overlaid on the potentiality of photography unconsciously to suggest death, creates a regime of disturbing and erotic photographs. Not only do they reinforce ideologies of sexuality as female submission to male force, but they also powerfully recirculate the connection between sexuality and death which is so cruelly played out in our society. (p. 18)

The circulation of this regime of definite meanings relates cruelty and sexual excitement. As Coward argues, this linkage is not confined to pornography: it is ubiquitous and, I would argue further, relates clearly to the meanings which are circulated in the comics and slide into those of the sexual representation of women. It is the relation between the representations at the level of fantasy and the production of meanings through which desire is understood and into which desire is invested which is important.

FICTION, FANTASY AND DESIRE

I want to begin this section by outlining the romantic resolution of desire for adolescent girls by citing Angela McRobbie's analysis of romance in

Jackie (1982). She lists several points. The first is that romance, not sex, is the key to sexuality: it is the moment of bliss as signified by the first kiss which is made predominant. Secondly, girls' lives are portrayed as dominated by their emotions: jealousy, possessiveness, and devotion. These spell out the conflicts which are produced between girls, making other girls into enemies, because the heroine has first to get a boy and then to keep him. McRobbie demonstrated the contradiction (which is underplayed in the magazine) that while getting and keeping men is a constant struggle for girls, the potential for romance is all over the place – from the bus stop to the disco. In this sense, then, what one girl can achieve in getting a man is constantly threatened by others with the same designs. So feelings of insecurity are constantly reproduced. The arrival of the prince is presented as the *final* solution which, of course, glosses over the problem that keeping a man is a serious threat to 'happiness ever after'. It is thus a fraught and fragile solution, but one that remains attractive precisely because it is the getting and keeping of the man which in a very basic and crucial way establishes that the girl is 'good enough' and 'can have what she wants'. It is because getting a man is identified as a central resolution to problems of female desire that it acts so powerfully.

The same fatalism which is apparent in the way girls in the pre-teen comics are supposed to suffer in silence is present in *Jackie* as a fatalism about *loss*: in this case the loss of a boy. Girls who lose their boyfriend to *another* are supposed to suffer in silence, certainly not make a fuss or get angry; and are supposed to work towards the next relationship in the hope of 'better luck next time'. The girl is therefore encouraged to put work into attracting the *next* boy rather than examining any aspects of the past relationship or, for that matter, relationships in general: the next prince might, after all, be the 'real thing'.

If fiction therefore presents fantasies by the use of textual devices which engage with the desires of the reader, this would suggest an understanding of the development of gender very different from one which is most commonly asserted. Those approaches stressing roles and stereotypes suggest a girl who is already rational, who takes in information, or takes on roles. By contrast, psychoanalysis offers a dynamic model in which no simple or static reality is perceived by children. Central to psychoanalytic accounts is the production of complex and tortuous conscious and unconscious relations, centred upon the girl's relations with her family. The account psychoanalysis offers presents a subject both more resistant to change than a rationalist account might suggest and engaged in a struggle in relation to the achievement of femininity and heterosexuality.

Recent advances in the study of texts have made use of psychoanalysis in understanding the production of textual identities. They provide a potential way forward for exploring the cultural practices which produce fantasies and the relation of those to the development of sexuality.

Freud himself located the production of sexuality in family relations. I have already mentioned some of the concepts he used – for example the way in which 'actual interactions' or family relations are lived by the participants through the framework of complex systems of psychic fantasy relations. Hence the importance of the working through in fantasy of certain wishes, particularly in relation to the mother. Freud insisted that the pain of separation from the maternal body experienced by the child pushes the infant into a struggle to possess the mother, to be dependent on her and yet to control her. The experience of psychic distress caused through the inevitable failure of the mother to meet the child's insatiable demands sets up a particular dynamic between them. Freud distinguished between need and wish (or desire). He recognized that the fantasy created in the gap between possession and loss was not made good by any 'meeting of needs' because the satisfaction would be only temporary and the object of desire would both constantly shift and be out of reach. The presence of siblings produced a rivalry in relation to the mother, setting up its own particular familial dynamic. However, the presence of the father, whose possession of the mother creates further rivalry, is of *crucial* importance to Freud's account of the production of sexual difference. Although the little boy struggles for possession of his mother, in competition therefore with the father, the little girl can never possess the mother. Freud therefore postulates the struggle for the transfer of desire from the mother to the father to account for female heterosexuality.

Subsequent schools of psychoanalysis (particularly Kleinian and Object Relations accounts) have tended to stress a difference from Freud along a variety of dimensions. The first concerns the countering of the emphasis on oedipal relations. Along with the stress on the mother in Object Relations accounts there is also the diminution of the emphasis on wish or desire. Such accounts move towards the possibility in practice of the adequate meeting of the child's needs by the mother.

The stress on the meeting of needs has been countered by the approach offered by Lacan. This has emphasized the gap between needs for bodily comfort and food, and the way in which demand always exceeds satisfaction. Freud demonstrated the way in which infants hallucinated the milk which had been withdrawn by the breast, or played games in which the presence and absence of the mother was controlled in fantasy. In this sense, Freud concentrated on the creation of fantasy in the gap between need and wish-fulfilment. Lacan developed this and argued that the satisfaction of need is an illusion, one sustained by practices which produce fantasy or imaginary resolutions. Although infants are clearly gratified by the mother, this gratification 'contains the loss within it'. The price paid for consciousness is the first recognition of the mother as Other, and therefore of the me/not me. Lacan uses the example of an infant's gaze at its own reflection in a mirror to stress the idea that singular identity is illusory. The infant is dependent and relatively powerless, but an illusion of unity and control is created by this mirroring. Lacan's account, then, stresses the importance of the child's acquisition of language as the means for control over both the initial loss of the mother and the capacity for self-reference, the illusion of control. He uses two terms: the Imaginary and the Symbolic. The Imaginary relates to the imaged state of self-recognition in the mirror. The Imaginary is the location of fantasy-resolutions, the illusion of the meeting of needs. This is why the fantasies of completion and resolution of psychic conflicts offered in children's fiction are so important. They proffer possible resolutions, held out as the meeting of needs and fantasies of identity (wholeness). The Symbolic Order is the site of control in language, which fixes meaning. The fixing of meaning offers certainty and knowledge: the idea that we can have control over our loss by knowing the truth. This truth is identified not with a 'real father' as such but by what Lacan calls the 'paternal metaphor'. Lacan uses the term 'phallus' to describe that in which the Symbolic is invested, the breaking of the mother–child dyad. If the child first imagines control through language, then it is the father – not as real father, but as imagined guardian of 'the Word' – who holds the key to the Symbolic Order, and thus to control.

The problem of sexual difference relates to the contradictory paternal and maternal identifications involved in being/having the mother, making good the loss, and having/being in control by having/being the phallus. It is in this sense that sexual identity is taken never to be a secure achievement because there is no easy fitting into available roles. However, because language and fantasy play such a crucial part, identities created in the everyday locations the child enters – in schooling, in texts, and so forth – offer locations for imaginary closure. They engage with psychic conflicts, identifications and resolutions. They are therefore both crucial to change and yet at the same time problematic.

In the pages of the pre-teen girls' comics, the heroines convey an overwhelming sense of loss, which is resolved by its investment into the selfless service of others. As we have seen, difficult feelings about that loss are dealt with in these comics by locating them in the 'bad' characters. They are displaced. Such displacements in psychoanalysis are dealt with by the defences, which are unconscious, so no fantasy engagement with loss is presented other than its displacement and rechannelling into service. Anger and aggression, then, are not so much not dealt with as dealt with in specific and important ways.

As we have seen in relation to the comics, the loss is not so much buried and denied – as, for example, Eichenbaum and Orbach claim (1982, p. 362) – as dealt with in particular ways. There are good girls and bad girls, naughty and nice, kind and horrible, and so forth. It is not so much the simple case of a repression or suppression, or inability to deal with loss (in pain, jealousy, anger, etc.) but *how* and *where* it is dealt with. We are not all 'good girls' who are selfless, and have repressed anger. Some of us are and were angry, jealous, horrid. But bad girls are punished, positioned in various ways. Identities are created to deal with those characteristics. Those identities are gender-specific. Being a naughty boy and a naughty girl is a very different matter (see Walkerdine, 1984). So it is not true that girls do not deal with loss, or that the culture denies the loss. Perhaps it is more the case that certain ways of resolving the loss are sanctioned and others prohibited and punished. Such sanctions and resolutions are presented in the fantasies created in these comics. They are also created in the practices which make up the daily lives of the young girls. Thus comics do not 'tell it like it is'; there is no psychic determinism which they represent. Their very groupings of meaning provide vehicles for the content of the gender differentiation and the resolution. If they did not do so they would not be successful as cultural products. This latter point is absolutely central to my argument. I am not arguing for a position in which psychoanalysis helps us to understand the internalization of norms of femininity through processes of identification. This would be to operate as though girls, in identifying with the texts of comics or with the position of their mother, 'became feminine'. Rather, my argument is about how to understand the relation of cultural products and practices to the production and resolution of desire. Such relations are not fitted easily on to girls, but are struggled over. What I am trying to demonstrate, therefore, is the way in which that struggle is lived and the relation of content to the proffered solutions to psychic and material struggles. Rose says:

> all this happens at a cost, and that cost is the concept of the unconscious. What distinguishes psychoanalysis from sociological accounts of gender (hence for me the fundamental impasse of Nancy Chodorow's work) is that whereas for the latter, the internalization of norms is assumed roughly to work, the basic premiss and indeed the starting point of psychoanalysis is that it does not. The unconscious constantly reveals the 'failure' of identity. Because there is no continuity of psychic life, so there is no stability of sexual identity, no position for women (or for men) which is ever simply achieved. Nor does psychoanalysis see such 'failure' as a special-case inability or an individual deviancy from the norm. 'Failure' is not a moment to be regretted

in a process of adaptation, or development into normality, which ideally takes its course (some of the earliest critics of Freud, such as Ernest Jones did, however, give an account of development in just these terms). Instead 'failure' is something endlessly repeated and relived moment by moment throughout our individual histories. It appears not only in the symptoms, but also in dreams, in slips of the tongue and in forms of sexual pleasure which are pushed to the sidelines of the norm. Feminism's affinity with psycho-analysis rests above all, I would argue, with this recognition that there is a resistance to identity which lies at the very heart of psychic life. Viewed this way, psychoanalysis is no longer best understood as an account of how women are fitted into place (even this, note, is the charitable reading of Freud). Instead, psychoanalysis becomes one of the few places in our culture where it is recognized as more than a fact of individual pathology that most women do not painlessly slip into their roles as women, if, indeed, they do at all. (Rose 1983, p. 9)

What seems to be at issue is not a series of roles or simple identities or images which are fitted on to girls. Nor is it a matter of certain behaviours being 'stereotypically feminine' and therefore allowed, and others not. Rather, we need to understand the relationship between those practices which not only define correct femininity and masculinity but produce them by creating positions to occupy. So it is not a case of unitary identities, but a question of those practices which channel psychic conflicts and contradictions in particular ways. 'Good girls' are not always good – but where and how is their badness lived? What is the struggle which results from the attempt to be or live a unitary identity? Much work is necessary to engage with such questions, but we might begin by exploring how different positions are produced and understood. In the comics good girls and bad girls are different personalities: they are mutually exclusive. So theories of 'personality' help to create a truth which informs those current practices which position girls in identity. Naughty girls might be maladjusted or juvenile delinquents, for example. In such practices relational dynamics and shifting identities are denied in favour of a fixed and measurable unitariness. Similarly, naughtiness in boys and girls is understood and lived in different ways. So there is a complex and important relationship between theories and practices which produce truth and identities, and the contradictory, multiple positioning of the little girls. I have examined one example of a practice: the fantasy of girls' comics. We might also look at the practices of schooling which produce positions for girls and claim to know the truth of such girls as singular beings: with personalities, intelligence, and so on (Walden and Walkerdine, 1983; Walkerdine, 1984).

TOWARDS THE POSSIBILITY OF
ALTERNATIVE PRACTICES

Finally, then, if we want to understand the production of girls as subjects and the production of alternatives for girls, we must pay attention to desire and fantasy. It is no good resorting to a rationalist account which consists simply in changing images and attitudes. If new content, in whatever form, does not map on to the crucial issues around desire, then we should not be surprised if it fails as an intervention. Unfortunately, when such interventions fail they leave the field wide open for reactionary explanations of femininity which, after all, 'must be true' if 'social conditioning' approaches fail to produce shifts in girls' actions and aspirations. Whatever we propose as alternatives, we have to recognize and deal with the production, fixing, and canalization of desire. Whether in this case we want to think about alternative cultural products or what form our intervention should take is an open question which must be urgently addressed.

Practices which put forward the possibility of alternative literature and images for girls create a set of conflicts and contradictions which often go unrecognized and may in fact make the struggle more difficult. For example, it is quite common in alternative or feminist literature for young children to display women and girls engaged in activities traditionally undertaken by men. In psychoanalytic theory, one problem for girls in the struggle for femininity is coming to terms with the recognition that the mother once considered all-powerful (the Phallic Mother) does not have the phallus. This becomes important in the move away from a simply located desire for the mother. Now, while shifts and transformations in practice mean that women can occupy positions which invest them with the phallus, they, too, are not coherent and non-contradictory identities. Just as Lacan has suggested that 'the phallus is a fraud' (that men also do not possess it, but rather struggle to achieve it), so women cannot be the Phallic Mother in any complete or total sense. This is not to suggest that those practices which position women are not important, nor that it is unimportant for girls to have powerful mothers. Rather, it is suggested again that such a simple image or appropriation is more problematic and complex than it might at first appear. In one feminist reworking of a classic fairy tale the princess, instead of marrying the prince, goes off to be a feminist decorator in dungarees! What we need to ask here is how such texts operate at the level of fantasy. For some girls they might well provide the vehicle for an alternative vision, while for others they might, by stressing the one as alternative to the other, feed or fuel a resistance to the feminist alternative. We are only just beginning to explore such issues in relation to texts and readings.

We could ask, therefore, what exactly fiction, along with other cultural practices, produces for girls. And in examining current practices we can begin to explore the constitution of femininity and masculinity as not *fixed* or *appropriated*, but *struggled over* in a complex relational dynamic. The question of alternative fictions for girls might then engage with the relational dynamic. How might other kinds of fantasies be produced which deal differently with desires and conflicts? What other fantasy-resolutions might be offered? What about characters who are not simply good or bad? Similarly, stories which engage with conflicts might relate to other kinds of resolution than a simple displacement to a future reward for present pain. It is not enough simply to present conflicts. If wish-fulfilment through fantasy is an important device for working through conflict, then resolutions will have to be engaged with, to create possible paths for action. By examining how present cultural practices deal with and offer resolutions to conflicts, we can understand both how they work and what they do and do not speak. By examining these alongside an understanding of the production of sexuality, we might begin to see what alternative fictions and fantasies could look like. If current fictions produce such powerful effects, such potent fantasies, we too must work on the production of other possible dreams and fantasies.

NOTES

1. In psychoanalysis the term *phantasy* is classically used rather than *fantasy*. This is because the term is intended to be wider usage than simple imaginary production, but relates to the 'world of the imagination' (Laplanche and Pontalis, 1973, p. 314).

2. It is significant that when I interviewed nine- and ten-year-old girls as part of my current research, the girls gave me anger and selfishness as bad qualities in themselves, some to the extent that they could not claim to possess any qualities which they felt to be good.

REFERENCES

Coward, R. (1982) 'Sexual Violence and Sexuality'. *Feminist Review*, no. 11.
Dixon, B. (1977) *Catching Them Young: Race, Sex and Class in Children's Fiction*. London, Pluto.
Eichenbaum, L. and Orbach, S. (1982) *Outside In, Inside Out*. Harmondsworth, Penguin.
Freud, S. (1909) 'Family Romances', in *Standard Edition of the Complete Psychological Works of Sigmund Freud*, vol. 9. London, Hogarth Press/Institute of Pyscho-Analysis.
Freud, S. (1933) 'Femininity', *Standard Edition of the Complete Psychological Works of Sigmund Freud*, vol. 12. London, Hogarth Press/Institute of Psycho-Analysis.
Henriques, J., Hollway, W., Urwin, C., Venn, C. and Walkerdine, V. (1984) *Changing the Subject: Psychology, Social Regulation and Subjectivity*. London, Routledge & Kegan Paul.
Lacan, J. (1977) *Écrits: A Selection*. London Tavistock.

Laplanche, J. and Pontalis, J.B. (1973) *The Language of Psychoanalysis*. London, Hogarth Press/Institute of Psycho-Analysis.

Lobban, G. (1975) 'Sex-Roles in Reading Schemes'. *Educational Review*, vol. 27, no. 3.

McRobbie, A. (1982) 'Jackie: An Ideology of Adolescent Femininity', in B. Waites, T. Bennet and G. Martin, eds, *Popular Culture: Past and Present*. London, Croom Helm/Open University Press.

Pinkerton, G. (1982) 'Challenging Sex Stereotypes: Ideas For the Classroom'. *Contact*, 12 November (Inner London Education Authority).

Rose, J. (1983) 'Femininity and Its Discontents'. *Feminist Review*, no. 14.

Walden, R. and Walkerdine, V. (1982) *Girls and Mathematics: The Early Years*. London, Heinemann.

Walden, R. and Walkerdine, V. (1983) *Girls and Mathematics: From Primary to Secondary Schooling*. London, Heinemann.

Walkerdine, V. (1984) 'Power, Gender, Resistance', in C. Steedman, C. Urwin and V. Walkerdine, eds, *Language, Gender and Childhood*. London, Routledge & Kegan Paul.

PLATE 1   Valerie Walkerdine as a Bluebell Fairy
PLATE 2   Projection/Introjection: Memories of Mother

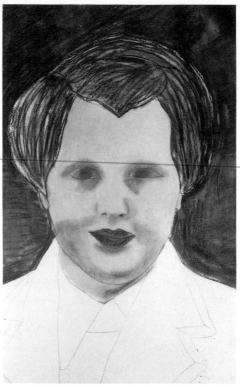

PLATE 3   Images from an Installation:
Behind the Painted Smile

PLATE 4   Toni Basil sings 'Oh, Mickey!'
PLATE 5   Textbook Children

"SHE'LL STAY A SLAVE!"

JENNY MOSS lived with her Aunt Mary and Uncle John. Her cousin Paula treated her like a slave and Jenny put up with it as she mistakenly believed that Paula had saved her life after an accident. Jenny was one of three girls being considered for a scholarship to Redpark College—but Paula tried to spoil Jenny's chances of winning as she did not want to lose her 'slave'.

The garden's much too dry—the only things growing are weeds! I wish I had more time to look after it.

I'll do some weeding for you after school, Mum.

Paula says she'll do some gardening for me—you girls are such a help. Thank you for doing the washing.

It's no trouble Aunt Mary.

I bet Paula gets ME to do the gardening! She never does any work unless Aunt Mary or Uncle John is around.

And after school—

Don't forget to put the hose on the flower beds after, Jenny. I'm going to see Brenda this evening.

If only Paula would give me a hand! I play Selma Thorpe in the first round of the Junior Girls' singles soon—but I shan't have time to go to tennis practice this evening.

I suppose I must put up with it and remember that Paula saved my life! But I do want to get that scholarship to Redpark.

Later—

Time for tennis now—your plants are looking healthy, Jenny.

Jenny's doing too well at everything.

I must think of more ways to stop Jenny getting that scholarship. I'm not going to be left at home to do all the chores!

SS1;

PLATE 6   Nice, Kind and Helpful: Girl as Victim

9

The meeting

(1985)

She could hardly sleep
    the night before
    the morning came

It had been so long
    and she had spent
    so many hours
        in tears
She was better now and stronger
Why then
    did she want to see him so much

Why did her heart pump
        blood through her veins
        at what seemed
            like time and a half
        or even double-time

She'd kicked and fought and punched
    the cushions till she thought there
    could really be nothing of him left
And yet
She wanted to see him more
        than she really cared to admit

Caution, caution, coolness is the order of the day
said her friends

And she knew that ambivalence
    coursed through every pore
           in his body

What a risk
Would she fail, give the game away
That really, truly
        she wanted to see him

Again and again
She'd made herself strong
Against the hurt
Just be friends – she'd agreed
So that when the time came
They could both
        go
          to their empty beds
              alone
And feel safe and secure
That their need
    the gaping desire
  had not shown itself
  for what it was

No, she said to herself
I will not lay myself open
    to his rejection
It will certainly be good
    to see him

The memories danced around her head
        And would not leave

I want him in my bed
She said to her friends
They knew that
  despite her coolness
  the longing did not go away

The memory of pleasure
    lingered
      sometimes catching her
        unawares

She wanted to relive that memory
so much

And yet she was prepared
to let him go
if that was what
he wanted

She was much stronger now!

10

Note written 29 July 1984

I am reading Lacan

    Suddenly I remember.

    I am thinking of my 'investment' in you and yours in me. The scene is the house in.... The day of my leaving. I am distraught. I cannot stop crying. The tears will not abate and I feel foolish. I feel frightened by your silence, sitting stiffly on the hard chair by the table. I want you to touch – and know that you cannot touch – me. That touch between us is impossible. That all you can do is watch the depths of my distress in horror, fear, anger. Suddenly I am sixteen and my father is dead. Died in the night. Here and then gone.

11

The Words To Say It*

(January 1985)

Words. Words to speak of our oppression, to tell stories of how and what have made us what we have become. Material for struggle. Building blocks for a future. In *The Words To Say It* Marie Cardinal reveals, with inspiring courage, her own history: a history of pain and terror, culminating in madness. Through psychoanalysis she makes the joyful, painful, terrible rediscovery of her own past, untying the knots of madness. It is one of the most moving histories I have read. Marie Cardinal seeks to be historian of her own past, but she is not a detached observer who turned to psychoanalysis for a method to do history. She was, in her own words, imprisoned by what she had forgotten. She was mad and on the verge of bleeding to death as a result of ceaseless menstrual flow, for which she had been hospitalized on countless occasions. Only when her psychoanalyst refused to treat the physical symptom as anything other than an outer sign of an inner struggle did the bleeding stop and the story of her healing begin. Cardinal spares us nothing in her miraculous story. She bridges, once and for all, the ridiculous gap between the normal and the pathological, the sane and the mad. For her strength is to show, by her own story, how much our own histories overlap with hers, whether or not we have lived through neurotic or psychotic crises, depressions, hopelessness, terror, loss, death. She shows us how, in the tiniest fragments of memory, lie the keys to open the secret doors to our own stories. In so doing she tells us so very much about psychoanalysis.

This little book, for me, helps to put flesh on statements of the radical potential of psychoanalysis, such as Jacqueline Rose's (see pp. 102–3). Our constant failure becomes a point of resistance, but also of pain, of forgetting, of struggle. Neurotics and psychotics all of us, then. For in

---

*Marie Cardinal: *The Words To Say It* (London 1984)

this account sanity and madness, normal and pathological, are shown up for what they are – not psychiatry's dividing line between health and illness, but there in our unconscious, our own formation.

Cardinal does not celebrate madness as though Woman, the Irrational being Other to Man, were something to gaze at in wonder. Neither, like some writers, does she pay homage to madness, as invested with either the spark of creative genius or the non-normalized consciousness, the revolutionary potential, of the schizophrenic. As one who has known madness, she finds, in the eyes of the neurotic, the terror which speaks of desperation, belied by an all-too-normal coping, while inside is a body tortured by a hidden and silent pain:

> ... this wandering, this despair, this cry for help, this powerlessness to express oneself that I know and understand well. Something poignant. The aliena-tion of the neurotic is tragic, because it is an alienation which doesn't tip the whole world into madness. There is only you, on the inside, who have tipped into the useless, into disorder. On the outside, everything is normal, you seem to be fit for society, while on the inside you don't understand anything about it. The more you plunge into neurosis, the less you can insert yourself into society, and not for political reasons or any other kind. For reasons you don't understand, don't know, you are surrendered to an unknown which wishes you harm and hunts you ceaselessly. It is hell.
> (*Autrement dit*, p. 30, my translation)

Such pain, such forgetting, while it remains, is not the road to any kind of revolution. It is the revelation of the history she recounts which is a revolutionary act. For to tell such stories is not to be normalized; it is rather to create new histories and therefore new places and strengths from which to struggle. It is to break the prison bars of forgetting, the forgetting which imprisons in its attempt to cover over traces of past pain. Memory, then, is unlocking the past; freeing the spirit. Memory is filling the gaps, breaking the silence, telling what could previously not be spoken, which was buried in the frozen silences of the history of women.

The tiniest fragments of past events become, in the eyes of a fright-ened child, the most self-destructive of fantasies. These are the events of Cardinal's life; the desires and fears of her mother, who tried unsuccess-fully, on the eve of her divorce, to abort the child she was carrying. Marie was the target of that terrible ambivalence, and she felt it. Yet, as she herself was to say later, any search for a simple causality in her history is fruitless. For her mother, too, devout Catholic that she was, was constituted by the conditions and the moment that formed her:

> To tell it [this history] it would be necessary for me to rework the whole history of Christianity, matriarchy, colonization, money, etc. Otherwise I'd

tell you totally personal anecdotes and one would reach the conclusion: it's because my father was like this and my mother like that that I was something else. That's not very satisfactory. It's true that it's because they were what they were that I am what I am. But they were carriers of what? It's what they transmitted that interests me.
(Marie Cardinal in conversation with Annie Leclerc, *Autrement dit*, p. 25, my translation)

What Cardinal manages to achieve so wonderfully is to show how the tiniest moments in that history – 'no matter how minuscule, how ordinary'; 'a scented sprig, a flash of colour, a flashing light, a fragment, a sensation, a shattering work. And less even than that, a rustle, an echo. And still less even: a nothing that is nevertheless something' – how these fragments can become an anxiety, a symptom, a hallucinated vision. She shows us how distress is produced and its origin forgotten. Her story is so rich that it is a pity to try to retell it here. Rather, I want to dwell for a moment on an incident which had many resonances for me – when Cardinal is first told by her mother about menstruation and what it means to become physically a woman:

'Don't lower your head, don't be afraid. All women go through this, you know; they don't die of it. I admit that men are better off than we are. They don't know troubles like these. It is true they go to war . . . I wonder which is worse . . .'
'And do you get it too?'
'Of course, I told you, all women do. One gets used to it. It's not painful apart from the dirt. It lasts only two or three days, four at the most.'
'Every month?'
'Every twenty-eight days as a rule. But having your period is one thing. Having children is another, although the two are related. The first is shocking at the outset but it can be easily concealed. It's like breathing or hunger, or any other natural function. You see what I mean? It's inevitable. It's the way we're made. . . . Also, from the moment you have your first period, you must never be alone with a boy again, still less a man. You who love boys' games will have to control yourself. No more rides in the forest with Barded's sons! Is that understood?'
(Cardinal, 1984, pp. 86–7)

JUNE 1984

Today in therapy I was ten.
For some time now I had been reading women's magazines. One advertisement told me that every day of the month could be wonderful with Tampax. What on earth could this miracle called Tampax be? After

all, what could transform every day of the month? Finally, curiosity got the better of me. I asked my mother. Later, she told me that this was the cue she had been waiting for, the key to my initiation. A neighbour's daughter had asked about the incinerator in the school lavatory. There was a terrifying sense of tension, of furtive secrecy. My mother led me into the garden. Clearly the house was too public a place to reveal what she had to tell me. We walked round the bits of crazy paving by the rose bushes, round and round, circle after circle. Three of those rose bushes still grow in my garden. I dug them out of the earth to remember by. She told me then what being a woman meant. Blood, pain, every month. I lay on the analytic couch and sobbed. No wonder, then, no wonder I had wanted to deny my sex for so long.

'I don't think men have anything like this.' Didn't she know? What was this thing which had to be concealed, not spoken of, blood to be endured, which nobody, but nobody, must know about?

And every month too. But why? What was it for? She told me nothing more. Merely that it would happen to me, soon. Yet everything about the episode told me so much more about the shame and secrecy attached to becoming a woman. So this is what Tampax was to liberate me from! That spurious kind of freedom that would allow me to swim, would liberate me from the hell of growing up.

Recently, a friend sent me a copy of a modern tampon advert. It showed a typewriter being thrown out of a modern office block. It was headed: 'Fems. Doing things your way ... Kotex Fems tampons are designed for today's woman. The woman who chooses to do things her way.' So now tampons give us the spurious liberation from the drudgery of being a woman, being a secretary. Like those from my youth, such tampons offer to liberate us by concealment, by helping us to deny to the outside the truth of our menstrual cycles. None but ourselves need to know. Only tampons can liberate us from the adult femininity of servicing others. What denial, what forgetting, what pseudo-liberation!

I was having a bath. Maybe I was about eleven. I no longer remember. My mother came into the bathroom. Out of the blue: 'Do you know what happens if you get too close to boys?' Actually, I had no idea. Was it bad, then, simply to get close to them? It was another episode marked by the furtiveness and shame of the earlier conversation. I blushed deeply and mumbled that I knew. It was a total lie. But I couldn't stand the tension, the embarrassment. No more was said on the subject. That constituted my mother's only attempt at sex education. My ignorance knew no bounds. My mother was very concerned about the transmission of disease from the toilet seats in public lavatories. We were taught never to sit on them, but to pee standing up. For a long time, at secondary school, I was terrified of sitting on chairs on which boys had been sitting in the previous lesson. Was THIS too close? What if I could get pregnant by sitting on their seats, or catch something? ... 'So THIS is what it means to grow up,' I wrote in my notebook, last year. And then I added the line: 'I liked the stories better.' Tampax stories. Fairy stories. Their version of growing up mentioned princes, beautiful maidens and happiness ever after. There was no mention of periods, shame or drudgery. Only the couple walking off into the sunset after the perfect kiss. Another sugary forgetting. Another painful denial. Isn't the memory which will free us so much more difficult than the balm which helps us forget?

Marie Cardinal tells stories. She explores, she feels and she unravels tiny secrets locked inside the silence. Fact and fantasy. Myth. All blend together. Suddenly, I feel angry – about that interest in psychoanalysis which denies this. Which is all science, objective. Theory. It is, of course, so clever to use psychoanalysis and never talk about yourself. Safer, too. Never to admit your own madness, while explaining that of others. Can we, then, only explain and not explore our own formation? Do we have no room for our contradictions? For the violence of our emotions? The sane disavow their madness by locking up the mad: keeping it at bay, safe where no one can see, let alone look at it inside themselves. It is so easy to project our bad feelings, to locate them inside others. They are safe there. They hold our badness for us, where we don't have to look. It is a good mechanism, along with forgetting. Let us demolish it.

> Each time I opened one of the dreaded doors, I realized that the mechanism of the lock was not as complicated as I had believed, and that, where I dreaded to discover terror, torture and horror, I discovered the little girl in all her moods: unhappy, infatuated and terrified.
> (Cardinal, 1984, p. 104)

References

Cardinal, M. (1977) *Autrement dit*. Paris, Grasset.
Rose, J. (1983) 'Femininity and Its Discontents'. *Feminist Review*, no. 14.

12

Schoolgirl fictions

INTRODUCTION

In this essay I want to begin to bring together a variety of fictions, uniting studies of popular culture, cinema and fictions for children with an engagement with those other powerful, scientific fictions: the fiction of the child.

In so doing I shall tentatively link the creation of fantasies of what we take to be the 'real', the scientifically constituted arena of modern education, and link it to a fictional constitution of the child as object of the pedagogic gaze. That scientific and pedagogic gaze may be described as creating a fictional image of 'the child' as an object of the adult desire, and thereby producing fictional spaces for children to enter: thus fictions of children and fictions for children may be examined together. In particular, in examining fictional spaces for little girls, I shall explore the fictions of a hygienic, sanitized child as compared with a covert, highly sexualized image entering the classroom only at its interstices: the forbidden, denied and suppressed production of children as heterosexual. I shall suggest that for little girls the fictional spaces open to them create a series of double-binds and contradictions such that certain positions become *overtly* open to them, while others have to exist only in the margins.

I want to begin by positing the primary school as an impossible fiction and therefore itself the site of the creation of a 'reality' which cannot exist, but is terrifyingly powerful in its implications. The British primary school has, since at least the mid-sixties, been the focus of attention in the Western educational world: it has become a paradigm of good practice with young children. But it was constituted on the basis of a dream: a hope of a moral order in which a fantasized 'nature' would invest in the innocence of children the hope of a better world – a world free from hate and fear. Children and childhood become the focus of this terrifying fiction – a fiction of freedom and safety and happiness – the progressive dream. Childhood then became created as a fictional space, with the family and school the major sites of its production.

What that 'nature' is has been the object of strenuous debate and considerable intervention: from Rousseau and Locke to the child study movement and modern child development, ethological psychology, and child psychotherapy. It can be 'instincts'; it can be innocent, full of love, or full of hate. Nevertheless the area in which the fiction is created, and the remedy, are all too clear. As I have documented elsewhere (Walkerdine, 1984), the child-centred pedagogy is the site for the production of the naturalized child, who progresses towards maturity within the nurturant confines of its walls.

Such practices also help to create the child they claim to be nurturing. The practices themselves, premissed as they are on the monitoring and observation (surveillance) of a natural sequence of development (in that sense), create what natural and normal means (Walkerdine, 1984). Instead, therefore, of being a place where natural development is watched, nurtured, monitored (a place for setting children free), the school becomes the place where overt regulation and government become replaced by covert self-government, self-regulation.

It is this fiction which is central to my exploration. In the short historical sketch I wrote in 'Changing the Subject' (1984) I pointed to the investment in the regulation and government of children as one aspect of the form of governmentality to which Michel Foucault refers in his analysis of the shift of forms of power and government from an overt sovereign power to forms of administration of the social body (Foucault, 1979), the administration of children. In the history of early education, the rise of scientific pedagogy – or education according to nature – went hand in hand with the concern that compulsory education as a device for ensuring a docile populace was failing and that overt regulation (constant surveillance and ceaseless activity) was to be replaced by education in which children were to be freed from coercion, and love was to replace fear. In this sense love was to ensure a more effective pedagogy, one in which incipient rebellion would be quelled before it began.

Central to those concerns was a school in which children would grow up 'free from hate and fear'. Although child-centred pedagogy had advocates from many political persuasions, it was centrally considered a safe space, a kind of greenhouse to which children would be removed from the squalor and degeneracy, the poverty and crime of cities in which implicit rebellion lurked, a 'natural' space where childhood could progress untrammelled, and children would become the self-regulating and democratic citizens, the hope for the world:

In the name of those who have died for the freedom of Europe, let us go
forward to claim for this land of ours that spread of true education which shall
be the chief guarantee of the freedom of our children forever! (*The Times*)

A powerful and passionate statement after World War II – the freedom
of our children for ever! If, by merely stating the right to freedom – not
only of children, but of the 'free world' – freedom could be guaranteed,
then democracy would begin in the cradle. Child-rearing and early
education both became the sites for ensuring that freedom, and central
was the motivating presence of women. Part of this fiction is the denial of
power. Covert regulation becomes typified by the image of the bourgeois
mother who nurtures, helps and understands. Schooling, therefore,
becomes a space in which inequality is denied, where the fiction is
perpetrated that equality can be produced by means of a new and better
'natural bond'. It thus becomes a powerful veridicality (see Foucault)
which has material effects on aid for children. In this fiction it is as
though this 'new mother' could take away the pain of deprivation, loss
and powerlessness, and thus create the basis of a democracy. We could
say that this fiction was itself created on a denial of pain – indeed, a
desire to conquer pain inscribed in the idea of freed and happy children,
playing in the safe space of the classroom. However, this and other
gender issues are hardly ever presented as central to the history of child-
centredness. The child-centred pedagogy at the heart of the primary
school is a powerful fiction because it is a fiction of freedom, democracy,
safety, nature – for ever.

The pedagogy of nature eschews all texts: it is taken to be realism
typified – there is activity, 'doing', the manipulation of objects and
natural materials. Language is used only as far as it reflects or represents
the underlying cognitive development of children. Such texts and
language as there are must closely approximate such nature. But very
central to the claim is that this realism is itself a pernicious fiction,
founded upon a denial of pain and loss and building upon it a desperate
desire at once for the safety of an enabling nurturance and for mastery of
nature, which can then be shaped, moulded and tamed into submission –
scientific mastery of a calculable universe. The twin and joint fictions of a
nurtured and mastered nature are unfolded and made fact in the classroom. The child whose nature we are to monitor with our all-knowing,
all-seeing gaze is to be calculatedly liberated, controlled into freedom.
This gaze constitutes the child as the universalized object of accounts of
universal language and cognitive development. Although the basis of this
approach is a kind of realism which is taken to be basic to 'nature' (only
play with objects, no clouding texts except realist ones), in practice it is a
powerful but impossible fiction. What do I mean by this?

The social and behavioural scientist, the teacher, the mother, all have roles to play in producing this child as the object of their benevolent but total gaze. However, I wish to argue that first, the total gaze is a powerful and impossible fiction. Secondly, it is the fantasy of the creators of this fiction, as well as those whom it inscribes within its orbit, that we must examine. Thirdly, we need to explore how children become constituted in this fiction.

I say that this fiction is impossible because it produces what it claims to describe – it is a powerful discursive formation which in imposing a reading upon the school produces the practices in its image. We need to look carefully, then, at this word 'produce', for I shall argue that the child which is the object is not coterminous with actual children or teachers. What the pedagogy does is produce *norms* of what is supposed to be, and to be happening: it therefore pathologizes the difference which it finds from the child it defines. The fiction is a production because it is embodied, built into the very architecture, the seating arrangements, the work cards. It helps to constitute the positions of 'teacher' and 'child'.

This impossible fiction is constituted on a set of differences – opposites – and a set of denials:

facilitating environment
teacher	child
passive	active
feminine	masculine

The child develops in the safety of a facilitating environment – it is its opposite and Other. The child is active, creative, doing, divergent, and so forth. The environment is passive, facilitating, nurturant: the teacher watches, enables, knows when to interest but not to interfere, knows each child as an individual. The teacher is part of the environment (part of the woodwork?). She is *there* – it is her watchful and surveillant presence which facilitates the mastery and independence, the self-reliance of the child. She must know thirty children 'as individuals'. She is passive; the child is an active body.

This distinction is repeated again and again; therefore femininity becomes encapsulated in an impossible fiction of a nurturant Other. It is the teacher who is to ensure the 'freedom of our children for ever' (*Times*). She is the price paid for autonomy, its hidden and dispensable cost.

SCHOOLING FOR GIRLS

The education of girls as children presents something of a dilemma – a dilemma about sexuality – suppressed in the pedagogic fantasy itself. What are girls to be educated for? To be mothers, teachers? Children are active, independent, achieve mastery. Little girls can become carers, or join the caring professions, serve others or join the service industries: they can be educated enough to care for the knowers but not enough to know. Elsewhere, I have argued that 'knowing' and 'mastery' are also impossible fictions – a desire, then, also invested in the social scientist and teacher who looks and can 'see it like it is' and in seeing it can control and shape destiny – playing at God? (Walkerdine, 1989).

What has all this to do with fiction? Powerful fictions create their own truth conditions: they create a veridicality of the present social order. In this way they have very powerful effects. But this is not enough. I am also saying that these fictions themselves embody powerful fantasies which try to produce the social world as a calculated and also a safe space.

Educational fictions of children are devoid of sexuality. Jacqueline Rose (1985) argues that children's literature since the development of compulsory schooling relies upon a hygienic, sanitized and desexualized concept of the child which specifically denies the desire of adults for children. The universal child is gender-neutral, self-disciplined, active. The desires invested in the production of this child displace any sexual desire of adults for children by displacing passion into nurturance in mothers – and investing the child with an active exploration of the world. I would add that the universalized, natural and gender-neutral child is very specific indeed. I have argued in Chapter 5 that such a fiction creates the idea, for example, of cognitive and linguistic universals, which then pathologize difference and render experience itself a sanitized category. In this sense, working-class experience is understood as bad, pathological, a danger to the moral order.

It is this moral order which is threatened by the sexuality of children and the desires of adults. The moral order sets up positions for children and adults to enter. Mastery and containment – the father and the mother – the ultimate fantasies of the civilized world. At least Freud, Lacan and Melanie Klein recognized that they were fantasies: Object Relations theorists in Britain and ego psychologists in the United States appeared to take fantasy for reality (see Denise Riley's excellent *War in the Nursery*). The moral order displaces this sexuality from its overt stage. The classroom fictions offer us only the facilitating 'teacher' and 'the child'. These are regimes of truth in which the signifiers 'teacher', 'child', make sense in the psychoeducational discourses, and therefore in the actual regulation of practices.

How do children become 'the child'? What is the relation between signifier and signified, discourse and materiality?

SCHOOLGIRL FICTIONS

What positions, therefore, are available for girls? Can they become the child? I have argued in Chapter 6 that people go to elaborate lengths to *prove* the intellectual inferiority of girls, and therefore that girls cannot achieve mastery. Such fictions are heavily invested with fantasies and fears that girls and women constitute a *danger* to the moral order – reasoning women, said Rousseau, are monsters. Girls present in the classroom those characteristics which are danger signs for the safety of the child-centred pedagogy: hard work, diligent rule-following – everything which is the antithesis of 'the child' and also speaks of the dangerous 'old ways' – 'chalk and talk' – which bred incipient rebellion. What lurks beneath the well-behaved passivity? Well, what lurks, hidden and subverted, is sexuality – there in the very fictions which are denied in the overt form of the pedagogy. The child whose safety and innocence are worshipped is a far cry from the sexualized child, object of an overtly sexualized heterosexual gaze. Yet they are not far apart. Such a sexualized child exists as another position, a heterosexual fiction present at the very interstices of the overt pedgagogy – its covert and dangerous shadow.

Juliet Mitchell (1983), suggests that there are three positions for women: the mother, the hysteric and the feminine. The mother has the 'child penis', the hysteric denies that she has lost or is lacking anything, and the feminine is the sexualized child. I want to suggest, very tentatively, that the *mother*, the *feminine* and the *hysteric* represent three positions for girls to enter the classroom: they can become quasi-teachers, or sexualized objects of an adult gaze. I do not for a moment think that for actual girls these are mutually exclusive, but that they present some important distinctions. The distinctions I wish to raise are these:

good	poor/bad
m/c	w/c
mind	body

because they come up in the fictional spaces which the girls can enter defined by the veridicality of the pedagogy and of the alternative fiction of popular cultural forms and practices.

I want to refer to a study of six-year-old girls in a school in London.

Here I undertook an intensive study of eight girls, four performing well and four performing badly – as chosen by teachers and tests. I am going to refer to the different fictional spaces open to them. I want to focus especially on four girls: Rachel, Janie, Joelle and Elishe. Janie and Rachel are doing well, whereas Joelle and Elishe are doing poorly. But first let me refer to all the girls. As part of the work, I audio-recorded them at home, at school, interviewed them and their teacher and parents. I examined and am still examining, in some detail, the popular cultural references which are made, as well as other aspects of their school lives. As part of this, I took photographs. When I looked at the photographs I had taken I noticed something I had not seen before – the way the girls were photographed.

If we compare these with photos from educational texts, an important distinction emerges – in the educational photos the girls look at their work and away from the camera. They are busy! (See Sharp and Green's analysis of education and social control, 1975.) They do not look *at* the camera. The camera is in the position of the observer, the surveillant Other, watching them work or play: it is a pseudo-, an asexual naturalism. The cartoon-type figures of the girls (and boys) from other educational texts are similar (Plate 5). If we compare these with other images, the position of the camera and of the viewer is of a different kind of voyeurism: the gaze is returned. We see the sexualized schoolgirl, whose childhood is a sign of her enticing eroticism, whether the image be from popular magazines or child pornography.

She returns the look: the look is erotic. She is captured by the heterosexual gaze of the voyeur. There appear to be two kinds of voyeurism: the voyeurism of the helping other or *detached observer*, whose desire is denied in the scientificity of the look, and that of the overtly sexual gaze of the 'popular culture'.

This latter gaze encompasses everything which the Other denies, and it is returned. Let us look, then, at the photographs I took of the girls. When I looked at them I noticed too what I had done – I had taken naturalistic shots of the children being 'schoolchildren' – that is, being busy. *But* all the 'good' girls carried on working. Note how they look away from the camera, are diligent, etc. – here 'good' connotes both academic performance and behaviour. By comparison, the poor girls rush to be photographed – they *pose* – their gaze to the camera is highly eroticized (and here, of course, 'poor' connotes academic performance and also poverty, lower class, animality, badness). One of the distinctions I want to draw here is between body and mind. There are ways of 'making it' (particularly for working-class girls) – one is the mind – being good, the other is the body. It is the opposite of the mastery/animal brute distinction for men (machismo/professor). The body/mind distinction here is invested in being the sanitized or sexualized schoolgirl. The good girl presents for herself and to us a diligence which is somewhat like that of the nurturant teacher. Where in this fictional space is the badness – is the child as innocent as she seems?

For all these girls, popular culture, with its explicit fiction of romantic heterosexuality, is present at the interstices of the practices (in the denied and marginalized spaces) where the sanitized images of children's fiction cannot reach. The girls present the *failure* of the attempts to create 'the child' as the centre of the safe, desexualized haven. No matter to what lengths the school may go, danger enters: the walls cannot seal off the outside.

The girls sing pop songs, talk about TV programmes, watch films. These fictions create other spaces. In the summer of 1982, when I made these recordings, one song was sung relentlessly by many girls in this and other schools, and by girls of all ages: Toni Basil's 'Oh Mickey'. Toni Basil (see Plate 4) is the epitome of the sexualized schoolgirl-turned-vamp. She is a cheerleader and wants Mickey to 'give it to her any way he can!' In a promotional video against huge, butch women, she stands out as sexual, wanting, angry – any way she can get it. The girls sang this song frequently. One 'good' girl, Rachel, held her own mock talent competition in the back garden: 'Oh Mickey' was the object of several teenybopper talent contests, full of pre-teen versions of Toni Basil in cheerleader gear. Another 'good' girl, Janie, is transformed in minutes from 'good' to 'bad' girl. The rendition of 'Oh Mickey' is sung in the privacy of the toilets. There in front of the mirror she sighs and poses: the child, the woman, the virgin, the whore, the harlot.

As she leaves the classroom she crosses the hall. In the toilets the suppressed aspect, that which cannot be revealed in her 'good girl' position, is the fantasy of being the object of that other look: the sexual gaze. She sighs in front of the mirror. Then, told to stop messing about, she returns to 'normality'; she steps out of one fiction and into another. As she crosses the hall to her classroom, some children from another class are dancing to a piece of classical flute music. The teacher shouts to a boy: 'You're not supposed to be running, you're a jumping frog – jump!'

High culture – flute music, and sanitized children playing at being little animals (far, far from the dangerous animal passions, of course) – high culture presents a similar part of that safety to which Janie returns in her place in the classroom. Later she and other girls talk about their experiences. Some others admit to having sung and acted out 'Fame'!

SCHOOLGIRL FICTIONS

CONCLUSION

I want to conclude this sketch by making reference again to the body/ mind distinction, to the production of desire and the living out of a fantasy. The fantasy is a fantasy of escape — from drudgery, the pain of being a woman, a mother, the pain of being working class. (For more examples see Chapter 19, 'Video replay'.) In other words, I am suggesting that the denial in the pedagogic discourses and practices, and the wider cultural denial of which they are a part, is lived out by these little girls in the way they are positioned and see themselves as good, poor and bad, and the splitting and denial which this engenders.

Uncovering the fictions of our formation is about examining our inscription within those fantasies. In that sense 'woman' and 'child' in all their guises are impossible fictions, yet fictions invested so powerfully in the practices which make up the veridicality of the present social order.

REFERENCES

Foucault, M. (1979) *Discipline and Punish*. Harmondsworth, Penguin.
Mitchell, J.L. (1983) *Women: The Longest Revolution*. London, Virago.
Riley, D. (1983) *War in the Nursery*. London, Virago.
Rose, J. (1985) *The Case of Peter Pan or the Impossibility of Children's Fiction*. London, Macmillan.
Sharp, R. and Green, A. (1975) *Education and Social Control*. London, Routledge & Kegan Paul.
Walkerdine, V. (1984) 'Developmental Psychology and Child-Centred Pedagogy', in Henriques *et al.*, eds, *Changing the Subject*.
Walkerdine, V. (1989) *The Mastery of Reason*. London, Routledge.

13

Breaking the Law of the Father:

Three films

In our male-dominated culture, women have always been considered strange, secretive and sometimes dangerous.
    (POLLACK, p. 149)

Violent, silent crime. Committed in one film by a mute woman, in another by three women, strangers to each other, one almost catatonic. There is no reason for words. There is no language to utter what these women have to say. For there are always others ready, willing to speak on their behalf, to excuse their badness, their madness. No words, then, can explain the terror, the smiling, fearful and silent response to unwanted advances, every day, everywhere. The response is silence. Just utter the words in reply, try as we have all tried it before, and the apparent adulation turns, fast as the switch-blade, into violence, hatred, fear.

'Come on, darling, give us a smile. . . .'

'Fuck off.'

'Whore, cunt, you stupid ugly . . .'

We cower, fearful, in corners, waiting for the sudden noise, the violation out of nowhere. But we are not the only ones who are afraid. Why, we might well ask, are men so afraid of women that they have to prove their superiority again and again with horrific acts of violence? Although, in our positivist culture, proof is usually considered the secure basis of certainty, on the contrary there is doubt, terrible doubt, lurking behind the relentless push to proof.

When in 1981 I wrote a paper about an incident which occurred in a nursery school, in which two four-year-old boys were horribly and verbally abusive to their female teacher (see Chapter 1), there were people who genuinely believed that the transcript I reprinted there was fraudulent, that such incidents simply did not occur. Where, might one ask, have these people been looking? In my current work, analysing transcripts from lessons in schools from infants' to secondary, and interviews with girls from six to sixteen, the violence towards the girls and female teachers is a fact of the everyday life of the classroom. There is hardly an interviewee who fails to mention it.

Violence and oppression. I want to explore the relationship between the production of desire, particularly the production of female paranoia, its relation to male sexuality, the suppression of violence, aggressivity and the fear of and identification with the oppressor, hoping desperately for the reward, the safe place in heaven, where the Heavenly Father gives the reward of his gaze, where we are safe at last from present pain.

In this exploration, feminine sexuality is central. I shall counterpose this to a position which would understand aggressivity as the central trope of human subjectivity, as in the work of Melanie Klein. I shall, however, be equally critical of the denial of violence and the pursuance of nurturance present in some Object Relations schools of psychoanalysis. Especially, I wish to make a link between the regulation of female sexuality, criminality and maternity. In so doing I wish totally to oppose the position that female criminality and delinquency are the product of the failure of maternal nurturance and criticize the view of female delinquency as linked with promiscuous sexuality, understood as the result of a desperate search for the security of missed mothering. While I shall certainly state that love, affection and desire are central, I shall argue that such accounts constantly blame women for their oppression, while constantly avoiding and downplaying the production of male violence and the regulation of sexuality.

Today, as I write this, I am filled with rage. You will have to take account of this as you read. My rage is the result of having to endure and be the target of a man in a senior position's bid for power, to put me firmly in my place. That place, it turns out, is to be the grateful recipient of his patriarchal reassurance, his benevolence. But he himself is actually filled with a terrible rage. He believes I let him down, humiliated him, by displaying fear and paranoid weakness when I should have displayed strength. Not that this would have revealed something about me, but rather his strength in having chosen me. And so, ever since, for nine months now, he has, in an underhand way, retaliated. There is a complete split between the benevolent father he wishes to present to the world, and the rage he feels inside. This renders me the overt target of his rage while he overtly claims to have my interests at heart, so that he can present himself to the world as making me the object of his helpful beneficence.

It is a very common story. Some time ago I would desperately have wanted to believe in the Good Father, who, unlike the brutal one, would be the benevolent God of Christianity, for whom I must die, not the vengeful God of Judaism. I would have been grateful for being chosen to love him; in his love, ever after, I would feel release, safety for ever. A wonderful example of Lacan's account of female paranoia, the story of the ecstasy of St Teresa (Lacan, 1983). Now, I do not feel that. I feel intense anger at being the object of this beneficent gaze, anger because of what it hides, how it produces me and my desire, how it covers over these terrible splits – that, more than anything else, it covers over the terror inhabiting male power and the desperate search in the eyes of the man for the woman who will make good his own lack.

In this scenario the two positions, masculine and feminine, sit there, complementary to each other, both responsible for each other's continued production. I shall not claim that it is the mother who is to cure all this rage by the adequacy of her nurturance. On the contrary, I shall suggest that the modern form of mothering covers over, and indeed supports, a fantasy of certainty, of the independent male child who is in omnipotent control over a calculable universe, who has the power to explore and explain. On the other hand, neither do I see the answer as simply accepting the circuit of exchange which places the father at the centre of an unchanging structure: the timeless Law of Exogamy. In the classrooms in which I have been researching, while girls' complaints of boys' violence might be a central feature, equally important is female teachers' denial of it. Again and again, female teachers downplay and ignore the reported violence of boys – violence which is frequently directed at them as well as the girls. This downplaying – indeed, downright disavowal – of boys' violence is endemic to the pedagogic and child-rearing practices on which it is based. That is, boys are independent, brilliant, proper thinkers. They are also naughty. There seems here to be a splitting. The teachers constantly downplay the violence of boys, transforming it into words like 'naughty', understood as a positive attribute, one at the very least to be allowed and probably positively fostered as the basis of independent thinking. On the other hand, girls are, by and large, described as lacking the qualities boys possess. They are no trouble, but then their lack of naughtiness is also a lack of spark, fire, brilliance.

So the practices themselves actually and positively permit this violence and, moreover, covertly link it to that other kind of mastery, the brilliance of the omnipotent theorist who can explain the workings of the universe and thus lay claim to controlling them and to the certainty of proof. Conversely, the girls appear to live in a chronic state of paranoia. They are constantly afraid to make the challenges to authority which would win for them the accolade 'brilliant'. The female teachers, too, in their adulation of the boys and dismissal of the girls, tell us something about the production of desire and the support of that Other which too claims to possess what we lack. But these are fantasies, fictions lived out in the powerful veridicality of the regulation of the present-day practices. Such practices create truths which are read back on to the boys, girls, men and women themselves, claiming often to be the incontrovertible truths about human nature, rather than elaborate fantasies masquerading as certain and true explanations.

I'd like to explore three films here which have women as their central characters.* In each the woman or women are the target of oppression and abuse, sexual, mundane, violent. But while one, *Liquid Sky*, offers the romantic resolution to this oppression, true love and the light of the Heavenly Father, the heroines of the other two films, just as assuredly, break the Law of the Father. They become criminals. In *Liquid Sky* the destructive acts are performed by the main protagonist, a young woman who, as it were accidentally at first and then with deliberation, 'kills with her cunt'. People she is having sex with are literally wiped out at the moment of their orgasm. But her cunt is merely the receptacle for the power of the God (in this case a space creature/ship in need of the chemical produced at the moment of human orgasm). It is her cunt which does the killing, but the power which works through her is that of the spaceman. Indeed, this superman is not like other men and in the end she is dazzled by the power he has given her and falls in love with him even though she has only ever seen the spaceship. At the end of the film she is transported away (literally; it is as though finally she is allowed her orgasm) into the spaceship, and here the link with the fantasy of eternal life basking in the light of God is evoked.

In the other two films the women commit their own acts of destruction and there is no man to save them – indeed, no romantic resolution at all. Both films involve silent women who will not, or cannot, speak about their violence and aggression. The Law of the Father which they break involves, in each case, killing men. In *A Question of Silence* three women in a boutique silently kill a shop manager for no obvious motive. They all go home afterwards and enjoy themselves. One has a good dinner; another a treat; the third gets considerable satisfaction when, after being mistaken for a prostitute, she does indeed have sex with a stranger for money; he is seen as the victim and she is very powerful.

Ms 45 Angel of Vengeance (Abel Ferrara, 1980, USA)
A Question of Silence (Marleen Gorris, 1981, Netherlands)
Liquid Sky (Slava Tzuckerman, 1981, USA)

When they are arrested, none of the women will speak or offer anything in mitigation. They refuse to be understood as mad in order to be excused. The only sound they utter in court is laughter. At first their female lawyer tries to 'understand' and therefore to pathologize them, but later she comes to see that the legal system has no way of understanding their act and the violence of their emotions, so there is no point in speaking. The legal system is presented as surveillant and regulatory, and therefore as having no way of understanding in its Symbolic Order just what it is they are trying to say. Their own violent rage at all the oppression they have suffered has no discourse for its articulation. Their silence, then, becomes the most aggressive act of all, but we are shown no resolution, no happy ending.

In Ms 45, the heroine is a deaf-mute who is attacked by a man, manages to kill him and then decides to wreak her own vengeance on other men who could oppress her. She goes out late at night dressed as a nun, and when she finds predatory men, shoots them. She is killed in the end simply massacring people at a Halloween party; it is another woman who finally shoots her. But it is the deaf-mute – a woman who is beautiful, but treated like a 'dumb animal'; who cannot speak and dresses as a nun, that apparently most chaste of women – who rebels; inside her wells up all the fury of the oppressed against the oppressor.

I want to explore briefly the relation between these films. All recognize women's aggression and violence, and in none of them is that represented as a product of the failure of nurturance. Liquid Sky is a masculine fantasy. The woman's power to kill is simply a product of a Higher Power, and it is that Power which attracts her even though it entails her own destruction. Or does it? The final shots show her liquidated by the spaceship, and it is unclear whether she has been beamed aboard or killed. But whichever it is, such an ending has strong resonances with the Lacanian idea of the safe place in the sky, the martyrdom of St Teresa, only to bask in God's everlasting love. The hidden trope here is death. Everlasting life is death. The gaze of that Other who will save her is one which in fact stops her from becoming strong, from breaking his law, from killing the Father. Although Liquid Sky may be seen on the surface as a story of female paranoia in the Lacanian sense, it can conversely be read as the story of an omnipotent masculine fantasy, or at least a belief in a safe place where we can dance in the safe gaze of the Other who protects us. What the heroine of the film wants is her own jouissance (Cf. Lacan) – to dance, to play like a child in the gaze of God. Indeed, at the end of the film she is presented as dancing as she is beamed up/liquidated by the spaceship. The director, Slava Tzuckerman, a Russian Jew, living in New York, longs for the place of freedom, of artistic creativity, for heaven. Anne's story is also the story of his desire –

which he sees as a feminization – to be transported to a romantic resolution, a heaven of artistic play. It is however, a false resolution: heaven doesn't exist. Lacan too seems to long to be a woman, fascinated with female paranoia and female crime, to take the female position and to be freed from the terrible burden of having to play God, to be the one who knows. He is obsessed by women who break the law when he believes in an incontrovertible Law of Exogamy, the exchange of women by men. He is trapped by the structure of his knowing, by being a law-maker, when he longs to know what it feels like to break the law, to be subjected, to be oppressed and then released into everlasting life.

In the other two films, killing the Father is punished – by death in Ms 45, by incarceration in A Question of Silence. In neither case is there a way in which women's oppression can be spoken or avenged which does not in the end destroy the victim herself. Yet none of these films denies the power and violence of women's responses to oppression. None of the women is simply a helpless and passive victim. Each acts where she has been denied the possibility of speaking. The opposite of the dream of the safe place in the sky, of freedom from oppression into everlasting life, is rebellion, breaking the Law, but here too the result is incarceration and death. Lacan leaves us with no way out except to become like the master, to take the Symbolic and then to tell us that anyway, for women, such a position is impossible. So then Symbolic is not the end, but the fantasy of a benevolent father produces the fantasy of a release, a paranoia, a longing to be made safe rather than fighting back. Breaking the Law means going beyond exogamy, refusing the exchange, but refusing also the other sop of maternal nurturance if it stifles our passion. Breaking the Law means beginning to struggle, to fight back. And that is why, in Ms 45 and A Question of Silence, that fighting back has to be shown as being ultimately punished as though there were no way out. Indeed, other women – the female lawyer in A Question . . . and the woman who shoots Thana in Ms 45 – become threats who might betray the struggle of the law-breakers, for they have to identify with the criminals – something which both resist.

We can move forwards, not backwards, to expose the historically specific modes of our regulation and subjugation. The scream becomes a roar, the roar a blood-curdling yell. No wonder men are so afraid of women's power. No wonder it has to be so forcibly suppressed.

Mock-up of Exhibit A::
Case for the defense.

Three glass cases, mounted in a triangle.

Defense of what, he asked?
She could not answer, only that someone else
felt he had to defend herself.
After all, she was a student of hers.
loved him, and of course failed
to think of anything … of her
case … any help. …
Something had to be defense,
didn't it?

Mock-up of
Exhibit A: Case for the defense

Rotania in Mexico?
Three glass cases
mounted in a triangle.

Defense of what, he asked?
She could not answer; after all she was
trying to give up being a psychologist.
Voices inside were associating freely: 'My case rests.'
She wanted to give it to him — after all she took
the photographs for her. Another voice reminded her
sternly that she'd failed to take any decent photos.
'It's the thought that counts,' said her mother, gently.

REFERENCES

Lacan, J. (1983) 'God and the *jouissance* of Woman', in J. Mitchell and J. Rose, eds,
    Feminine Sexuality: Jacques Lacan and the École Freudienne. London, Macmillan.
Pollack, O. (1961) *The Criminality of Women*. New York, A.S. Barnes.

14

Femininity as performance

INTRODUCTION

As girls at school, as women at work, we are used to performing. We are used, too, to dramaturgical metaphors which tell us that life is a performance in which we do nothing but act out a series of roles,[1] or indeed that these roles can be peeled away like layers of an onion to reveal a repressed core, a true self, which has been inhibited, clouded by the layers of social conditioning which obscure it.[2] Such views form much of the common sense of ideas about gender socialization in relation to education. Girls are conditioned into passivity, the story often goes; this is why they do badly at school: implicitly, femininity is seen as a series of roles, often imposed by agents of socialization, of whom the worst offenders are taken to be women: mothers and female teachers. But I want to tell a different story – one of female success, one which criticizes the idea that socialization works to render girls and women wimpish, feminine and passive.

Let me begin with an example, one which can be multiplied many times over. A woman teacher, one of my students, receives a well-deserved Distinction for her Master's degree. She received more or less straight As for all her work, but still she cannot believe that the Distinction belongs to her; it is as though the person with her name exists somewhere else, outside her body: this powerful person whom she cannot recognize as herself. Instead, she feels that she is hopeless, consistently panics about her performance and appears to have little confidence in herself. She can, however, express her views clearly and forcefully and the external examiner in her *viva* thanked her for the tutorial! I am sure this story has resonances for many women. Indeed, I am sure I related this story because I too have been constantly aware that the Valerie

Walkerdine whom people speak well of feels as though it belongs to someone else, someone whom I do not recognize as me.

How is it that for many women, the powerful part of themselves has been so split off as to feel that it belongs to someone else? Here is no simple passive wimp femininity but a power which is desired, striven after, yet almost too dangerous to be acknowledged as belonging to the woman herself.

In this essay I shall explore this phenomenon, using work from both post-structuralism and psychoanalysis and data from my research on gender and schooling (Walkerdine et al., 1989) to illustrate my arguments.

PERFORMANCE IN SCHOOL

There is a widespread myth that girls and women perform poorly in school. In the Girls and Mathematics Unit we investigated this issue in relation to mathematics in research, spanning several years and with children aged four to fifteen (Walkerdine et al., 1989). The first way in which I want to deal with the issue of performance is to challenge the idea that femininity equals poor performance and to concentrate rather on the ways in which femininity is read. What I am concerned to demonstrate is the discursive production of femininity as antithetical to masculine rationality to such an extent that femininity is equated with poor performance, even when the girl or woman in question is performing well. In other words, I am talking not about some essential qualities of femininity, but about the way in which femininity is read as a constellation of signs which mark it off as antithetical to 'proper' performance to an incredible degree. When we first became aware of this, Rosie Walden and I called it 'the just or only phenomenon' (Walden and Walkerdine, 1982). By this, we meant that whenever a positive remark was made about girls' performance in mathematics, particularly the strong sense that girls performed well in school up until the transfer at eleven, a remark would be brought in which suggested that the performance was to be accounted for by 'something which amounted to nothing'. In other words, no matter how well girls were said to perform, their performance was always downgraded or dismissed in one way or another. These pejorative remarks usually related to the idea that girls' performance was based on hard work and rule-following rather than brains or brilliance (in other words, what was supposed to underlie real mathematical performance).[3] This reading of girls' performance was consistent across schools and the age-range. In the younger age-groups it was common for teachers to talk about boys as having 'potential', a term often used to explain their poor performance. Throughout the sample of thirty-nine classrooms, not one teacher mentioned 'potential' within a girl. Quite the contrary, if a girl were performing poorly there was no way she could be considered good – indeed, if she were performing well it was almost impossible for her to escape pejorative evaluations, while boys, it seemed, no matter how poorly they performed, were thought to have hidden qualities:

> Very, very hard worker. Not a particularly bright girl ... her hard work gets her to her standards.

This typical example of a comment about a girl can be compared with the following comment about a boy, of the kind that was never made about girls:

> ... can just about write his own name ... not because he's not clever, because he's not capable, but because he can't sit still, he's got no concentration ... very disruptive ... but quite bright.

Indeed, it was as though boys did indeed in fantasy possess the 'phallus'[4] while girls represented a fictional 'lack' or absence. For whatever was said, again and again, the presence of certain attributes, like good performance, was read as an indication of a lack of something much more fundamental even when, as in the case of many boys, they did not perform well academically (see the quote above).

This led me to point out that in engaging with issues concerning the 'truth about women' it is necessary to avoid being caught in an empiricist trap in which we are led to attempt to prove the mathematical equivalence of girls (Walkerdine et al., 1989). For here we are not presented with something as straightforward as 'the evidence of our own eyes'. Here, girls are doing well yet they are said, in one way or another, 'not to have what it takes', while many boys, whose performance is poor, are said to possess something even when it is not visible in their performance. In order to examine and to understand such a situation I believe that we have to move away from a simple empiricism to a position in which we understand fact, fiction and fantasy as interrelated. It is to post-structuralism that I turn for an account which will allow us to examine how it comes about that gender difference is produced in fictional ways which have power in that they are part of the truth-effects of the regulation of children in classrooms. They form a basis of the 'truth about women', in this case the truth that women do not have rational powers of the mind. Such a truth, I shall go on to argue, has to be desperately reasserted for fear that it is not true; only the paranoia of the powerful keeps it in circulation.

RATIONAL POWERS OF THE MIND

In Chapter 6 I argued that counting girls' performance as evidence is not distinct from the issue of which it is taken to be evidence of. We have not only to debate about the data but also to engage with why this decision is made at all, what it means, and what its effects are in terms of practical consequences for girls' education. Classically (within philosophy, for example), the truth of such statements has been the subject of epistemological critiques. But the latter treat truth as though it were a timeless matter, separating the conditions of the production of truth from truth itself. The question that I want to pose is not 'Are the arguments true?' but 'How is this truth constituted, how is it possible, and what effects does it have?' Such questions, derived from the methodology of genealogy utilized by Foucault, can help us begin to take apart this truth about girls. Only if we understand its historical production and its effectivity can we begin to go beyond it. We shall argue that we can chart the historical antecedents of the position that females do not possess a capacity for reason or have 'mathematical minds', and so document how and why the arguments in support of that position have such a force now, and how we might challenge them.

As we also saw in Chapter 6, ideas about reason and reasoning cannot be understood historically outside of considerations about gender, and the development of science from the seventeenth century was intimately connected to the control of nature by man.[5] Discussions about female failure have focused on a minority of girls.[6] Of course, it is not surprising that later science 'discovered' the 'female intellect'.[7] Thus women, taken also to possess the capacity to reason, were allowed to enter the competition – if they had *enough* ability. But this means that the terms of the debate are never changed; women must still prove themselves equal to men. I have tried to show why we should not unquestioningly accept these terms but should question their very foundation. We are not duty-bound to accept existing truth conditions. We would argue that showing the truth about girls to be a production in which there are no *simple* matters of fact is a central and strategic part of our struggle.

In the same chapter I discuss specific concepts within the development of education which I have outlined elsewhere[8] – 'the child' (gender unspecified) taken to develop with a 'facilitating environment'. The two terms form a couple; a *child* developing in an *environment*. Further analysis suggests that the mother and the teacher both become part of the environment. They are defined by the very qualities that are opposite to those of 'the child', who is active, inquiring and whose activity leads to 'real understanding'. The teacher and the mother, by contrast, are not necessary to instruct but to watch, observe, monitor and facilitate development. Teacher and mother are defined as 'passive' in relation to the child's 'active'. They are nurturant, facilitating, sensitive and supportive, and they know when to intervene but not to interfere.

This opposition is necessary to support the possibility of the illusion of autonomy and control upon which the child-centred pedagogy is founded.[9] In this sense, then, the 'capacity for nurturance' grounded in a naturalized femininity, the object of the scientific gaze, becomes the basis for woman's fitness for the facilitation of knowing and the reproduction of the knower, which is the support for, yet the opposite of, the production of knowledge. The production of knowledge is thereby separated from its reproduction and split along a sexual division which renders production and reproduction the natural capacities of the respective sexes.

The central concepts in the child-centred pedagogy and early mathematics education may themselves be regarded as signifiers – that is, aspects of discourse. That discourse claims to tell the truth about the universal properties of 'the child' which 'has concepts'. In this view, the attempts within psychology and mathematics, for example, may be seen as aspects of the attempt to construct a rationally ordered and controllable universe. We have argued that such an attempt is deeply bound up with the modern form of bourgeois government and the emergence of the modern state. It is also deeply involved with the attempt to describe and therefore regulate 'woman', 'the child', 'the working class', 'blacks' and 'the mad'.

The purpose of examining the conceptualizations which form the bedrock of modern practices is to draw out the key terms to the regime of truth which is constituted in and by the practices. My claim is that the discursive practices themselves – in producing the terms of the pedagogy, and therefore the parameters of practice – produce what it means to be a subject, to be subjected, within these practices. It can be stated that the terms in the discourse, such as *experience*, *discovery*, *stage*, etc., are signifiers which take their meaning from their position and function within the discourse itself: they enter as a relation. But this does not mean that there is a simple relation of representation between the material and the discursive. The discourse itself is a point of production and creation. When we say, then, that *experience* is created as a sign within the practice, or *the child* is produced as a subject, what we are talking about is the production of signs. If language does not represent reality, but rather the regulation of a practice itself produces a particular constellation and organization of the material and discursive practices, then it can be argued that something is produced. It is in this sense that Foucault's power/knowledge couple can be applied here.

By means of an apparatus of classification and a grading of responses 'the child' becomes a creation, and yet at the same time provides room for a reading of pathology. There are no behaviours which exist outside the practices for producing them, not at any rate in this particular sequence constellation and with these particular effects. The discursive practice becomes a complex sign system in which signs are produced and read and have truth-effects: the truth of children is produced in classrooms. 'The child' is not coterminous with actual children, just as Cowie (1978) argued that the signifier 'woman' is not coterminous with actual women, but central to the argument is the specification of that relation that is between the signifier and signified. If children become subjects through their insertion into a complex network of practices, there are no children who stand outside their orbit. I use the concept of *positioning*[10] to examine further what happens when such readings are produced and how children become *normal* and *pathological*, fast and slow, rote-learning and real understanding, and so forth. In other words, the practices provide systems of signs which are at once systems of classification, regulation and normalization. These produce systematic differences which are then used as classifications of children in the class. It is the meaning of *difference* which is a central feature in the production of any sign system in terms of the relations with other signs within the discourse. Similarity, that is, those signs which are linked within the discourse also pile or heap together to provide *evidence* of a related classification. Thus *activity*, *doing*, *experience*, *readiness* and so forth operate in relations of similarity, while *rote-learning* and *real understanding* are signs of contrastive opposition, of difference. I will attempt to demonstrate that these signs are produced and that often one sign may be taken as an indicator of the presence of another (similarity). Thus, for example, *activity* heralds a signal system, a complex discursive practice, whose terms and limits may be specified. Within this, then, children become embodiments of 'the child', precisely because that is how the practice is set up: they are normal or pathological, and so forth. Their behaviour, therefore, is an aspect of a position, a multifaceted subjectivity, such that 'the child' describes only their insertion into this, as one of many practices. But the behaviours do not precede the practice precisely because their specificity is produced in these practices. This is why discourses of developmental psychology themselves can be understood not simply as providing a distortion of a real object, but may be read as evidence of *real understanding*, while *passivity* may be read as coterminous with, or similar to, *rote-learning*, *rule-following*.

These produce the practices in which 'the child' becomes a sign to be read and a normal is differentiated from a pathological child. 'The child' develops through active manipulation of 'objects' in an 'environment'. Here all the practices become objects existing in a biologized environment. The Plowden Report is full of illustrations, all of which describe the school, the classroom, as an 'environment'. This sets up another aspect of the readings which are to be made. 'The child' is a unique individual, developing at 'his' own pace in an environment. The class-room therefore becomes the site of such development. However many children there are in a classroom, each is an individual – there is no sense of 'a class'. Indeed, it will be remembered that 'the class' forms a signifier in contrastive opposition to 'the child'. In this way, examining both the texts and practices themselves, it is possible to produce a reading of the pedagogy pre-existing object, 'the real child' which they fail to represent or describe adequately. If they are points of production, they have positive and not simply negative effects. In this sense they are our 'raw material'; the 'real' of a child is not something which can be known outside those practices in which its subjectivity is constituted. The signified forms a sign only out of fusion with the signifier. The signifier exists as a relation within a discourse. The material can be known as a relation only within a discursive practice. To say, therefore, that 'the child' is a signifier means that it must be united with a signified. Particular children therefore both become children – but also present behaviours to be read – which may be normal or pathological.

The question remains, of course, what precisely is it that produces these current truths? I have argued that current claims themselves rest upon a constant 'will to truth'[11] which, investing certainty in 'man', constantly seeks to find its Other and opposite in 'woman'. This truth is constantly reproven within classrooms in which the very apparatuses differentiate between success and its posited causes. This has profound material effects upon the life chances of girls.

It is suggested above that within current school mathematics practices, certain fantasies, fears and desires invest 'man' with omnipotent control of a calculable universe, which at the same time covers a desperate fear of and desire for the Other, 'woman'. 'Woman' becomes the repository of all the dangers displaced from the child, itself 'father' to the man. As I have argued, the necessity to prove the mathematical inferiority of girls is motivated not by a certainty but by a terror of loss. In all these respects, I have wanted to suggest a story in which these very fantasies, fears, desires become the forces that produce the actual effectivity of the construction of fact, of current discursive practices in which these fantasies are played out and in actual positions in such practices which, since they can be proved to exist, literally have power over the lives of girls and boys, as in Foucault's power/knowledge couple.

In this case, we could take the signifiers 'child', 'teacher' and 'girl', or the dichotomies 'active/passive', 'rote-learning/real understanding' as examples. We can ask how the contradictory positions created within

these practices are lived, and how these effect the production of subjectivity – for example fears, desires, and fantasies (see Chapter 19).

The first and most important thing to state is that there are no unitary
categories 'boys' and 'girls'. If actual boys and girls are created at the
intersection of multiple positioning, they are inscribed as masculine and
feminine. It follows, therefore, that girls can display 'real understanding'
or boys 'nurturance'. What matters is the effects of these positions.

At first sight, it seems curious that such qualities could be displayed
inside a pedagogy designed not only specifically to produce their opposite
but also to avoid their appearance at all costs. It is important that in this
respect the pathologization of these qualities, linked to the fear of totalitarianism and authoritarianism, has related to certain developments in
post-Freudian psychoanalysis, notably the work of Klein. However, as we
saw in Chapter 6, much as their appearance is dreaded, it is also needed.
Such ascriptions are frequently correlated with 'helpfulness', in which
helpful children become an important part of the maintenance of calm,
order and the smooth regulation of the classroom. Our research demonstrated that it is common for female teachers to fear such qualities as much
as they want them.

In the classroom discourse itself, there appears to be an *overt* message
concerning activity, exploration, openness, and so forth, derived from
the child-centred pedagogy. However, our work in the primary classrooms suggests that the discourse of good behaviour, neatness and rule-
following exists *covertly* alongside overt messages. It would have to be
covert because it is the exact opposite of what is supposed to take place.
Moreover, all those aspects – good behaviour, neatness and rule-
following – are taken to be harmful to psychological and moral development. Thus they act as a fear- and guilt-inducing opposite. It is not
surprising that teachers cannot afford to acknowledge the presence of
such qualities in the classroom – if they do, they pathologize their
appearance in girls, while failing to recognize that they are demanding
the very qualities they simultaneously disparage. This possibility allows us
to explore how girls come to desire in themselves qualities that appear
the opposite from those of 'the child' that the pedagogy is set up to
produce. Clearly, further investigations would have to engage with the
classroom production of such contradictions, examining both the overt
pedagogy and its covert shadow.

It is common in some psychoanalytic discourses, for example, to
counterpose 'fantasy' to 'reality', yet it is this division that appears most
questionable. After all, if it is true that some girls respond to the covert
regulation of the classroom, we cannot say that such behaviour is pathological with respect to the real. It is precisely that certain aspects of the
regulation of the practices are themselves suppressed. Simultaneously,

the 'reality' of the child-centred pedagogy seems to be the object of an elaborate fantasy. It appears that here in the practices there circulates a vast and complex network of meanings, in which the play of desire, of teachers for children, of children for each other, envy, jealousy, rivalry, and so forth are continually created and re-created. It is not necessary to counterpose fantasy to reality, but to demonstrate how fantasies themselves are lived, played out and worked through in their inscriptions in the veridicality of discourses and practices.

I have begun to explore what this might mean elsewhere[12] but here we can take the analysis a little further, using the distinctions *work* and *play*, *rote-learning/rule-following* and *real understanding*. *Work* forms a relation in the 'old discourse'. In the new, children learn through doing, activity and *play*. *Work* forms an opposition of this. Work is bad because it relates to sitting in rows, regurgitating 'facts to be stored', not 'concepts to be acquired' through active exploration of the environment. Work, then, forms a metaphoric relation with rote-learning and rule-following. Each describes a practice, a mode of learning which is opposite and antithetical to the 'joy of discovery'. Play is fun. There are also other aspects of work, which could be further elaborated – it leads to resistance. Children regulated in this way do not become self-regulating. But *work* is also a category to be outlawed by a system of education set up in opposition to child labour. It constitutes a category which frees 'the child' to be something distinct, playful, not an adult, outside the field of productive labour, innocent, natural. Related therefore is a series of values, fantasies, fears, desires which are incorporated into the discursive practices. It follows that *work*, as constituted as an opposite of *play*, can be recognized as a difference, as everything which does not signify play. It can also be recognized as a danger-point, a point to be avoided. It is pathologized. It is learning by the wrong means; it is not 'natural' to 'the child'. If any child is observed 'doing work', this is likely to be understood as a problem. Hence the distinction between 'rote-learning' and 'real understanding' discussed earlier. First, what happens when a child produces high attainment as well as producing behaviour to be read as *work*? If play is the discourse of the school, through what discourse do children read their performance? If 'real understanding' is coterminous with the fantasy of possessing total power and control, how is it distinguished and what is the relation of this to 'getting the right answer', 'being certain', etc.? How does *possession of real understanding* provide fantasy, a chimera which has to be constantly and continually proved to exist out of a terror that lurking around every corner is its Other, rote-learning, work? Why is there such pressure, remorseless and unrelenting, to 'prove' that real understanding causes real attainment, and moreover that certain children have 'it' and that others just as surely do not, despite high attainment? What is invested?

One of the features of the apparatuses and technologies of the social, the modern production of truth through science, is that *proof* and practices for the production of evidence are central to the production of a truth; certainty of 'real understanding' is ceaselessly proved in practices even though the evidence is often ambiguous. Here we want not so much to dwell on the evidence itself as to question the motivation to provide proof, in particular of the opposition of *work* and play, rote and real.

Now, if the power of control over the universe invested in mathematical discourse is a fantasy, I am not setting out to demonstrate the *real* of the proof that girls *really can do* maths or boys actually do not have real understanding. Rather, we are interested in how those categories are produced as signs and how they 'catch up' the subjects, position them and, in positioning, create a truth. For is not girls' bid for 'understanding' the greatest threat of all to a universal power or a truth that is invested in a fantasy of control of 'women'? Teachers will often go to great lengths to demonstrate that boys have real understanding. By the metaphoric chain created, *activity* is frequently read as a sign of understanding. Understanding, then, is evidenced by the presence of some attributes and the absence of others. It is activity – playing, utilization of objects (Lego, for example) rule-breaking (rather than following) – and so this can encompass naughtiness to the point of displays of hostility and conflict towards the teacher. All these and more are taken to be evidence. Conversely, good behaviour in girls, working hard, helpfulness, neat and careful work, are all read as danger signs of a lack. The counter-evidence – hard work in boys and understanding in girls – is also produced as evidence, but when it is, other positions come into play (see Walkerdine, 1984). Evidence of real understanding, therefore, depends first upon a set of practices in which real understanding is the goal of an explicit framework of the 'activities' set up, as in all the examples given here. Secondly, it is possible to read the correct accomplishment as the result of understanding, and failure produced through a lack of requisite experience, readiness, concepts. Thirdly, the likelihood to favour one explanation of success over another depends upon other characteristics which define a real learner. However, boys frequently do not achieve terribly well, yet evidence of failure is itself produced as evidence in support of understanding.

Chapter 6 showed how, in these pedagogic practices, facilitating and nurturant Others (teachers, mothers) are necessary to the facilitation of a 'natural' sequence of development in 'the child'. These contradictions are lived out by girls in pedagogic practices. The very contradictions in the practice set girls up to achieve the very thing which is simultaneously desired and feared – passivity. It is feared in 'children', yet it is the very quality desired in nurturant care-givers, women as mothers and teachers.

SPLITTING THE DIFFERENCE

If women being powerful within mathematical and pedagogic practices is so threatening, it is hardly surprising that many women are fearful of recognizing power within themselves. No wonder the woman I mentioned in the Introduction has such difficulty in establishing that the person with a Distinction is actually herself. What she lives as a psychic problem is a profoundly social one, but a social one in which psychic processes are at the heart of the matter. Women's success appears to present such a threat to masculine rationality, and to the bourgeois and patriarchal power which it underpins, that it is very dangerous for women to admit their own power. How is that deep contradiction lived for such women? Is femininity a performance, a defence against the frightening possibility of stepping over the gender divide?

In this section of the paper I shall explore this issue, first with reference to the work of Wendy Hollway (1982, 1989), who has discussed splitting in couple relations, and the work of women psychoanalysts who have attempted to address this point, particularly Joan Riviere's (1985) work on womanliness as masquerade.

Wendy Hollway analyses adult heterosexual couple relations in terms of the way in which rationality and emotionality are split between partners, with the woman being taken to 'hold' the emotionality for the couple, a quality which the man also projects into her so that she can be the emotional one, meaning that as long as it is located in her, he does not have to come to terms with his own emotional vulnerability. Similarly, the man can hold rationality for the couple. Hollway analyses in great detail how this is achieved by the couple. The concept of splitting which she uses is derived from Kleinian psychoanalysis.[13] In Klein the split-off part of (in this case) 'man' is projected into and held by 'woman'; similarly rationality in woman cannot easily be accommodated and therefore has to be experienced as though it belonged to someone else. To put the argument in this way is completely different from the essentialist view of femininity in which certain characteristics simply do not belong to women, or a socialization account which treats the social as though it were added on to the psychic rather than seeing them as produced together.[14] Lacan[15] argued that 'woman' exists only as a symptom of male fantasy. What he meant was that the fantasies created under patriarchy (or the Law of the Father or Symbolic Order, as he calls it) create as their object not women as they really are but fantasies of what men both desire and fear in the Other. Women, then, become the repositories of such fantasies, and the effect for the psychic development of women themselves is extremely damaging and complex. Many psychoanalysts have attempted to engage with the problem presented by femininity under patriarchy. Freud tended to naturalize women's procreative function as a normal solution to the problem posed by the gendered splitting of rationality and emotionality. He did not investigate in great depth the elaborate fantasies which uphold the patriarchal and bourgeois order, and which I am suggesting are projected on to women. It is not surprising, then, that many women analysts who discovered the terrible confusions in their women patients around their power tended to essentialize them. The analysis I am suggesting here makes the essentializing tendency impossible. It is also true that there is no easy division between fantasy and an observable reality, since the social contains the elaborate fictions and fantasies of which I have written.

If masculinity and femininity may both be seen as defences against the qualities held by the Other, then there can be no natural division of the sexes, but a complex order through which difference is held in play. Joan Riviere (1985) presents an interesting analysis of femininity in relation to cases of women patients. In her paper 'Womanliness as Masquerade' she gives the example of a woman academic who, after giving an academic paper, has to flirt with men, often picking a 'fatherly' type as object of her flirtation. Riviere suggests that such flirtation provides her with reassurance that she is, after all, a woman. It acts as a masquerade, an elaborate defence against her fear that her femininity is a mere charade. If the male gaze, in Lacan's terms, constructs the object of the gaze as a masquerade, what lies beneath the mask? Lacan would have us believe that there is nothing, or a confusion. However, we could equally well ask what it is that the fantasy of the phallus holds up. In the academic scenario it appears that the fantasy of femininity is kept in place by the discursive truths which define and regulate the evaluation of women's performance. The struggle both to perform academically and to perform as feminine must seem at times almost impossible. No wonder some of us split them apart in various ways, or have different conscious and unconscious methods for dealing with the unbearable contradiction.[16]

To maintain this requires a tremendous amount of social and psychic labour. Luce Irigaray (1985) points clearly to these phallic fantasies and suggests that there is another libidinal organization for women that cannot be spoken in the present Symbolic Order. However, where Lacan presents women as a lack, Irigaray presents her as having Other desires screaming to be spoken. The feminine performance in this view is a defence not only against masculinity, but also against a powerful and active sexuality quite unlike that defined under patriarchy, although of course precisely that which is pathologized as bad or mad. Irigaray celebrates the plurality of woman as the plurality of sexual pleasure which does not have a goal of a single orgasm nor a single site of pleasure. Bronwyn Davies (1988) has explored women's sexual fantasies and also suggests that those fantasies are unlike the ones to which women are subjected. I am arguing, therefore, that to become the object of those fantasies – the ones which render women as the object of the male gaze – requires a tremendous amount of work to cover over not an essential femininity but a different set of desires and organization of pleasures (cf. Foucault) from those which can either clearly be articulated at the moment or are sanctioned in the practices in which femininity circulates as sign.

PEDAGOGIC STRATEGIES

If girls' and women's power is a site of struggle, constantly threatening the tenuous grasp of male academic superiority, then any engagement with these issues in practice cannot rest upon a rationalistic base of choice or equal opportunities. Not only must the fiction of the gendered splitting be taken apart, but the psychic struggle engaged in by girls and women to live out the impossibly contradictory positions accorded to us must be addressed, as must the paranoias of the powerful that understand women's success as a (conscious or unconscious) threat to their position of superiority, shaky as it is. This requires a strategy which engages with the educational politics of subjectivity, a politics which refuses to split the psychic from the social and attempts to understand the complexity of defence and resistance, and to find ways of dealing with them for teachers and students alike. Equal opportunities and models based on choice simply cannot engage with the complexity of the issues I have tried to spell out in this essay. Indeed, the danger is that when such strategies fail, as they do, educators will resort to existentialistic arguments, as they do, to explain, for example, the failure of girls to take 'non-traditional' subjects. Such essentialism is completely unwarranted, but working on fiction, fantasy and contradiction is to work in dangerous and threatening territory. It is that territory that we have to move into if we are to proceed in the struggle which recognizes that women, after all, can be very powerful indeed.

NOTES

1. See, for example, Hartnett et al. (1979).
2. Social conditioning is a term which is commonly used, and although it may once

have referred to social learning theory, I think its roots in behaviourism are often forgotten.

3. This idea is discussed more fully in Walkerdine (1988) and Walkerdine et al. (1989).

4. This is a term used by Lacan (1977) to indicate not the real penis but the idea of male and patriarchal power invested in the possession of a penis. Possession of the phallus is both a metaphor and a fantasy.

5. In Walkerdine et al. we discuss at greater length the way in which physiological evidence is used to support the contention that educating girls would be physiologically dangerous by, in the end, affecting their capacity and desire to have children.

6. Of course, not all girls fail. (The discussions about failure concentrate on the failure of girls and women to enter higher-level careers requiring maths and to obtain higher-level passes in the subject, but the issue is generalized so that explanations for this are sought with respect to all girls; see Walkerdine et al.)

7. Higher education began to be open to women when the caring professions began to be based on the idea of the amplification of the capacities for maternal nurturance (see Walkerdine et al.)

8. Walkerdine (1984).

9. Walkerdine and Lucey (1989).

10. See Walkerdine et al. for a further discussion.

11. Cf. Foucault (1979).

12. Walkerdine et al.

13. See for example, Mitchell (1986).

14. Henriques et al. (1984).

15. Lacan.

16. One example of a little girl coping with the contradictions of being both her father's feminine little baby and a tomboy are discussed in Chapter 19.

References

Cowie, E. (1978) 'Woman as Sign'. m/f, no. 1.
Davies, B. (1988) 'Romantic Love and Female Sexuality'. Unpublished paper.
Department of Education and Science (1967) Children and their Primary Schools (The Plowden Report). London, HMSO.
Foucault, M. (1979) Discipline and Punish. Harmondsworth, Penguin.
Hartnett, U., Boden, G. and Fuller, M. (1979) Sex Role Stereotyping. London, Tavistock.
Henriques, J., Hollway, W., Urwin, C., Venn, C. and Walkerdine, V. (1984) Changing the Subject. London, Methuen.
Hollway, W. (1982) 'Identity and Gender Difference in Adult Social Relations'. Unpublished PhD thesis, University of London.
Hollway, W. (1989) Subjectivity and Method in Psychology: Gender, Meaning and Science. London, Sage.
Irigaray, L. (1985). This Sex Which is not One. Ithaca, NY, Cornell University Press.
Lacan, J. (1977) Écrits: A Selection. London, Tavistock.
Mitchell, J. ed. (1986) The Selected Melanie Klein. Harmondsworth, Penguin.
Riviere, J. (1985) 'Womanliness as Masquerade', in V. Burgin, J. Donald and C. Kaplan, eds, Formations of Fantasy. London, Methuen.
Walden, R. and Walkerdine, V. (1982) Girls and Mathematics: The Early Years. London, Heinemann.
Walkerdine, V. (1984) 'Developmental Psychology and the Child-centred Pedagogy', in Henriques et al.
Walkerdine, V. (1988) The Mastery of Reason. London, Routledge.
Walkerdine, V. and The Girls and Mathematics Unit (1989) Counting Girls Out. London, Virago.
Walkerdine, V. and Lucey, H. (1989) Democracy in the Kitchen. London, Virago.

15

Behind the painted smile

INTRODUCTION

In 1985 I wrote an autobiographical piece about growing up in the fifties. As part of that I explored a photograph of myself, aged three, entered for a local fancy-dress competition, dressed as a bluebell fairy (see Chapter 17). I spent some considerable time discussing my desire to hang on to the image of myself as a pale, sickly and eroticized child: the fairy with the superhuman powers, especially, in this case, relating to my father. The fairy is not a strong and powerful woman, but a frail and fragile object of wardship. When I wrote that piece it was as though I had said all there was to say, but I knew at one level then, and see more clearly now, that there are far more disturbing images to explore, which are hidden and covered over by the erotic allure of the bluebell fairy. When I wrote the piece I sent the publishers two photographs: one of the bluebell fairy and another, a school photo of me aged about seven, looking puffed out, sickly and fat. They wanted to publish the latter. I, having sent it to them in the first place, adamantly refused to let *this* image be the object of public scrutiny. I might have mentioned becoming fat in the article, but clearly I did not want to let the actual image escape into the public gaze. I continued to hide behind a wall of words, academic words, which kept me from exploring the traumatic effectivity of that and other reviled images of myself.

Much has been written about femininity as object of the male gaze.[1] But what I want to explore here is the relation between acceptable and unacceptable images – the ones we tear up or hide away in cupboards – and what lurks behind them. I explored before how the image of the bluebell fairy was one which I always treasured, and a view of myself from which I could not escape. I do not feel the same now, and it is the mark of a set of moves made therapeutically that I do not feel the need to hold so strongly on to *that* image. However, it linked in with a set of fantasies* in relation to my father, which meant that he played on the bluebell-fairy theme when he called me Tinky, short for Tinkerbell, as his pet name. Now, Tinkerbell was a fairy who was small, not-quite-human, and used her powers to save Peter Pan from death by poison. I was often ill with tonsillitis and was therefore quite small and sickly, but the fantasy of the bluebell fairy carried an enormous allure. A fairy, through her very frailty, has magical powers. My father's vision of me tied in with his own fantasies and nightmares of the disabling heart condition which finally killed him.

I explore in Chapter 19 just how these visions by men of women and of fathers of daughters, especially in the working class, crystallize an infantilization in which the child-woman is to be protected by male wardship, and often relates to illness and death. Indeed, many comics for girls (see Chapter 8) are full of stories in which the heroine is ill, disabled or oppressed and secretly has to bring out the good side of herself to fight against the injustice to which she is submitted. These stories, like the bluebell fairy and other fantasies, further the idea that good girls are those who, through selfless helpfulness, triumph over the powers of evil. Similarly, the little fairy is a tiny creature, good and beautiful but with enormous power. She is on the side of the angels, but contrasts markedly with the vision of the witch. I have also argued that these fantasies are particularly important for working-class girls because they play into a kind of 'good-girl' femininity which is associated with upward mobility and for me, at least, with success in school.

Now, however, I think that issue is more complicated than my original formulation, because there is another side, another set of fantasies, which are much harder to explore. On one level, the idea that we are constructed in the male gaze is reassuring. We remain somehow not responsible for our actions, as though we were mere puppets to masculinity. I say that this is reassuring in the sense that the images of the bluebell fairy remained a treasured image; that is, they were an indication that I *was* feminine and attractive and loved. No matter how much we might take apart those fantasies as part of the male gaze, I think they prevent us from coming to terms with the negative emotions which are covered over by all this sugar and spice. Here I am referring both to the fragility of the assumption of femininity and to the covering over of negative emotions. In other words, take apart *this* image as I might, this did not mean that I was prepared to look at the other one, the reviled image of me as fat. It strikes me as easier to take apart a beautiful image,

---

*Although I use 'fantasy' here, an unconscious dimension must also be implied.

blame patriarchy, and yet hold on to that image (Yes, yes, I am that really) or to point to a void as its other side) than to examine what else may lurk beneath.

WORKING BENEATH THE SURFACE
OF THE IMAGE

If the bluebell fairy and my father's associated nickname for me, Tinky, were the stuff of my dreams, then these other images provoke fantasies of a more nightmarish kind. Lurking behind the pretty, quiet and well-behaved little girl is the terror of a monster who can never be let out to public view. Recently, I began to explore these representations of myself. I made slides out of family snapshots of myself at different ages. I projected these on to a wall, placed a piece of paper on the wall and drew and coloured the projected image, so that with the slide the image looked like a tinted slide, but without the slide the image itself became another and separate representation. On the first image of myself as a smiling and pretty little girl I first wrote the caption 'as pretty as a picture'. But I knew that was not all there was to say. I drew a second. I crossed out the mouth and stuck a piece of tape over, obliterating the mouth alto-gether. As a caption I wrote 'all mouth'. This was a profoundly shocking piece of self-mutilation to the image, since the one thing I worked hard at not being was a talkative and cheeky child who could possibly be described in the negative connotations of 'shouting her mouth off'. I think what I achieved was a kind of censorious silencing of myself, without ever necessarily having an adult to tell me to keep quiet. I mean that I have no recollection of being told to keep quiet or even of being told off. I suspect, then, that what I was doing was censoring myself so that I could not possibly be in the position where I would have to be told off.

One of the crucial issues in psychoanalytic work which has been important to me in the process of development that I am describing is that the unconscious can work in ways which do not relate clearly to an actual event.[2] Thus the superego itself can provide a censoring device as a defence against a set of fears. In this case, I think I was guarding against the fear of what might just slip out of that mouth – or indeed, what might be put in it. . . . For when I turned to another photo – in this case an image of me at about eleven, standing rigid and trying to smile in somebody's garden – I began by crossing out the mouth and the abdomen and then drawing a ring round my abdomen (my tummy). I could hardly bear to work on the image, so hateful did I find it. I directed considerable venom at myself, writing captions like 'fatty', 'ten ton

Tessie' and then, colouring the dress I was wearing green, wrote, 'green for greedy'. I remembered then how I always hated the colour green, except for one image of myself standing, aged about thirteen or fourteen, next to my father, wearing a green jumper. It was the only green garment I ever liked. But of course, green is not just for greedy, it is for envy, too. I have discovered in my therapy that greed and envy form important aspects of my psychic and social formation, and both are inflected in relation to class and femininity in ways that I do not yet entirely understand.

GREED AND ENVY

In *Democracy in the Kitchen*[3] I wrote about a phrase my mother used, which I remember as being particularly salient when I left home and went to college in London. The phrase was 'much wants more'. It encapsulated for me aspects of greed and envy in my desire for something more, something different from the opportunities never open to my mother and for a life that she could never have dared hope for. This produced inside her great envy of me, and to this day I still have great difficulty with the idea that something I have or am might produce envy in others: especially being powerful. Now this issue, crosscut by class inequality and oppression, in which there is what Carolyn Steedman[4] has called 'a proper envy' among working-class people, relates also to issues of accepting one's lot, of not asking for too much; but it also relates to greed for food and greed for love and envy of the mother, as Melanie Klein has remarked.

Klein argues[5] that the infant's envy of the mother stems from earliest experiences. The mother possesses breasts which can satisfy the infant, but these can be seen as both good and bad because the infant has to exist during periods when the mother's body and milk are absent as well as. while needs are being satisfied. Freud first suggested[6] that fantasy begins when the infant 'hallucinates' the breast, producing wish-fulfilling fantasies of self-satisfaction. Klein added to this the idea that such fantasies can be negative as well as positive, and that the infant fantasizes both a good and satisfying breast and a bad, absent breast. Klein links greed and envy, suggesting that 'greed is an impetuous and insatiable craving' which aims to suck dry and devour the breast, whereas envy aims not only at robbing the breast but also at putting bad parts of the infant inside the mother. Because the feeding breast contains everything the infant desires and has a limitless supply of milk and love, the feeling of envy can become hatred. The good mother and the bad mother can exist in the infant's fantasy as split off from each other, and the infant can feel such intense guilt about the negative emotions, which need not emerge as anger or aggression but as delusions of both a perfect mother and trying to be a 'good little girl'. In my case I was excessively good, in sharp contrast to my younger sister, whom I remember as being always the naughty tomboy. My mother often used to remark that my sister had been a greedy baby and was always wailing tears of rage. By contrast, then, I was a model baby and a good little *girl* (not a tomboy). But I was sickly and underweight as a child until I had my tonsils out at the age of seven, put on weight, and became the object of my own hatred in the 'greedy' photograph.

There appear, then, from my initial reactions to my photographs, to be two areas of my body which became the source of anxiety and hatred: my mouth and my abdomen. I used to have terrible problems about speaking, about 'saying the wrong thing', especially in public, which faded only when I began to explore my own anger at what was silenced; my dilemmas about eating to keep quiet and eating which made me fat. I also think that there was a strong link between the fatness of my abdomen and my own fears about sexuality. Women's abdomens can, after all, be fat from eating, or they can be large through pregnancy. At the age of eleven, when I was showing a considerable amount of 'puppy fat', I remember being taken to the doctors, who pointed out stretch marks on my thighs and buttocks, saying that women had these after childbirth. I came away secretly profoundly traumatized: what had I done? What did this mean? Growing up, then, meant both growing bigger and becoming a sexual adult woman (split into good and bad, the virgin and the whore?).

When, at the age of seven, I had my tonsils removed, this put an end to the reason for my sickly fragility. Of course, it did not touch the reasons that had led to this malady of the throat (not far, after all, from my mouth). I began to eat – indeed, I think that my very depressed mother virtually stuffed my sister and me full of food. I started to put on weight. When I look at these images they present to me not the dreamed-of feminist tomboy but a passive overweight child who is depressed and terrified that something has been lost with nothing positive to put in its place. The terror was the stuff of my nightmares, the fears and fantasies; the anxieties which had to be kept at bay (stuffed down my throat?) at all costs. So, the negative side hardly dared emerge to dent the surface view of the nice little girl or the depressed fatty or, later, the desperately slimming young woman, but I am going to argue that its shadow existed as a struggle in the unconscious which led to the anger being turned upon myself in self-mutilating and destructive ways, and later to health problems centred on my abdomen.

BENEATH THE SURFACE OF THE GAZE

What I am suggesting, therefore, is that even when the images of myself present me as the feminized object of the male gaze, a pretty little girl who smiles for the camera, there is a terrible rage underneath, a depression and anger that have been entirely split off. In other words, then, the surface of the images is not all there is to be read. Like dreams, images are the manifest content which is only the surface cover for what lies latent beneath.[7] Thus, although much radical work on photography has shown us how to read the semiotics of photographs, it has not ventured much below the surface, except for the pioneering work of Jo Spence and Rosie Martin using phototherapy. Similarly, feminist approaches to femininity in filmic representations, following the pioneering work of Laura Mulvey,[8] have read the latent content as an oedipal drama, whereas I am suggesting that negative fantasies and pre-oedipal relations are important too.

When I further extended my exploration of the projected images discussed above, I tried to get away from using word associations and concentrated on making more careful drawings and pastel colourings from the images. What began to happen was dramatic I started carefully to shade in the shadow on the photographs. I noticed that under the eyes of one sweet little image were shadows. I shaded these in heavily. I continued with other areas of the face and worked on all the images in this way, so that what emerged in the end was a series of highly disturbing portraits. I had become transformed from a sweet little girl or blank-faced fatty into a depressed, demanding and angry child. Every woman who has seen these images in progress finds them extremely disturbing. Yet what I had done was work with what was there, as signs, as traces, in the photograph.

What is the relation between these issues and my mother's envy and the 'proper' class envy discussed by Carolyn Steedman (1986)? My mother seemed to envy a me who had so much but wanted more, was greedy. To many working-class people the middle classes, 'rich people', appear to have everything: so they feel deprived and envious. Now, it would be quite wrong in my view to pathologize all such working-class people as themselves deprived of appropriate mothering, as was fashionable in the post-war period and in some approaches to crime and delinquency.[9] Such approaches deny material differences and pathologize the working class using strategies of regulation designed to 'normalize' them.[10] It is not easy, however, using Klein's framework, with her innate drives, to reconcile the social and psychic aspects of envy and greed without reducing one to the other. I can only say that from examination of my own fantasies 'rich people' become both the objects of envy – wanting to be them, to be like them – and the objects of hatred and contempt because they appear to be withholding riches from us, to be arrogant, posh and prissy.[11] This ambivalence is exactly what Klein describes. However, working-class people seem too to be the object of middle-class fantasies, also containing good and bad parts; they are the salt of the earth, full of community spirit; as well as stupid and authoritarian and bigoted. Some collective fantasizing is going on which surfaces in the representations of class with which we are familiar. Perhaps it is necessary to explore more fully the link between negative and positive fantasies and power and powerlessness, between aggression and violence.[12]

NEGATIVITY AND SEXUALITY

I remarked earlier that I still had difficulty with others' envy of my power. It is still so much easier to see myself as the good girl, who is looking for the good place, the good Other to save me – so much easier than letting out all that rage and becoming a powerful *woman*. It is still, then, in some ways easier for us to see ourselves as objects of the male gaze, with male definitions of ourselves, than to take on the negative fantasies, replete as they are with images of witches, oversexed and insatiable women, castrating bitches and the like. It is not as if those 'other' images do not exist in the social, but they certainly need to be reclaimed. Angry women are hateful as well as good, demanding and active: qualities naturalized in men and pathologized in women.

I want to argue, therefore, that it is precisely those 'other' images which I was so steadfastly guarding against presenting to the public arena. The male gaze was the acceptable and dreamed-of fantasy. But my attempts at being active, angry and sexual were indeed pushed into psychic and bodily[13] symptoms visible to the camera only as traces; the depressed look, the forced smile, the fat tummy, the closed mouth. Covered over, I suggest, was the fantasy of the angry child, actively shouting out loud, crying and screaming; the all-consuming, rapacious woman with a large (sexual) appetite. The passive little object of the male gaze covers over the possibility of the actively sexual woman, the strong and powerful woman.

But I am suggesting too that, following Klein's analysis of splitting, male fantasies of the feminine, the objects of the male gaze, can also be taken apart as the good and bad splittings which relate to the mother. It is so reassuring for masculinity to produce a fantasy of a dependent child-woman who, above all, will always *be there*. The fantasy that hides is one of terrifying dependency upon powerful mothers who will not always be there to satisfy them; men therefore feel rage and terrifying dependency.

The envy and greed of boys may be projected on to women in order to make us the 'good' object.

For both women and men, then, the positive desire, the desiring gaze, covers over darker and more dangerous negative fantasies, fears and anxieties. The desperation to keep myself the object of that gaze must have been matched only by an equal male desire to keep me looking that way, so that the myth could be terrifyingly kept in its place and circulating in the vast array of public and private representations of the feminine.

This negativity is, as I said at the beginning, so very much more painful (it is the site of failure, after all) and harder to get at than the pretty little images. In *Democracy in the Kitchen* Helen Lucey and I examined transcripts of conversations between thirty four-year-old girls and their mothers. We discovered how hard it was to face growing up and growing big for most of the girls, and for their mothers too. Many of the girls actively resisted their mothers' attempts to make them behave in a more 'grown-up' way. They did this often by expressing desires to remain a baby, *the only* baby, not wanting their place usurped by younger siblings. They expressed considerable jealousy and violence towards siblings. What they appeared to want was to remain their mother's baby for ever, looked after, the only girl in the world, little and adored. Becoming a big girl and a powerful grown-up was not easy, and for some of the mothers was presented as a frightening option, for these women were not powerfully in control of their world either. Active, sexual motherhood is not an image easily validated, nor is being strong and outspoken and demanding.

I never managed to show much of my anger – the anger at my mother for having another child, the anger and desire to speak my own mind, the active, sexual and desiring adolescent. What I revealed instead were the pretty little girl and the fat and depressed teenager who then went on to slim and still be terrified of opening her mouth (never mind her legs). The overt position got me a long way; it produced many significant gains in my path out of the working class. Anger got turned inwards to self-mutilation. One of the ten-year-olds whom I interviewed expressed forcibly the view that she had no good qualities except to feed the pets at home, that she was too big and that she was sometimes horrible to other people. She was having a lot of trouble with her school work too. It seemed to me that this girl had almost entirely turned her violent feelings in on herself, and that these could easily lead her to be a victim of eating disorders like anorexia. For me, anything wanting and demanding had to be suppressed as 'pathetic'.[14] I so wanted the little girl back, to be loved, and I could find little way to be strong except through rigid control, still wanting so much not to be the strong and active woman, but the loved object of the male gaze. Hegemonic representations of the 'bad woman' often present her as dark, evil and actively sexual. But all too often, in the movies at least, she gets killed off.

BEHIND THE PAINTED SMILE

I am therefore trying to explore the relationship between the desired and reviled images of myself, between small and big, thin and fat, smiling and angry, powerful and powerless. I am trying also to explore what can hardly be seen, but remains as traces upon the photographed body. The active, angry and desiring girl was not seen. To let her out would have been too much of a risk. We are not constituted only as the object of the male gaze. The gaze itself is built also upon a fantasy of what is desired and what rage and anger and violence are suppressed. The Other images of ourselves challenge the very foundations, the overt premisses of male heterosexual desire. For it brings to the surface the male fears and desires that can hardly be articulated for fear of annihilation by powerful women, women who will go away and leave them. I believe that investigating these issues takes us beyond a deconstructive examination of the constitution of the feminine in representations. It takes us to an exploration of the powerful fantasies and anxieties which keep those representations circulating and provide us with the basis of other narratives of our histories and the claiming of our power.

NOTES

1. The classic article here is Laura Mulvey's 'Visual Pleasure and Narrative Cinema', *Screen*, vol. 16, no. 3, 1975.
2. See, for example, the discussion in *History Workshop Journal*, no. 26, 1988.
3. V. Walkerdine and H. Lucey, *Democracy in the Kitchen: Regulating Mothers and Socialising Daughters*. London, Virago, 1989.
4. C. Steedman, *Landscape for a Good Woman*, Virago, 1986.
5. M. Klein (1956) 'A study of envy and gratitude', reprinted in Mitchell, J. ed., *The Selected Melanie Klein*. Harmondsworth, Penguin, 1986. See also *Envy and Gratitude*. London, Virago, 1988.
6. S. Freud, *The Interpretation of Dreams, Standard Edition*, vols. 4–5.
7. Ibid.
8. L. Mulvey.
9. See, for example, the work of Bowlby and Winnicott and N. Rose, *The Psychological Complex*. London, Methuen, 1985.
10. J. Henriques *et al.*, *Changing the Subject*. London, Methuen, 1984.
11. Walkerdine and Lucey.
12. Ibid.
13. By bodily symptoms I mean what is called somatization. That is, I am saying that the anxieties associated with my abdomen and my greed, for example, become the basis of physical illness, just as my mouth and tonsillitis had been.

14. Jacqueline Rose has argued in 'Femininity and Its Discontents' (reprinted in *Sexuality in the Field of Vision*, London, Verso, 1987), that symptoms breaking through to the surface are an indication that socialization does not work. But when they do break through they do not surface simply as illness, but as pejorative designations. In the study described above Helen Lucey and I discovered that girls who were active and outspoken in class were often described in terms such as 'she's a madam' or 'she's selfish'. Thus, we also need a reading of how these public discursive positionings of women are the object of regulation (cf. Foucault).

PART III

Working-Class Rooms

In 1984 I wrote what for me was one of the most painful essays of my life. 'Dreams from an ordinary childhood' was a 'coming out' as working-class, a realization that for years I had been frightened to reveal my past in academic circles and had engaged in a kind of masquerade in which I had not only felt ashamed of my background, but had come to the Left and to feminism entirely through academia. The shocking fact is that the Left in which I became involved was entirely theoretical and I found no space, ironically, either there or within feminism, to address the formation of my own subjectivity: a working-class girl who became a teacher and then an academic.

It was black women who first began to raise within feminism differences between women, and they did so in a way which was not like that of most current ways of talking about class. They were angry, emotional, not dry and rationalist like many male academics raising class as an issue as though it had nothing to do with our own subjectivities. In the post-war period in which I grew up, children of my class could be 'chosen' for the first time to go to grammar school and to higher education. What class meant then and means now is quite specific. Just as it is argued that there is not one black struggle but many black struggles, so the struggles of class are many, varied and full of contradictions.

What I want, however, is to be able to raise something as an issue which was spoken about in one way when I was 'educated out': a discourse of mobility, of embourgeoisement, of the pathology of working-class families, the specific fictions functioning in truth to describe and regulate the working-class girl in the period in which I grew up. But now we seem to be faced with another set of truths: those constructed by a Left which has been disappointed by 'the working class' (as though it were a homogeneous group). In recent years, while gender and race have become common currency, it has become almost impossible to speak about class. While there may be many problems with the old discourses, now I have learnt to speak, now I have stopped being a schoolgirl, have uttered the words which would shock the teachers, I am no longer prepared to be silent. I call myself an 'educated working-class woman' (a term I owe to Pam Trevithick). This may be a fictional identity like all the others, but it allows something to be spoken and some things to come together: educated, working-class and woman – three terms which I thought were hopelessly fragmented. Terms which assert my education and my power with pride and claim back my education, not as alienation and a move to another class but as part of a narrative which allows me a place from which to struggle, a sense of belonging.

In 'Video replay' (Chapter 19) I describe what happened when, in 1983, I went into the home of a white working-class family to conduct some research. Where and who was I: the working-class child of my fantasies or the middle-class researcher who was part of an attempt to tell a truth about 'The Working Class'? Fact, fiction and fantasy mingle together, and instead of trying to work out 'what really happened' I am beginning to see the place of the construction of all those fictions in producing me. But I am fighting back. The things a little girl would once not have dared to say are being spoken. They may be confused and contradictory, but they have turned from the painful screams of a child who is frightened to speak to the discourse of a woman who demands to be heard.

16

Working-class hangover:

workaholic haze

(March 1984)

You kill me with your gentle oppression
The subtle insinuation
                working itself inside my mind

You cannot see it
    Its lines flicker softly across my face
You cannot know how I got here
and the incarcerating pain of survival

Try harder
    keep going
    You tell me.
    That was quite good, but we
Still need more
            effort

Gentle oppression, fighting its way out
                        into madness

'You are compulsive, depressive, hopeless'
    Well, what do you expect
No longer will I hide behind
    the terror of my failure
No longer will I say, quietly, pleading
    let me in
    I'm good enough really
No, today they will have to see
                        power

Its fraudulence is going to be opened
                                    now

No more, I will accept no more
                    be sorry no more

Be quiet no more
They will have to hear my story
and they will not dare to say it
                        made me mad
Of course it made me mad
After all, they pathologized
                    my history

No more, no more
    my shouts today will be
        so loud
My tears drops of pure fire

You will no longer take away
                        my past
for today I take my life
    into these two hands

I am a time-bomb
and I have started ticking

17

Dreams from an

ordinary childhood

It was the summer of 1983. In a suburb of Derby I sat in the car and looked at the interwar semi that had been my childhood home. A little girl on a tricycle cycled along the drive and out on to the pavement. It was as though I were seeing myself in a time warp.

This was the first time I had been able to go back and look at this place, the house that was the basis of my childhood memories and dreams, the last remaining testament to that secret past of a proletarian provincial childhood. I had wanted to keep its nooks and crannies, its supreme ordinariness, safe as a place I could remember, where the past would not be lost.

Yet everything about it, its sense of safety, had felt for so long like a trap, the site and origin of an ordinariness both hated and desired. It was the place in which, if I were not careful and being so vigilant, I might turn into my mother.

In the fifties I felt set up, set up to want, to want to be different, special, when I was chosen to be one of the children of the post-war boom, who would leave the safe innocence of the suburbs for the stripped-pine promises of the new middle class, for the glamour of the metropolis and the desperate lure of the academy.

For years, in the midst of other people's confident sophistication, I felt trapped by a wall of silence about the very ordinariness of my past. I imagined that my new-found acquaintances in the intellectual élite had different and exciting childhoods. Indeed, casual conversation at parties always seemed to act as confirmation of this, making me sink into a depression, feeling that absolutely nothing about my childhood was worthy of comment – but more: that the embarrassment of my past was a topic to be kept well hidden. I didn't have an affair at fourteen, join the Communist Party at sixteen, go off to paint in Paris, or live in an ashram in India. Childhood fantasies of getting out, of being rich and famous, abounded, but in the circles I moved in there had been only two ways to turn the fantasy into the dream-lived-as-real of bourgeois life, and they were to marry out or work my way out. It is the latter which, for that first moment of the fifties, lay open to me. For that moment of the post-war educational expansion fuelled my puny and innocent little dreams as I grew up, the epitome of the hard-working, conservative and respectable working-class girl.

Becoming middle-class in the seventies was like entering a new world peopled by those who designated themselves as special. I felt split, fragmented, cut off from that suburban semi, where I couldn't tell my mother what was happening. Where nobody knew what academic work was (and where it would have been better to announce that I was going to produce a baby, not a thesis). I felt, in the old place, as in the new, that if I opened my mouth it would be to say the wrong thing. Yet I desired so much, so very much, to produce utterances which, if said in one context, would not lead to rejection in the other.

But in all of this, it was the supreme ordinariness which I found so difficult to talk about in the circles in which I had begun to move. My version of a working-class childhood simply did not fit the illusion of the proletariat as a steaming cauldron of revolutionary fervour. The suburban semi could hardly be described as a backstreet slum from which I could have claimed a romantic poverty. I came from among the serried ranks of what my mother was fond of describing as 'ordinary working people'. It is that conservative and respectable ordinariness which I want to reclaim. The ordinariness of manners, of please-and-thank-you'd politeness, of being a nice girl, who went to Brownies and Guides, and for whom the competitions in the annual Produce Association show provided one of the most exciting occasions of the year. Reclaim that, name it, speak it, for in it lies a childhood like so many, and yet all too easily explained away in a pathologization of difference. It is as though those stories which are 'nothing to write home about', in all their ordinary obviousness, were not themselves both constituted by, and constitutive of, a history which has to be told. It was the pattern of daily life which gave this adult that I have become her specificity.

There, caught in the threads of that ordinary life, is the basis for understanding what my subjectivity might be about.

Proto-fascist organizations are embarrassing to those who stand outside the familiarity of one of the mainstays of suburban life. Yet it was the church, the school, the Brownies, the Guides and the fêtes and competitions which helped provide the building blocks of my formation. Or holidays in Skegness, brought sharply into focus one day in the early seventies when, walking with friends in another seaside town, we passed a row of cafés, watching the ordinary working families eating fish and chips inside, off plastic tables, with tomato sauce.

'How can they do it?' How could I reply that that had been me, that I liked tomato sauce (indeed, it was from brown sauce that I got a first French lesson: *Cette sauce de haute qualité est une mélange d'épices orientaux . . .*)! How could I evoke the happy holiday memories here at once disdained as nothing? But what I failed to recognize was the fascination of gazing at the working class, and the question these friends so very much wanted an answer to: what was it like to *be* like that, the fantasized Other, repository of simultaneous fears and dreams of radical subversion? Yet gazing further, looking through the window of the past, I glimpse the happiness of sunny days at the tea table, laughter, hopes and fears and pain: pain of loss, pain of leaving, of wanting. Fear of the reproduction of that ordinariness inside myself. To be ordinary is to be a woman; to be ordinary is to be a worker: terror and desire.

I have a terrible fear of the suburbs: I cannot bear the provinces, and especially the edges of conurbations. Just like home. The safe familiarity of the bay windows, the neat gardens, safety like a trap, ready to ensnare in its enfolding arms. The price: having to live in London, the fear and lure of elsewhere, of always working, never stopping, for working was the way out, the only guarantee, the safeguard against the necessity to accept, to return, to give up. I cannot explain what it feels like to be in another place because of that work, for embedded in it is the necessary fear of giving up, the terrifying doubts that very soon they will find out that you have no talent. To stop is to turn, like Cinderella, from splendour back to rags. But my home is paid for by my mental labour. What else, except the slippery slide-path back to being ordinary, at home with children in a suburb?

But they set me up to want, fashioned my desires, and then held out the promise that if I were a good girl, by dint of my own efforts, it could all come true. And here, the dreams of the prince, of being rich, of the exotic, the different, and being clever, mingle into one.

> Three-year-old Valerie Walkerdine, one of the 'fairies' in the fancy dress parade at Mickleover children's sports and field day last night. (*Derby Evening Telegraph*, summer 1950)

There are many versions of the press photograph accompanying this text among our family snapshots. It is one of my favourites, an image I cannot erase from my mind. It shows a little girl dressed as a bluebell fairy: a pale blue dress with puff sleeves and a frilly skirt, a bluebell hat, fairy wings and wand. She smiles, hesitantly, towards someone near the camera but not holding it. Whose gaze? In whose vision was I created to look like this, to display the winning charms, so that when I posed before the judges, they too, like the camera, would be won over? It is my first memory of what winning meant. But towards whom am I looking, who dressed me like this? Like all the fairy fantasies rolled into one? I wanted to be like one of the Flower Fairies in the book of that name, of which I still have a copy. How I too gazed at those fragile and ethereal little fairies, who were not quite of this world; the sickly and underweight child, object and source of those fragile and yet devastating fantasies. It was somebody's dream, their fantasy, my fantasy, meeting in the mutuality of the returned look; the gentle and uncertain smile created there, too. Charming little fairies who have good and beautiful powers to transform, fuelling the flames of an omnipotence, to cast spells, work magic. But then, the magic might fade ... for if some central piece of myself was formed in the crystallizing moment of that gaze, were not the will-o'-the-wisp charms threatened by growing up, growing big?

'A day-early birthday present.' The day of my birth was the day before my father's birthday, and so here I was, in the circuit of exchange, given by my mother to my father. Tinkerbell, he called me: Tinky, the bluebell fairy, not quite of this world. A sick man's dream – he was always ill – of another who would make him well, whole again, give him life, the laughter in the soul, to take away the ever-present threat of death. Tinkerbell, who so lived for the life of Peter Pan that she drank his poison, and whom only the belief in fairies would keep alive:

> Hook poisoned it.... He lifted the glass, but Tink still hovered over it. There was no time to argue. She perched on the rim, her light shone inside it, and dropped down and down until the glass was empty. Down to the very last drop, Tink drained the glass ...
> It was poisoned, she repeated faintly, and I think I'm going to be dead now.... All of you out there, if you believe in fairies, clap your hands. Clap them hard and go on clapping. If you don't, Tinkerbell will die.
> There was hardly a moment before, suddenly and miraculously, the silence was broken by a tremendous clapping of hands.

He wanted me to be a doctor, the magician of science, substituting medicine for magical cures, but still with the wish-fulfilment of my capacity to cure him, to make him whole, complete. I never wanted to be a doctor. I remembered toying with the idea of being a nurse, but I didn't like blood. A casual remark. The wish of a working-class father for his daughter. But how else can I explain that 1975 found me telling his shadow in a corner of the churchyard that I had got my PhD? I was a doctor, yet the kind that couldn't have cured him even if he were alive.

Nothing would succeed in bringing him back, for wherever he seemed to be, in whatever guise, there around every corner was loss. When I was sixteen, a month before I took my O levels, he died suddenly in the middle of the night, there and then gone. And I struggled with those O levels, wanting somehow to show him that I would not give up.

I must have been about six. They took me into hospital. I had always been a rather sickly and underweight child, constantly absent from school with tonsillitis. I am told that in hospital I was a model patient, who sang to the nurses. But this charming episode was to mark the end of the reign of the bluebell fairy (see also Chapter 15). Delicacy was to make way for an awkward lumpiness, a terror of my body that has always stayed with me. But I felt cheated in the hospital. They told me that I was ill and would be better, that I could eat what I liked. But who was to know the terrifying gains that had been made from that illness?

They told me that I could have jelly and ice cream after the operation – the kind of food reserved for special treats like parties, birthdays and Christmas. So they set it up to be a celebration, the triumph over illness. But they didn't tell me that the pain would be so great that the jelly and ice cream was all I would be able to swallow. I had lost a lot more than my tonsils.

After that I seemed to eat a lot. I certainly put on a lot of weight, so that I find it almost unbearable to look at photographs of myself from that time on. They called it 'puppy fat', attributed it to my glands. The charming little girl, who was so frail and fragile that she could not be expected to be physical, had turned into a huge and clumsy lump. I could no longer be excused physicality through illness, but in fact lived in a state of terror about my body. I couldn't do the kind of sports that were expected. So instead of the active young girl of the pre-adolescent feminist myth, I was frightened and clumsy and seemed to have lost, with my tonsils, the magical powers; the capacity to be a fairy. Just because you are big, they imagine you are not afraid. Big and small, active and passive. The longed-for femininity. But that lumpen docility could be put to good use in the classroom. It was still possible there to win, to become the object of that other, laudatory gaze, in the place from which once again I might be chosen.

They don't just sell you a dream in school, they pin you down with truth. In the classroom the truth of a position is produced, holding you fast and steady, keeping the wanting going. When you have a position to keep up, winning and losing take on an altogether different meaning. When I was six, Miss Wedd, the class teacher, told me that if I didn't get a scholarship they would enter me for an Art Scholarship. I spent all my spare time drawing. It fitted well with the quiet and well-behaved little girl. She could let her imagination run riot with a pencil and paper. Where other people read books, I filled in the hours with this kind of solitary occupation. 'Valerie seems quite gifted,' said my school report. Gifts, it seemed, were everywhere; on my birth I had been a gift and now I had a gift. It was given and I was chosen. I don't think I knew what an Art Scholarship was, but my desire to be a teacher seemed to date from that time. It was an art teacher at first. Later, in that other dream of difference, it became a French teacher. I became neither, I became that much more acceptable thing, a teacher of young children. Nevertheless it was a teacher I wanted to be, like the teachers who had chosen me. I knew no other teachers except my own, and had no sense of an ambition outside the possibility that if you were good at something, then one day you might be good enough to teach it. When it came, later, to the point of applications for college, I put down six choices, all of them in London, for teaching was to be my passport out of the suburbs.

Reading my reports of that time, I find everywhere the facticity of those choices:

Junior 1   No. in class: 52   Age: 8.4
Position in class: 3rd
Conduct: excellent
Progress: most satisfactory in all subjects
Remarks: a very good report. Valerie is a steady, reliable worker, with an
    ability above the average. If she continues as she has started she should do
    very well indeed.

But when I read it now I could tear it up. I have spent enough time studying the ways in which girls' and boys' performance is understood to recognize the pejorative as well as positive connotations of being a 'steady, reliable worker'. Later, my head teacher was to call me a 'plodder'. Boring, ordinary, lumpish, snail-like. Yet the phrase steady, reliable worker, could have been written by a personnel manager in a factory. Reliable doesn't rock the boat; and yet, and of course, the position: third out of fifty-two. Conduct, excellent: what else to keep you there, thinking, dreaming, one day, one day, the reward would arrive, the dream come true? They pin you down with facts: 'an ability above the average'. A dream, a fantasy to be sure, but so powerful in its effects and implications.

Psychologists claim that it is possible at a very early age to predict with some degree of accuracy the ultimate level of a child's general intelligence.... Since the ratio of each child's mental age to his chronological age remains the same, while his chronological age increases, the mental differences between one child and another will grow larger and larger and will reach a maximum during adolescence. It is accordingly evident that different children from the age of eleven, if justice is to be done to their varying capacities, require types of education varying in certain important respects. (Board of Education, Consultative Committee on Secondary Education, 1938, pp. 357–8)

Psychologists may well make claims, but teachers have to put into practice those fragile illusions of truth. They classify and position. But let's make no mistake: the double-bind of this double standard is that it got me where I am today. Those little moments in the dream: of being a teacher, third in class, the excellent conduct. Contradictory, painful, alluring. There, but not quite yet. The constant search, the constant fear of rejection. But what, in that system, would I swap? Could I honestly say that I would rather have been forty-third than third?

Trying, crying, gaining, winning and, of course, ever present the barely whispered fear that I might not be good *enough* to avoid and evade failure and loss. But you told me, you told me if I tried ...

But everywhere there was competition. Together, my younger sister and I competed. The most memorable competitions were on holiday. At the seaside there were always competitions sponsored by children's comics and food manufacturers. We tried our hardest to win these, and usually did. Often they were artistic, such as making castles and pictures in the sand. The local Produce Association annual show always had sections for children: 'posy in an eggcup' or, more difficult, 'design a cup and saucer'. I still have the prize certificates.

One form of winning which knitted together money and the dream of riches was Purpose Day. This was the Brownie and Guide equivalent of the Scouts' Bob-a-Job week. We got only a day. The main aim was to collect as much money as possible by doing simple household chores. My sister and I worked out fairly quickly that if we stayed around where we lived we wouldn't get much money, but by walking quite some way to a private avenue of very large houses it was possible to earn much larger sums. Here lived what we took to be the wealthy. Not only did they have more money, but there was a double and even more enticing bonus: we could get to see how the other half lived. In cleaning the shoes and washing the floors of the rich, there was a vicarious pleasure. We could find out what it was like to live like that. And so the dreams of being like that too were given some substance – a bit like the upstairs parlourmaid. Ironically, being inside the houses was in some sense enough. It was to be included. It is not difficult to understand how the mixture of desire and resentment should render occupations inside well-to-do households glamorous. Sharing in the magic is almost like possessing the magic yourself.

It was my granny who most fed these dreams. My maternal grand-mother, who lived with us, had her own fantasies and dreams of grandeur. The arch conservative of the working class, who hated every-thing to do with proletarianism, she spent at least part of most evenings as the centrepiece of the local pub, drinking Double Diamond like an early version of Ena Sharples at the Rovers Return. But while she might have looked like Ena, her aspirations were more in line with those of Annie Walker.

The Midland Drapery was the largest department store in Derby. I loved it when she took me there for tea. They had waitresses, music, and mannequins swirling around between the tables. Granny and I played this little game together. We had sandwiches in little triangles with the crusts cut off, toasted teacakes and tea in heavy pewter pots. Then we would look around the shop and fantasize about what we might have bought. Granny seemed a funny old lady, but she had class!

She seemed almost to perform the function of a fairy godmother. One of the things she made happen was visits to the home of her brother, who lived in Chesterfield. The family story had it that he had worked his way from rags to riches, from office boy to managing director of a local firm. We used to go sometimes to the large house, set in its own grounds, which had the ultimate in decadence, a revolving summer house. You could turn it round to catch every last flicker of the sun's warmth. Everything there seemed to be tinged with sophistication. I had never before eaten biscuits sandwiched together with real chocolate, or tasted ravioli.

The suburb of Derby was not always a suburb. Mickleover was once a village. That is how I first remember it. It is the village I want to preserve inside my imagination. Everyone knew everyone else. But gradually, the suburban expansion of the post-war reconstruction began to encroach on the fields in which I had once played. New housing estates sprang up. The old Victorian school building burst at the seams. A new school was built, which I moved to while in the Juniors. This was the 1950s. When I made that journey home in 1983, it still seemed like the 'New School'. It was on the 'New Estate'. Its architecture was modern. I could not fit this time of post-war expansion of thirty years ago with the idea of the new school. The *Derby Evening Telegraph* reported the new school along with the year's award of swimming certificates:

> Mr J.W. Best, the headmaster, spoke of the growing number of children (425) attending the school, and said that with the opening of the new school at Mickleover the position would be eased.

The encroachment of the new housing estates seemed to match the waning both of the countryside and of my childhood. But things were changing; we felt it in the new estates, we heard it on the radio, we saw it on the television, bought especially for the Coronation. Separation was difference. Change was moving out.

In my school they asked me what my father's work was. I replied with some pride that he was a mechanized fettler. It had taken me a long time to learn that. The teacher wrote down 'Works for Rolls-Royce'. Most fathers worked there or for British Railways, the two major employers in Derby. Some people's mothers were nurses and domestics at the county mental hospital in the village. My grandmother worked there until she was seventy-two, when they forced her at last to retire. She died a year later. My mother did no paid employment until after my father died. In the post-war respectable working class, it was clear where a mother's place ought to be.

To be special and to be ordinary: the home, the safety, the woman, the worker, the difference, there held out sparkling in the palm of an outstretched hand. To be clever is to be chosen. To leave the safety for the lure of those promises.

As part of the expansion, new grammar schools were built in villages further outside Derby. In 1958 I passed the eleven-plus. Ten years later I became a teacher. To want to be clever is to desire to win. It is both to be different and to long for acceptance. To be attractive enough, to be clever enough, to have enough money. I wanted them all. The new grammar school was part of what winning and being chosen meant.

They held out a dream. Come, they told me. It is yours. You are chosen. They didn't tell me, however, that for years I would no longer feel any sense of belonging, nor any sense of safety. That I didn't belong in the new place, any more than I now belonged in the old. So, around every corner of apparent choice lurked doubt and uncertainty.

Leaving one's class was to be both admired and scorned. My mother described its pejorative connotations as typified by a change of accent which she referred to as 'lasting and pasting'. The fear in this working-class morality of putting on airs and graces was the fear of being found to be an imposter. The terror was not a simple matter of working-class pride. It was all right to talk like that if you had a right to belong to that class. In 1983, I lasted and pasted it. Few would have recognized my accent as local. In London they still constantly remark on my 'northern accent', as though it were a mark of quaint and charming working-class authenticity.

To be neither, in no place, with no sense of belonging. For if the long vowel sounds are fraudulent, so would be the continued maintenance of the inappropriate authenticity. Valerie, the clever working-class girl from

Derby, the trumped-up little teacher. These personages lurk fearfully in the insecurities of imagined failure and rejection. What if winning in one place is simultaneously always a loss? What if the fear of losing so fires you that you never dare to try? Other lives, other stories, but tangible and important histories.

And finally, where shall I look for cause in this history? The circuit of exchange in which a sick man accepted a gift? (To Stan and Rosemary the precious gift of a daughter.) But who gave it? The Lord giveth and the Lord taketh away. The man who wanted so desperately to hang on to the possibility of life that he found in his daughter. The woman who gave her children everything, hoping to find there some fragment of herself. My mother in this history has no history. She lurks silently in the kitchen. She is safety. She is danger. She is the suburbs. She is morality. I cannot find her in my dream because the kitchen is where I am most afraid to look.

Or what about that moment in history, the dream held out in the palm of an outstretched hand? They held out the knowledge, the position to me, and told me that I could claim it as mine, if I worked for it and had the ability. So what of that dream? Should I have adapted to reality? If so, which of the realities would you have me adapt to? The dream of difference, of the exotic, out of my class, out of my gender? The reality of the factory, the office, the kitchen, the cradle, workers and women, ordinary people? Did anyone really expect me to adapt to those realities, to swap poverty for wealth, when they faced you with a dream? Who in their Valium-induced haze would want to swap that version of reality for the glittering landscape of the dream?

Look, children of the post-war boom, over there at the new day dawning, the sun rising over the bright future of the new housing estates where, by our abilities and aptitudes, we would be chosen to take our place in the land of opportunity. But how can we hope if we do not have dreams; how can we build if we do not have a future? What dream, what future, what here, what now? You should never have educated us, the ordinary girls of the fifties, for we are dangerous. We are set on becoming, and you will not stop us now. But it is not the individuals you sought to make of us who believe we have made it, leaving all the pain and uncertainty behind in that other place. No, not that. We are beginning to speak of our histories, and as we do it will be to reveal the burden of pain and desire that formed us and, in so doing, expose the terrifying fraudulence of our subjugation.

18

'We never forget you have a choice'

(Notes written around 1980)

I remember pondering on 'dropping out' and the fundamental unfairness of it. Not only did you have to drop out of it, give it up, but you could always drop back into a secure position.

I had struggled and struggled against exclusion, and now they were telling me that what I had struggled for was worthless. But what is more, they said it from a position of a success which I badly wanted and had never achieved. It is relatively easy, therefore, apparently to give up something you take for granted, but for those on its margins, it is excruciating. I remember feeling intense anger that people would give up a PhD, say it wasn't 'where they were at', when it had taken me years of battling to prove that I was good enough to do one, years of refusing to give up. How could I drop out of something I'd struggled so long to have? So it is a position which seems possible only if you are inside (a white, middle class-male?), someone who has never been excluded and can therefore give it up. If you've always had the desire, got what you wanted, how easy then to think you can offer it to everybody else (progressivism) or say that it is worthless!

'You can't have everything you want,' said my mother – often. There we are, set up to want and we can't have it. And we blame our parents. And those mothers who do not give their children choice, let them be free, autonomous – restrain them – are punished. They are keeping their children down. Yet they know they cannot have what they want. This was the lesson of the time when my father told me that I could not go with the school to Nottingham to hear the Hallé orchestra. I knew you were supposed to want that culture. They didn't. My parents saw it as a way to teach me that you cannot just ask and expect to get. 'You don't know, you don't understand, this is what I *have* to want!' I cried. They 'kept me down'. To them the matter was a simple lesson – to people like

171

me desire is not fulfillable. Choice ends. And we feel hurt, angry and deprived. Yet they were right. 'Go and tell your teacher I like the Donkey Serenade', said my mother, 'not the Hebrides Overture.' How could I tell him *that*? The making of me as a bourgeois individual was painful, a struggle not to put a foot wrong. They laughed at what you brought from home, as teachers now deride parents' attempts to help their children calculate. It is as though they shouldn't help at all, but of course that would be wrong too.

So they tell you that you can pull yourself up by your bootstraps and then, when you've done it (got the job, become clever, got the 'things you wanted', 'married the prince'), they tell you it's all bad. You were bad to want to own your own home, or they want to deprive you of your ownership at exactly the time when things are getting bad. Not for nothing was it called the Depression. But Thatcher offers choice, the promise, if we work. . . . But we always knew we had to work, to struggle – that's what got us the things we've got. Labour wants to take them away. Thatcher tells us that times are bad but we'll pull through. We know that, we have always known that. And in the end, in the end, she'll promise us our choice back. Our choice, just when we were fearing that we'd lost it for ever: people dropping, like flies, their jobs disappearing, the threat of deprivation. And she's giving us our power and our glory just when we were being emasculated, and so she seems to have given us what we've always felt deprived of: power and autonomy. We always had to fight, and we never give up without a struggle. . . .

19

Video replay: families,

films and fantasy

I am seated in the living room of a council house in the centre of a large English city. I am there to make an audio-recording as part of a study of six-year-old girls and their education. While I am there, the family watches a film, *Rocky II*, on the video. I sit, in my armchair, watching them watching television. How do I make sense of this situation?

Much has been written about the activity of watching films in terms of scopophilia. But what of that other activity, film theory, or, more specifically, what about this activity of research, of trying so hard to understand what people see in films? Might we not call this the most perverse voyeurism?[1] Traditionally, of course, observation – like all research methods in the human and social sciences – has been understood as, at worst, minimally intrusive on the dynamics and interaction unfolding before the eyes of the observer, who is herself outside the dynamic. My argument is that such observation, like all scientific activity, constitutes a voyeurism in its will to truth, which invests the observer with 'the knowledge' – indeed, the Logos. The observer, then, should be seen as the third term, the law which claims to impose a reading on the interaction. This is offered as an explanation to which the observed have no access, yet it is crucial in the very apparatuses which form the basis of their regulation. In addition, the observer becomes the silent Other who is present in, while apparently absent from, the text. Clearly, I cannot escape the contradictions and effects of my own need here to produce a reading, an analysis, an account of what happened. But in order to insert myself explicitly into the text, I shall attempt to speak also of my own identification with the film I watched with this family.

My concern is therefore not just with the voyeurism of the film spectator, but also with the voyeurism of the theorist – in whose desire for knowledge is inscribed a will to truth of which the latent content is a terror of the Other who is watched.

From this perspective I shall explore, in a preliminary way, the relationship of families to television and video and, more particularly, the effectivity of the films they watch upon the constitution of family dynamics. Within film theory concepts from psychoanalysis do not seem to have been used to examine how specific films have been read in practice, nor how they produce their specific effects. Identification, for example, is often discussed in terms of the effectivity of representation as distorted perception – the viewer is accorded no status which pre-exists the film. Psychoanalysis is used, in the end, to explore the relations within a film rather than to explain the engagement with the film by viewers already inserted in a multiplicity of sites for identification.

The family I shall be discussing did not watch *Rocky II* as ideal, acultural viewers, for example, but in relation to complex and already constituted dynamics. And these dynamics cannot simply be reduced to differences of class, gender and ethnicity – although the question of how these enter into the divided relations of domestic practices is nevertheless central.

Such differences themselves exist within a regime of practices, in which 'fantasy' and 'reality' already operate in a complex and indiscernible dynamic.[2] In trying to understand the domestic and family practices in which adults and children are inscribed, therefore, I examine the play of discourses and the relations of signification which already exist. And I approach the viewing of the film in the same way, as a dynamic intersection of viewer and viewed, a chain of signification in which a new sign is produced – and thus a point of production or creation in its own right.

In discussing families watching films, I try to show how aspects of the filmic representations are incorporated into the domestic practices of the family. This explains the themes and emphases in my argument. First, there is the question of how to understand the act of *watching*. I shall describe the watching of families as a surveillant voyeurism, a 'will to tell the truth' about families which contains a set of desperate desires – for power, for control, for vicarious joining-in – as well as a desperate fear of the Other being observed. Secondly, I want to challenge the 'intellectualization of pleasures' which seems to be the aim of much analysis of mass film and television. In opposition to the implicit contrast between the masses narcotized by the mass fantasies produced by the consciousness industry and the intellectual unbefuddled by the opium of ideology, it seems to me that we should look at the desire for forms of mastery that are present in our own subjectification as cultural analysts before rushing to 'save' 'the masses' from the pleasures of imaginary wish-fulfilment. Thirdly, therefore, I stress the materiality of power and oppression. Politics, in other words, are central to the analysis.

ROCKY II

The Coles are a working-class family. They live on a council estate and have three children – Joanne, aged six, Robert, nine, and James, thirteen – together with a large Alsatian dog, named Freeway.[3] I am seated in their living room. The video of *Rocky II* is being watched, sporadically, by the whole family. I sit there, almost paralysed by the continued replay of round 15 of the final boxing sequence, in which Mr Cole is taking such delight. Paralysed by the violence of the most vicious kind – bodies beaten almost to death. How can they? What do they see in it? The voyeuristic words echo inside my head, the typical response of shame and disgust which condemns the working class for overt violence and sexism (many studies show, for example, how much more sex-role stereotyping there is amongst working-class families). In comparison with a bourgeois liberalism it seems shameful, disgusting (key aspects of voyeurism) and quite inexplicable except by reference to a model of pathology.

I do not remember if I saw the whole film then. All I recall now is the gut-churning horror of the constant replay. Much later, when beginning to do the work for an analysis, I hired the video of *Rocky II* and watched it in the privacy of my office, where no one could see. And at that moment I recognized something that took me far beyond the pseudo-sophistication of condemning its macho sexism, its stereotyped portrayals. The film brought me up against such memories of pain and struggle and class that it made me cry. I cried with grief for what was lost and for the terrifying desire to be somewhere and someone else: the struggle to 'make it'. No longer did I stand outside the pleasures of engagement with the film. I too wanted Rocky to win. Indeed, I *was* Rocky – struggling, fighting, crying to get out. I am not saying that there is one message or reading here for all to pick up. On the contrary, the film engages me as a viewer at the level of fantasy because I can insert myself into, position myself with, the desires and pain woven into its images. Someone else might have identified with Rocky's passive and waiting wife. But Rocky's struggle to become bourgeois is what reminded me of the pain of my own.[4] The positions set up within the film then create certain possibilities, but it seems to be the convergence of fantasies and dream which is significant in terms of engaging with a film.

One aspect of the popularity of Hollywood films like the *Rocky* series is that they *are* escapist fantasies: the imaginary fulfilment of the working-class dream for bourgeois order. And they reveal an escape route, one which is all the more enticing given the realistic mode of its presentation, despite the very impossibility of its realism.[5] Such are popular films, then, not because violence or sex-role stereotyping is part of the pathology of working-class life, but because escape is what we are set up to want, whatever way we can get it. For the majority of women and men, the escape route open to me, that of the mind, of being clever, is closed. It is the body which presents itself either as the appropriate vehicle for bourgeois wardship (all those women starlets, beauty queens and 'kept' women) or for the conquering champion who has beaten the opponents into submission.

What is important for me about watching a film like this is the engage-ment, the linking, of the fantasy-space of the film and viewer. Watching *Rocky II*, to be effective, necessitates an already existent constitution of pains, of losses and desires for fulfilment and escape, inhabiting already a set of fantasy-spaces inscribing us in the 'everyday life' of practices which produce us all. This does not imply a concept of a unitary subject, whose location in a 'social totality' determines the reading of a film, but rather a fragmented subjectivity in which signifying practices produce manifest and latent contents for the inscription of fantasy. Such wishes cannot be understood outside signifying activity – which is itself also discursive and involves aspects of power and regulation.

The magic convergence, therefore, is an act of signification, the fusion of signifier and signified to produce a new sign, a new place, desire leaping across the terminals, completing the circuit, producing the current. These multiple sites of my formation, these dynamic relations, are the diversity of practices in which power and desire inscribe me. The reader is *not* simply in the text, not then the spectator in the film, motivated simply by a pathological scopophilia. The *position* produced for the reader or spectator is not identical with an actual reader constituted in multiple sites and positions. Perhaps the 'desire to look' belongs with the film theorist and social or behavioural scientist who disavow their own engagement and subsume their own fantasies into a move into the symbolic, the desire for the mastery of explanation. Just as there is no 'reader' (simply and exclusively) 'in the text', nor is there a pre-formed subject whose experience is reflected, biased or distorted in the film. If fantasies of escape are what we are set up for, then any amount of cinematic fantasy posing as realism about the drudgery of our lives will not convince us to abandon our enticing fantasies.

There is, in this watching, a moment of *creation* – if it is effective and successful as a cultural product for the mass market whose desires it helps to form. There is certainly an aesthetic or a pleasure, yet each of these terms is more redolent of an up-market art movie in which there are taken only to be acceptable, not nasty, pleasures. An aesthetic is cold. What I am talking about is red-hot. It is what makes the youths in cinema audiences cheer and scream for Rocky' to win the match – including many black youths, even though the Mr Big of boxing, whom he defeats, is black. It is what makes Mr Cole want to have the fight on continuous and instant replay for ever, to live and triumph in that moment. And it is what makes me throb with pain.

Rocky II, like *Rocky I*, was a great box-office success. It brought in huge cash returns and Sylvester Stallone as Rocky was said to live out the part of the poor Italian-American who makes it in his 'real' life. The films tap into the classic working-class image of boxing as an escape route for tough young men. Boxing turns oppression into a struggle to master it, seen as spectacle. In Stallone's later films this is transformed into a one-man defence of 'America' (against Russia in *Rocky IV*) and the 'forgotten heroes' of the Vietnam War in *Rambo*. Although it is easy to dismiss such films as macho, stupid and fascist, it is more revealing to see them as fantasies of omnipotence, heroism and salvation. They can thus be understood as a counterpoint to the experience of oppression and powerlessness.

Rocky II tells the story of a successful fighter who, after a successful career in the ring, tries to go straight. Despite his attempts to achieve respectability and a 'decent' lifestyle, he can find no way out of the misery of menial manual labour (working in an abattoir) except a return to boxing. Rocky is portrayed as a 'trier', a 'fighter', a small man who beats the black, villainous Mr Big by dint of his perseverance, his 'sticking power'. The story thus engages the fight for the bourgeois dream of the small man who has 'brawn not brains'. Rocky's attempts to get a clerical job or to become an actor in television commercials are doomed because he cannot read. It is the woman he marries, the quiet girl, who equally struggles for him, who bears and nearly loses 'his' child, who, like the good-enough bourgeois mother, teaches him to read. Yet, failing all else, in order to become respectable, he has to return to fighting and he has to fight to win, nearly killing himself in the process. The struggle to be respectable is therefore also to be able to 'provide for' and 'look after' a wife and child/ren who will not need to work, suffer or go short of anything. The film itself is replete with such fantasies. What is important for Rocky's story is the presentation of the *necessity* of fighting for survival. Certainly here the fight pays off and the hero wins. But it validates trying and fighting and therefore the singular effectivity of bodily strength and the multiple significance of 'fighting'. Understood in this way, 'macho-masculinity' becomes no mindless sexism but a bid for mastery, a struggle to conquer the conditions of oppression, which remain as terror. It also throws into sharp relief the effects of the bourgeois mastery of the mind. These do not require the *overt* forms of physical violence or shows of strength, which are replaced by symbolic violence and displays of logocentric pyrotechnics.

Intricately tied in with the necessity for fighting, and therefore for aggression, is the necessity to protect a 'good woman'. The wife is both to be protected from other men (with more money and more glittering prizes?) and to be protected from the 'streets' – from being the bad woman, the whore, the tart. She has to be kept pure and virginal. In this respect Rocky is represented as a 'big man' at home. The sets are made especially small so that he looks giant-size and yet remains a 'small man' in the outside world: a man who has to fight and to struggle therefore 'to be' the big man at home. This shift is especially significant for Mr Cole.

As well as being portrayed as bodily big at home and small outside and in the ring, Rocky is also presented as an outer spectacle, hiding inner pain. Rocky is a public hero who provides good entertainment. 'The crowd' and 'the public' do not see the inner suffering and struggle which produce this entertainment; only his wife does. In the opening minutes of the film, when Rocky has won a match after almost being beaten to death, he screams 'Adrienne, Adrienne', like a desperate child; her protector is in reality dependent upon her. Against a musical crescendo on the soundtrack they slowly struggle to reach each other. Finally, when he is safe in her arms, they say 'I love you' to each other. This shot is held for several seconds, before a cut to the titles for *Rocky II* – this narrative image provides the lead-in from, and flashback to, the first film.

Fighting, as a key signifier in the film, is related to a class-specific and gendered use of the body (as against the mind). Masculinity as winning is constantly played across by the possibility of humiliation and cowardice (that he is 'chicken'); Rocky's body is constantly presented as beaten, mutilated and punished. The film always presents this body as spectacle and triumph, triumph over and through that mutilation, which is the desperate fear which fuels it. Although such a reading of masculinity is now common within film analysis,[6] it is the *class-specific* aspects of this masculinity that are important. Physical violence is presented as the only way open to those whose lot is manual and not intellectual labour, and another aspect of this classed masculinity is the wardship of a woman who does not have to work (like a man) but whose domain is the domestic.

The fantasy of the fighter is the fantasy of a working-class male omnipotence over the forces of humiliating oppression which mutilate and break the body in *manual* labour. Boxing as a sport is a working-class-specific development of fighting, in which young poor men break their bodies for prize money. It is a classic working-class spectacle in that sense, in which the boxer's mutilation provides the sport for the spectators. What is to be won is both the symbolic conquering of oppression and monetary gain – although of course, young men are as exploited in boxing as anywhere else.

Echoes of upward mobility recur throughout the film, and not just in Rocky's attempts, despite his wife's protests, to display the 'proletarian flash' of cars, jewellery and clothes. Particularly significant is the way his attempts at respectability are seen to be thwarted by his failure at school. Asked what he was thinking about in the last round of his fight as he is loaded into an ambulance, he replies, 'I don't know – that I should have stayed at school or something.' His interview for a clerical job goes like this:

> *Interviewer*: How far did you go in high school, Mr Balboa? ... Do you have a criminal record? Would you be interested in manual labour?
>
> *Rocky*: Well, I've got nothing against honest manual labour, it's just that I'd like to see if I can make a living sitting down, like you're doing over there.[7]
>
> *Interviewer*: Can I be honest? No one's going to offer you an office job: there's too much competition. Why don't you fight? I read somewhere that you're a very good fighter.
>
> *Rocky*: Yeah, well, when you're punched in the face five hundred times, it kind of stings after a while.

And at a later interview, he is told:

> Hey, look pal, you've got to be realistic. You've got no high-school diploma, no qualifications, wouldn't you be better with a good-paying menial job?

'Adapting to reality' is presented as the most punitive of options, for it condemns him to a life of misery and poverty. It is bourgeois dreams which provide a way out, and the body which is the vehicle, given an absence of 'brains'. Constantly, the 'assurance' of a secure gender and class identity is subverted by Rocky's terror, struggle and failure – in fighting and reading, for example. A coherent identity, a sense of having 'made it', is presented as a sham, not something easily achieved.

Meanwhile Adrienne works and suffers in silence, having got a job in a pet shop to help out. She gives birth prematurely through overwork and goes into a coma. No wonder Rocky needs to box, because he is saving her from death. She is a key figure: she simultaneously prevents Rocky from boxing and spurs him on to win. The struggle is thus also a specifically gendered struggle, in which positions relating to domestic and waged work are played out.

THE COLES

I have chosen to explore the term 'fight/ing/er' because it figures centrally in the *Rocky* films, not as a celebration of masculinity in a positive sense, but as something Rocky is 'driven to', a last resort.[8] I now

want to consider how 'fighting' enters as a relation into domestic discursive practices and produces a certain effectivity with respect to the
family members, linking this to my presence as an observer and thus to
the monitoring of pathology (correct language, for example) and to
moral regulation.

Let me begin by outlining briefly how the observation was experienced
as my surveillance of them. When I entered the house for the first
recording, Mr Cole shouted to his daughter, 'Joanne, here's your psychi-
atrist!' I had never mentioned psychiatry, let alone psychology, yet it was
evident to him that I was monitoring normality/pathology. In addition to
this, on several occasions he made reference to the monitoring of 'correct
language'. Joanne would at first not wear the microphone and Mr Cole
was quite clear that if nothing was said into it, 'they' would think she had
nothing to say. Quite.

> Do you know you're wasting the tape, you are, missy? Gonna go back to
> school and say what did Dodo do at home? And they'll say 'nothing'. Here's
> the proof – a blank tape.

In addition, he tells his daughter to 'do nothing, just act normal', yet
tries to encourage her to speak by saying 'The rain in Spain falls mainly
on the plain' or 'How now brown cow' (phrases often used in elocution
lessons, of course) into the microphone. On other occasions, moral
regulation centres around the dichotomy 'rude v. respectable' behaviour.

How did the family watch *Rocky II*? I shall begin with the final, bloody
rounds of the boxing match at the end of the film. At this time Mr Cole
(F), Joanne (J) or Do, and her brother, Robert (R), were watching,
together with the three-year-old child of a friend, called Jonas. Mrs Cole
(M) was in the kitchen, working, and thirteen-year-old James was elsewhere in the house. I reproduce below an annotated transcription of the
sequence.[9]

Rocky II, the video

Fight scene, possibly the fifteenth
round.

000
R: (untranscribed)
F: Watch, watch. Cor, he ain't
half whacking him, ain't he, Do?

Watch, here.

010
F tells J to go and ask M to make
some tea. J goes to the kitchen.

M's friend is with her – Scottish accent – with her young child. They talk about karate.

050
J is back in the TV room. She brings in the doughnuts. Film is on in the background.

J goes out again. She talks to M in kitchen.

090
J is back in TV room. There is general conversation going on, 'Do you want a doughnut?', etc. J is not saying much.

M's friend comes in with younger child.

112
J is sitting on the settee, eating a bun.

115
No one is saying much.

118
F: Hey, watch this, Rob.
R: Does he kill him?
F: Watch.

125
F pauses video or winds back to the closing round, because M is handing out the tea and cakes.

Rocky fighting championship round, pitched against huge black opponent. Things aren't looking good. Rocky is taking a bearing. The crowd is going wild, cheering, shouting.

R: Mum, hurry up.
F: You ready?
M: What?
F: We've yet to see the end of this.

Rocky is in his corner with his trainer, Chris, who is warning him.
Rocky: I know what I'm doing.
Chris: Listen. You're getting killed
        out there.
Rocky: It's my life.

Both fighters are in their corner with coaches. They are both badly beaten.

The commentator favours Rocky's opponent. He says 'All he has to do is stay awake to steal the title'.

There is talking in the background. M asks R to get something for her (?her slippers). R is put out.

R: Dad, stop it for a minute.
F: Ohhh, June.
M: Well, I wasn't to know. I thought you'd stopped it just for me.
F: No, we didn't stop it just for you. He's been trying to watch it.

The video is stopped again and wound back to the fifteenth round.

145
M and F are talking.

148
Getting ready to switch video back on.
F: Are you ready? (? to R or M)

149
Video is switched on.

This is the fifteenth round again. Rocky takes lots of punches from opponent. Then he fights back for a bit.
The crowd is shouting and cheering. Who for?
Both fighters are in a bad way – no one seems to be winning at the moment

J talks about Jason:

J: He's got all jam down him.

Rocky begins to punch opponent, who is too weak to retaliate by this time.
Both men's faces are a bloody mess. They both stagger round the ring, exhausted, but Rocky just has the upper hand.

155
Everyone is quiet, all watching the film.

The crowd chants 'Rocky, Rocky'.

Suddenly the film switches to slow motion.

161
F asks J if she likes her cake.

F hands round custard tarts.

There is slow, dramatic music. Rocky and his opponent fall.

All the while Rocky's wife has been watching the fight at home with her brother.

172
R: They both fall down.

All very quiet in TV room.

She seems to feel every punch herself, she looks distressed. Her brother is enjoying the fight, cheering and jumping up and down. Rocky's wife gasps 'Oh'. She has her hands up to her face.

175
Author and M talk about cakes.

In the ring everyone is shouting for Rocky and opponent to get up. The crowd is still going wild. Rocky's coach is yelling for Rocky to get up.
Rocky just about manages to stagger to his feet before the countdown ends.
Film cuts to wife and her brother at home. They are both jumping up and down with joy.

179
F says something to R about the film (untranscribed).

Crescendo of triumphant music.

Rocky's face is a bloody mass as he accepts the prize.
He is very emotional.
He speaks to the TV cameras.
Rocky: Thank you, thank you, I can't believe this is happening.

Rocky says that this is the greatest moment of his life, 'apart from when my kid was born'.

He begins to cry.
He says to his wife at home 'I did it'.

We see her crying as she quietly says 'I love you, I love you.'

There is much triumphant cheering and music.
End of film.

185
Child (unidentified) talking.

190
M and author are talking.

199
R: (? to F) I've gotta see, err, Rocky I.
F: So have I. You saw Rocky II today.

201
F: (untranscribed) ... after the last film (laughs).
M(?): They're only messing.

208
M: He says to Paul (untranscribed) ... no, he said, you're Rocky II and I'm (untranscribed) ...
F: Paul said that? (laughs)

214
Turn over to television.

I would like to pick up several points from this. First, there is the specific way in which a videotape is watched. This differs from the fascinated concentration of the spectator in the darkened cinema, and also from the way television is often used as a backdrop to domestic routines. The video has been deliberately selected and hired. More important, because – as here – it can be stopped and replayed, it allows for more overt connections to domestic practices and relations. Thus, secondly, Mr Cole is able to point excitedly to the fighting – once to Joanne ('He ain't half whacking him ...'), later to Robert. Thirdly, Mr Cole both 'sends out for' tea from Mrs Cole, who has to service the family, and also emphasizes that they have not stopped the video to replay it for her. She is told in no uncertain terms that 'we didn't stop it just for you', but for Robert, who's 'been trying to watch it'. The fighting (linked to control of playback on the video machine) is in this way most clearly presented as masculine, and something from which women are excluded.

The theme of fighting came up many times in my recordings and interviews with the family. Fighting is the key term for Mr Cole in particular. He sees himself as a 'fighter' – against the system and *for* his children, whom he also encourages to fight. In my second recording, he urged Robert and Joanne to fight each other, telling Joanne to give as good as she gets: 'Well, bash him hard.... You've been told, you whack him as hard as him.' Mr Cole also commented to me: 'It's surprising really, they're like this at home, but in school, if someone's whacked her, she's crying for about an hour after.'

In an interview with me, Mr and Mrs Cole also referred to Joanne as a tomboy, relating this to fears for her femininity. As Mr Cole observed: 'Obviously, she plays with dolls ... [untranscribed] with any luck ... [untranscribed] ... she might get married and away we go ... if we can find somebody.'

This concern for her future in terms of femininity is crosscut by issues about class, in which fighting is a key term. When I commented that Joanne is quiet at school, Mr Cole saw the solution in terms of standing up for herself: 'Well, I think she needs to have a good row with one of the kids in school, give them a good hiding', adding that the two boys were 'the same, until they started like'. The fear would disappear if she could 'hit just as hard or harder'.

Other aspects of Mr Cole's relation to Joanne are salient here. His nickname for her is 'Dodo'. In this instance, although 'Dodo' might relate to an infantile mispronunciation of Joanne (Jo-Jo: Dodo), it also has links with infantilization and death. Dodo, says Mr Cole, is an extinct bird. Dodo is therefore an anachronism, something which no longer exists (a baby?) but is kept alive in Mr Cole's fantasy of his daughter as dependent. It may also keep alive for Mr Cole a feminine which is opposite from, and Other to, himself.

Mrs Cole revealed her own reticence and similarity to Joanne when I questioned her about her own activities as a shop steward for NUPE. 'Well, I wouldn't have done it, not unless I got roped into it,' she says; and 'I think if I had to stand up there and talk in front of a whole load of people I'd crack . . .' Mr Cole systematically encourages and undermines her, commenting that 'we're not talking about thousands of people'. He, conversely, is on the executive of the local Labour Party. He also 'fights for his children'. Mr Cole is the 'big man' at home. He 'talks for' his wife and systematically stops her talking. He is the 'fighter'. Like Rocky, he is a 'big man' at home who is 'small' and has to 'stand up for himself' in the world outside. Mr Cole is physically very small and the necessity for a fighting masculinity might therefore relate here to a terror of femininity (invested in Dodo?).

Two incidents illustrate this combativeness. The first was the Coles' successful struggle with their local education authority to get the elder son, James, into a prestigious school. The other was their campaign for the removal of asbestos from their daughter's school. For Mr Cole 'The point of fact is though, as any layman knows, asbestos kills'; unlike other parents and teachers he would not put education above physical health and life. The Coles were the only parents to keep their daughter home until the asbestos was removed – the only ones who 'had enough fight'. According to Mr Cole: 'we're Evil. . . . We like to go against the system. . . . I think they've got a little black book on me somewhere.' Indeed, the Coles are not liked by the school, where their fighting is perceived as 'trouble-making'. The notions of fighting stressed by the Coles also make Joanne's 'nurturant' teacher see her as a problem child.

Here the signifier 'fighting' enters into a different relation as it forms for the teacher a characteristic of combative and troublesome parents. It is read as a threat to her position and therefore relates to her reading of the Coles and her own fears of professional powerlessness. Joanne, for her part, stresses the need to 'work hard' and not to 'jaw'. She is largely silent in her interview with me and wants to go and 'get on with her work'.

Mr Cole also encourages his sons to fight and had Robert tell me a story of how he was banned from the school coach because he 'beat up' another boy. In addition, during one recording, he stopped the play-fight between Robert and Joanne with 'no fighting downstairs, eh? . . . Yes, sir, I'll kill you'. At the end of the recording, because of my presence, James managed to go off swimming without really getting permission. Mr Cole's response was, 'Wait till this lady goes, you've had it.' Here, 'fighting' is both an aspect of a bid for power over the body and yet a desperate struggle in relation to it. Fighting can be turned into a celebration of masculinity, but its basis is in oppression. This should also be understood, as in *Rocky*, as the desperate retreat to the body, because the 'way out', of becoming bourgeois through the mind is not open to Mr Cole.

Talking (saying 'the right thing', surveillance) is also crucial to aspects of power and regulation. As in *Rocky*, it establishes the place of the body and its place in relation to class and gender. Always there is a sense of surveillance of what is said, what can be said outside my hearing, its wrong and pathologized character, as well as the silence and silencing of Mrs Cole and Joanne, the combative talk and fighting. Fighting and power/powerlessness therefore seem to me especially related to an experience of oppression and present a picture of the very 'failure' in covert regulation, the reasoned/reasoning avoidance of conflict which is the object of psychoeducational discourse and which therefore pathologizes them.[10] Although Mr Cole stressed his concern that Joanne should fight (like the boys), fighting remains an aspect of a gendered practice. It is the masculine body which is invoked even when Joanne fights, as a 'tomboy'. Mrs Cole's only role in this is to service. She performed domestic labour throughout the recordings and very rarely spoke. Mr Cole 'ordered' cups of tea and stressed that he likes times when his wife is on holiday best because 'she bakes every day'. Robert picks up Mrs Cole's status as a 'servant' in relation to Joanne, at one point calling her his 'slave'.

Fighting enters into the Coles' domestic practices as a relation in a way which is totally consonant with its presentation in *Rocky II*. That relation was crystallized in the watching of the film and the repetition of the final round. In terms of 'forwards' movements, therefore, I am placing the relations of signification within history, and within an experience of gendered and class-specific lived oppression. Fighting is a key term in a discourse of powerlessness, of a constant struggle not to sink, to get rights, not to be pushed out. It is quite unlike the pathological object of a liberal anti-sexist discourse which would understand fighting as 'simply' macho violence and would substitute covert regulation and reasoning in language as less sexist.

It is in this way that I am aiming to demonstrate the *fixing* of fighting in that lived historicity – the *point de capiton* (cf. Lacan, *Écrits*). I am stressing too that 'fight/ing/er' as a relation is quite specific in its meaning and therefore *not* coterminous with what fighting would mean in, for example, a professional middle-class household where both the regulation of conflict and the relation to oppression are quite different. This is an argument *against* a universalism of meaning, reading and interpretation. However, having examined the manifest content in which the relations of signification are historically fixed, this is not all there is. If we are to explore the latent content, it is necessary to ask what is suppressed/repressed/forgotten beneath the term? The working-class male body is a site of struggle and anxiety, as well as pleasure. Mr Cole is a very small man. Fighting is a way of gaining power, of celebrating or turning into a celebration that which is constituent of oppression. Power in its manifest content covers over a terror of powerlessness, an anxiety beneath the pleasure.

Mr Cole is afraid of being 'soft', of a femininity lurking beneath the surface. This is referred to while the family watch the musical film *Annie* on video. It is seen as a 'women's film', and its fantasies, its dancing and singing, are constantly held up for ridicule. It is as though Mr Cole cannot bear to be seen (by me?) as liking such a film, as having passive, romantic fantasies. In this analysis, masculinity as fighting is a defence, a defence against powerlessness, a defence against femininity. The backwards movement can be articulated in relation to several points. The fear of being watched or monitored (counterpointed by my voyeurism), the expectation of female servicing (when his wife is at home), the *struggle* to fight against a fear: all these suggest that fighting represents a triumph over, repression of, defence against, the terror of powerlessness. This powerlessness, as in *Rocky II*, is presented as the humiliation of cowardice – of the man who cannot work, fight, protect women, and who is therefore feminized. Latent beneath Mr Cole's conscious self-identification as a fighter may lurk the fear of a small man whose greatest dread is his cowardice and femininity. It is this which has to be displaced by projection on to, and investment in, others (his wife, Joanne) who can be the objects of his protection and for whom he fights.

In psychoanalytic terms, such a reading keys into the necessity for – but also the fraudulence of – the phallus as a sign of power. Whether one finds in this an oedipal struggle or an ominpotent, pre-oedipal one might be a point of dispute. However, my aim is not to suggest that the historical 'fighting' is really about a psychic relation. Far from it. It is to demonstrate the centrality of sexuality and power in the lived historicity of current struggles and the interminable intertwining of present and past, of material conditions and psychic relations. What is being fought for and fought against by Mr Cole can therefore be understood as having a manifest and latent content. But since Mr Cole's (childhood) anxieties were and are produced in specific historical conditions, it is quite impossible, and indeed dangerous, to separate the one from the other.

PSYCHIC REALITY

In suggesting that the practices in which Mr Cole is inscribed locate him as a 'fighter', I have argued for a reading of the manifest and latent content of the term. In understanding the relation between the manifest content of *Rocky II* and that of the Coles' domestic practices, it is necessary to examine the chains of signification produced which link the two. This is particularly possible with a video-recording, since it is watched partly as a backdrop to other practices rather than in a darkened cinema.

Identifications, like those of Rocky and Mr Cole as fighters, may be fictions inscribed in fantasy, set and worked out in the film itself, but they are also lived out in the practices in which Mr Cole is inserted. There is no 'real' of these practices which stands outside fantasy, no split between fantasy as a psychic space and a reality which can be known. If such fictional identities become 'real' in practices, they must have a psychic reality which has a positive effectivity in the lived materiality of the practices themselves. Such fictional identities must be created in the plays of power and desire. They are also, therefore, created in relational dynamics in which others can project fantasies on to, and invest them in, subjects within the family and other relations. I want to point up the psychic reality of such projections by dwelling for a moment upon Mr Cole's nickname for his daughter, Joanne: Dodo. Although I have suggested that this may well be derived from a childish mispronunciation 'Jo-Jo', it has other associations, which Mr Cole makes, of the Dodo as an extinct bird.

It is not uncommon for men to give baby names such as Dodo to women and girls in their wardship. Deborah Cherry and Griselda Pollock, for example, have analysed Rossetti's use of 'Guggums' for his model and mistress, Elizabeth Siddall.[11] They make reference to Lacan's statement that 'woman does not exist' except as a symptom and myth of a male fantasy. As in his later statement that the 'phallus is a fraud', Lacan sets up there the possibility that subjectivity is created not in a fixed and certain gender-identity, but in shifting and uncertain relations. The desire of the Other, the fears and fantasies inscribed in and projected on to that Other, help to fix what 'woman' and 'man' are taken to be, not the essentiality of their nature. In addition, actual men and women strive and struggle to be 'man' and 'woman' within specific regimes of representation.

Cherry and Pollock's concern is to demonstrate that Elizabeth Siddall, as the object of a regime of representation (i.e. Rossetti's paintings), is a fiction. They make a strong distinction between Rossetti's representations and the historical individual, Elizabeth Siddall, suggesting, for example, that, renamed Guggums by him, this fiction itself constituted the object of male fantasy.

In using the idea of a 'historical individual', however, they seem to me to elide the issue of psychic reality and the material effectivity of such fantasied representations. It is as though they understand this fictional identity as, in some sense, not claiming a part of her lived historicity. This tends to deny the issues of wardship and patronage in which poor women become 'kept' women and their objectification consisted in the utilization of their bodies to keep them, as it were, from the streets. Elizabeth Siddall, like many other women of her class, used her body as her means of survival. Her infantilization as Guggums by Rossetti was a fantasy of protection played out right to the point of the romanticization of her death as a consumptive.

Let me take this further by recapitulating a number of representations from my own history (see Chapters 15, 17). The first image is of Valerie Walkerdine, dressed as a bluebell fairy in a local carnival. There are a number of similar representations: a press photograph from the local evening paper, the *Derby Evening Telegraph*; another press photograph (possibly from the same edition) in which Valerie Walkerdine poses with other entrants. 'Children waiting for the judging of the fancy dress parade at Mickleover branch of the British Legion Carnival Sports', runs the caption. The first photograph singles Valerie Walkerdine out from the other entrants, to be photographed alone. It does not mention that she won the competition. There are numerous other photographs of the bluebell fairy. Some appear to have been taken by the same press photographer, others are amateur photographs, posed in the front and back of Valerie Walkerdine's home. In addition to this extraordinary and multiple validation of a single image, the bluebell fairy, we could add other dimensions to the creation of the fictional representation. Clearly the costume itself is a construction, made by a neighbour from, I assume, a store-bought paper pattern. My father, who was at that time a semi-skilled worker in the machine shop at Rolls-Royce aero-engine division in Derby, made the metal wand at work. Relatedly, as with the representations of Elizabeth Siddall, my father had a nickname for me, itself clearly related to the fairy fantasy. This was 'Tinky', abbreviated from Tinkerbell. It is perhaps relevant that, out of the female characters in *Peter Pan*, it is Tinkerbell, not Wendy, which was chosen. By examining the regime of representations in which Tinkerbell enters as a relation, we can therefore begin to understand the constitution of Tinky and the bluebell fairy as fictions, representations constructed in the fantasied image of the Other. 'Valerie Walkerdine' was, in this guise, to be gazed at, dressed up to look like this and designated, in naming, its object.

In *Peter Pan*, Tinkerbell is certainly not the mother, this ascription being given to Wendy. She appears therefore to be another and opposite designation of the feminine. Perhaps then she is, in Juliet Mitchell's terminology, the hysteric.[12] That is, Tinkerbell is tiny, childlike, even smaller than the children in the story, much smaller than the eternal child Peter Pan. She is charming, mischievous, constantly comes between Peter and Wendy, and works magic. She is a fairy who, at one point, saves Peter's life by risking her own, and who is saved only by the audience's being told to believe in fairies to keep her alive. Wishes, wish-fulfilment, then, keep this representation a living symbol. But of what?

A fairy is not a human woman. She is tiny. She works magic, casts spells, charms, is not quite of this world. She does not grow up to be a woman. There are several similarities here with Elizabeth Siddall. Tinkerbell is feminine, but she is safe – the perpetrator of childhood charm, magic. She is a sexual object and yet totally safe. She is *not* a woman and not quite human. She seems to be the opposite of the mother. Feminine and powerless, the object of the male gaze, she is that Other created in his image, which is not the mother or the wife, but the one which he has power to construct, his Other, his forbidden femin-inity, the powerless child, object of his protection and wardship. The child who 'casts a spell' is magic, does not grow up, is doing the magic herself and yet is all dressed up to *be* charming, the construction and representation of a fantasy. However, this archetypical femininity, this object constructed in the male gaze, as femininity, is rather strange. It is a sexualized childhood certainly, but it seems to be a narcissistic image of the femininity of man, the hysteric, denying castration, the female constructed in man's narcissistic image. The representations of Elizabeth Siddall, the 'Guggums' created by Rossetti, were said to resemble the artist. When I examine these representations of myself, they are the site of an anxiety that I closely resemble my father. But is not the bluebell fairy saved by her feminine charms? The fairy is unattainable, not quite human, charming. Desire, passion and incest are thereby displaced and hidden.

Clearly, this vision and creation of three-year-old Valerie Walkerdine was much admired. There are *so many* photographs. The problem for me, in relation to these representations, comes in precisely what Cherry and Pollock invest in the historical individual. Although the point they are making is crucial and well taken – that it is a fiction which is constructed – nevertheless, we cannot simply displace the 'historical individual' as though she were no part of, or in no way related to, this regime of representations. How did Guggums become one aspect of her fractured subjectivity? How did she become inserted as a subject into particular sexual and artistic practices such that these representations were produced? It seems to me necessary to move towards an investment of desire, in which Elizabeth Siddall, like myself as the bluebell fairy, *wants* to live that fiction, basking in the gaze of the Other who constitutes it. Similarly we cannot set Rossetti, or my father, or those other Others, outside the fictions in which their own desire is created. The phallus too is a fraud.

The fantasy of Tinky and the bluebell fairy designate me, and I want to be there, to *be* that fairy – small, protected, adored and never growing up. Therefore to enter that fantasy. At what cost, though? The gaze is to be returned. To this day I can feel surging through my body the effect of the smile necessary to pose for such a gaze. Still, statuesque, frozen in the look, the light shining in the eyes of the Other. Only recently have I been able to understand its incredible investment of a fantasy in me, and to wonder what is hoped for in that image, to go beyond the safety of that gaze to anger at its patronage. A fantasy of childhood charms for ever, remembered as I searched that book treasured by so many little girls, called *Flower Fairies*,[13] each ethereal little fairy painted, dressed like a flower in delicate watercolours. Such representations form an important site for the investment and creation of my desire. Tinky was not all I became, but it related to a mutually lived-out fantasy. I wanted to be and to remain Tinky. The affirmatory gaze in its narcissistic reflection confirmed the positivity of that site of subjugation. Let me elaborate simply, then: certain aspects of this fiction seem relevant and salient to the constitution of the feminine as the hysteric in these two examples. First, it may be relevant that it was my father who manufactured the wand, precisely that which is waved to cast a spell – a fairy with a phallus?[14] Secondly, this gaze, this representation, crystallizes wardship. As in Lacan's 'God and the *jouissance* of Woman', the gazing, watching Other provides safety – the child who never grows up and, as in Lacan's vision, the moment of *jouissance* is the moment of death.[15]

For the safe place is an impossible location. In both the Tinky and Guggums representations, the child-woman is given a baby-name. In my case illness was a central trope. I was constantly ill with tonsillitis (passivity, diminutive size, not quite of this world). Elizabeth Siddall was more than a sickly child. She was consumptive: she died, playing out the sadomasochistic regimes. The haunting, ethereal quality of the pale femininity of the Rossetti paintings, the romanticization of death, celebrate the production of a femininity whose goal is death. And who, in those representations, lives on as in Rossetti's fantasy? Not a strong and healthy Elizabeth Siddall, capable of moving beyond the artist's protection, which also effected her rags-to-riches transformation from working-class girlhood to artist's model. However, such death-inducing representations are central to our culture of the child-woman, where slimming and anorexia retain the hysteric with the phallus in the protection of the father.

The important point is that such fantasies have a psychic reality which has positive and material effects when its significations are inscribed in actual practices. When Mr Cole calls his daughter 'Dodo', for example, that suggests not only his desire to infantilize her, but also his identification of himself as a 'fighter' for her and on her behalf. He becomes her Other – the big man, the protector. This is then inscribed in the semiotics of their relating and their positioning within practices. But Joanne is not only infantilized as Dodo. She is also positioned, in contradiction, as a 'fighter' like her father – Dodo and yet a 'tomboy'. This reveals the complexity of his identification with, and investment in, her as he makes her simultaneously his feminine ward to be protected and later 'married off' and his masculinized working-class fighter, like her brothers. Joanne's fractured subjectivity is therefore lived not without some pain produced by this splitting.

RECOGNITION AND LATENT CONTENT

I argued at the beginning of this essay that psychoanalytically orientated film theory, despite its many strengths, still elides certain problems about subjectivity when it implies that subject-positions are produced *within* the discourses of filmic representations. To some extent that should be read as a self-criticism too. Like many other people, I have drawn on the work of Althusser, Lacan and Foucault to understand the relation between 'positioning in discourse', 'modes of signification' and the 'semiotics of the psyche'.[16] Although the centrality of plays of signification to the formation of subjectivity has been emphasized within such modes of analysis, very little empirical work has been done on how the process actually works in the regulative practices of daily life. As a result of concentrating on the dynamics within regimes of representation, we risk ending up with a sense of the determined and passive subject we had hoped to avoid. Hence the question I have tackled here: how do we reassert the importance of the creation of subjectivity as active, even if the subject is caught at an intersection of discourses and practices?

The subject is positioned or produced in multiple sites. These are not all-embracing, but may work with or against each other. The person watching a film, for example, will always be already inscribed in practices which have multiple significations. That is why the film cannot in and of itself produce a reading which 'fixes' the subject. Rather, the viewing constitutes a point of dynamic intersection, the production of a new sign articulated through the plays of significance of the film and those which already articulate the subject. This sort of approach should make it possible to deal with the issue of specific readings, and the location of readers/viewers, without collapsing into essentialism. Thus Claire Johnston has argued for:

a move away from a notion of the text as an autonomous object of study and towards the more complex question of subjectivity seen in historical/social terms. Feminist film practice can no longer be seen simply in terms of the effectivity of a system of representation, but rather as a production of and by subjects already in social practices, which always involve heterogeneous and often contradictory positions in ideologies.[17]

As I say, though, the problem has been that, however clearly this agenda has been set, there has been little empirical work to back it up so far. My account of how the Coles (and I) watched *Rocky II* is an attempt to show the effectivity of filmic representations within the lived relations of domestic practices – signifying and discursive practices which are historically constituted and regulated.[18]

This means attempting to examine the relations between domestic practices (and other practices and discourses) in a number of ways. We need to understand how these 'lived relations' are formed through regimes of meanings which position the participants and 'lock into' relations of signification in the media. But more than this, we need to go beyond the present use of psychoanalysis. That is, by using psycho-analysis to understand relations *within* a film and then using voyeurism to understand the viewer, we are left in a sterile situation which assumes that all viewers 'take on' the psychodynamic of the film as far as it relates to the oedipal conflict. As Laura Mulvey and others have pointed out, this leaves women as viewers in a difficult position. As ethnographic studies such as those of Janice Radway have shown, it also imposes universalistic meanings on particularistic viewing situations.[19] Radway and others, however, are almost forced back on to an 'effects' model because they end up having to understand readers and viewers as pre-located and pre-determined. Cathy Urwin has pointed out that children's use of figures from the popular media in their therapy is not necessarily oedipal.[20] Using a Kleinian framework, she finds pre-oedipal struggles. Importantly, she suggests that the use made by the children of these figures, although it relates in some ways to the dynamic in the film or television programme, particularly relates to their own struggles in therapy. Hence a young boy can use the figure of Superman, not in relation to an oedipal resolution but as a carrier for his fantasies of omnipotent power. This suggests that different readers will 'read' films, not in terms of a pre-existing set of relations of signification or through a pathology of scopophilia, but by what those relations *mean to them*.

Although we have to understand the dynamics within which the viewer is already inscribed in order to engage with viewing, I do not wish to resort to an essentialistic reading, nor to a notion of a pre-formed subject. It is important not to reduce each viewer to some 'stage' in the analytic move from infancy to maturity. Rather, the viewers are themselves created in dynamics which are understood through, and inscribed in, historically specific practices and relations of power and oppression. The fantasies, anxieties and psychic states cannot be understood outside that history.

This, as I have stressed throughout this essay, applies as much to the position of the researcher as to the families or viewers being observed. I have already considered my own relation to *Rocky II* and to fathers' infantilization of girl children. But what of my position as researcher? As I suggested in the introduction, this itself constitutes part of the dynamic I was studying. It has to be understood not as a problem of 'intrusiveness', but in terms of the power/knowledge couplet.

As observer I became a 'Surveillant Other', not only watching but also producing a knowledge that feeds into the discursive practices regulating families. The 'social scientist' is the producer of a 'truth' which claims to 'know' those whom it describes. Together, observer and observed constitute a couple in the play of power and desire. We therefore need to examine the response of the observed to their experience of surveillance. Equally important, however, is the theorist's 'desire to know', for this contains both a fantasy of power and also a fear of the observed. (Scientific objectivity might therefore be seen as the suppression or disavowal of this desire.)

Humanistic forms of social science often attempt to escape this inevitable power dynamic by reducing 'power-differentials' or by 'putting subjects at ease'. Despite these patronizing attempts to get 'beyond power', I would argue that most therapeutically and psychoanalytically orientated work on families and films or television clearly remains normative and regulative.[21]

However disguised, the observer's account is a *regulative* reading which pathologizes the participants' actions. The knowledge it produces will inevitably differ from the meanings ascribed to them by the participants – meanings they produce as they live out the practices in which they are formed. But the struggle between them is not simply about the 'values' attached to meanings. Nor is it about validating people's interpretations. It is a struggle about power with a clear material effectivity. One might therefore ask how far it is possible for the observer to 'speak for' the observed.

The families I was studying in my research (which, as I have noted, concerned the education of six-year-old girls rather than film or television watching) clearly indicated on many occasions that they experienced me as surveillant Other. Their responses to my presence cannot be understood without taking this into consideration. Equally I was struck by the fantasies, anxieties and pain triggered in me by being perceived as a middle-class academic confronting a working-class family. Although I invested considerable desire into wanting to 'be one of them' at the same time as 'being different', no amount of humanistic seeking for the 'beyond ideology' would get them to see in me a working-class girl 'like them'. Rather than disavow that dynamic, therefore, it became necessary to work *with* it and to acknowledge the clear effectivity of their reading of me as middle-class in the data I collected.

But I also wanted to examine my multiple positioning as both middle-class academic *and* working-class child, to use my own fantasies in exploring how the participants perceived me and how they understood their experience. In this work I developed the term *recognition* as a reworking of Althusser's concept of 'mis-recognition'. Rather than engage with its negative connotations for the study of ideological (i.e. always-already distorting) interpellation, I wanted to use the idea of recognition *positively* in my work on domestic practices. Recognition is what places the subject in the historical moment. It is achieved through the circulation of the signifier as a relation in present discursive practices. Like Lacan's *point de capiton*, recognition acts as a nodal point (involving also forgetting and the repression of what went before): it provides the post-structure. In my own research, therefore, I wanted to use my own fantasied positions within those practices as a way of engaging with their unconscious and conscious relations of desire and the plays of anxiety and meaning. Often when interviewing the participants I felt that I 'knew what they meant', that I recognized how the practices were regulated or understood what it was like to be a participant.[22] Using this 'recognition' to explore the positivity of how domestic relations are lived seems to me an important step beyond assertions that academics should side with the oppressed, that film-makers should see themselves as workers or that teachers should side with pupils. Such rhetoric may represent *our* wish-fulfilling denial of power and responsibility – a way of disavowing our position instead of accounting for it.

To take a rather mischievous example, Paul Willis's *Learning to Labour* could be interpreted from this perspective as the story of an ''earole' who wants to become a 'lad', a male academic vicariously becoming one of the boys. What is missing from such work is any account of the ethnographer's own position in the web of power/knowledge/desire. Another problem with much ethnographic work (my own included) has been the way it takes discourse at face value. In working with a transcript, for example, of what can we take it as evidence? Ethnographic interviews with adolescent working-class girls are often used to justify theories of girls' resistance, as is their anti-school behaviour and taking on of femininity (through using make-up or subverting uniform). Yet could these discourses and actions not equally well hide pain and anxiety in relation to academic failure? The problem of ethnographic work is how to take adequate account of the psychic reality of both observer and observed.

This means disrupting the common-sense split between 'fantasy' and 'reality'. Fantasy is invested in domestic relations just as much as it is in films — that is the point I have been making in drawing out the intersection between the fantasy-structure of *Rocky II* and the domestic dynamics of the Cole family. The fiction, the fantasy, is created in this interaction, not only in the projection and introjection between the voyeuristic observer and the observed.[23] This emphasis on the inscription of fantasies within family practices raises the question of the power relations within those practices and their regulation. Power, however, as Cathy Urwin has demonstrated,[24] is inextricably intertwined with desire. If positions created within the regulation of domestic practices also generate fantasy and desire, it becomes necessary to dig beneath the surface of the discourse — its manifest content — to find the latent content behind it.

Here, for example, I have attempted to analyse the constitution of subjectivity within a variety of cultural practices, of which watching videos is one. I have tried to avoid either essentializing social differences between viewers or reducing the relations of fantasy and desire inscribed within a film to any one reading without engaging with the family relations and domestic practices into which the video is inserted. Instead, I have asked how people make sense of what they watch and how this sense is incorporated into an existing fantasy-structure.

The basis for this approach is to be found in Freud's analysis of dreaming, where he explores the relationship between dreams as fantasy-scenarios and the inscription of those fantasies in everyday life. He takes their manifest content, as consciously described by the patient, and then focuses on the dream-work — the chains of associations, the changing patterns of condensation and displacement — to discover their latent content. Just as Freud drew on associations made by the patient and also on issues which had previously surfaced in the analysis, I have taken certain key signifiers which feature both in the film and in the domestic practices and examined how associations, either of equation or opposition, are made by the participants at various points in the dialogue.

Although this mode of analysis remains to be developed, I would like to stress two kinds of movement within these relations of signification. One, which I call the forwards movement, anchors and fixes the signifier within current practices, producing the regulative effectivity of the term as it operates as a relation within a regime of representation and truth. The other is a backwards movement which traces the associations of the signifier into the unconscious. This may relate not only to the history of the subject, but also to the forgotten relations inside the practice itself.

(Some working-class domestic practices, for example, may have developed in relation to defences against poverty, yet they may persist as
cultural practices even when poverty is no longer a threat.) By focusing
on the relation between these two movements, it is possible to identify
latent content without implying (as happens in certain forms of psychoanalysis) that there must be a psychic Originary Moment which is not
also social-historical. Equally, my approach acknowledges the effectivity
of the manifest content: manifest/latent is not the same as phenomenal/
real. It therefore engages with the positivity of recognition as it is lived.
The signifiers generate their meanings from the living out of historically
specific relations, not from the internal rules of a Saussurean sign system.
Meanings inscribed within power/knowledge relations provide a basis for
surveillant and regulative practices; other meanings are produced in
opposition to them from people's lived historicity. Meaning thus
becomes a site of oppression, contestation and political struggle. The
subject cannot therefore be positioned in a single textual location which
can be put under erasure to reveal the infinity of traces. As Derrida
remarks, this activity contains a fiction of mastery over the process of
uncovering, the deconstructing of the truth beyond the telling of the
truth.

The examination of latent content would involve an infinite historical
regression, were it not for the forwards movement which anchors the
subject in history. We might make our own history, but in conditions
which are not of our choosing – that is, in relations of domination and
subordination/subjectification. Derrida accuses Foucault of forgetting
that the subject is to be put under erasure. But if we are to produce a
history of reading of the present and a political practice that is adequate to
it, then we need to understand how surveillance functions, how power
works, where the buck stops. We need to examine how existing discursive regimes function 'in truth' and have a positive effectivity in positioning the subject. The quasi-Foucauldian approach to how the truth
operates is an attempt to produce the forwards movement of which I
have spoken.

FANTASY AND INTELLECTUALIZATION

How, finally, are we to come to terms with the voyeuristic social
scientist? The 'space' of observation, I would argue, like that of watching
videos, is a fantasy-space in which certain fictions are produced. One
effect of these fictions is to constitute a knowledge, a truth that is
incorporated into the regulation of families. At the same time, the 'claim
to truth' designates the social scientist as an expert in the bourgeois order

which produces this intellectuality. But it also, I have suggested, hides the fear that motivates it. The masses must be known because they represent a threat to the moral and political order; the theorist/voyeur expresses shame and disgust at the 'animal passions' which have to be monitored and regulated – and which she cannot enjoy. This logic of intellectualization is evident in many studies of audiences. I therefore want to consider how the fantasies and fictions embodied in academic accounts, as well as in films, are inscribed in the daily lives of ordinary people.

Modern apparatuses of social regulation, along with other social and cultural practices, produce knowledges which claim to 'identify' individuals. These knowledges create the possibility of multiple practices, multiple positions. To be a 'clever child' or a 'good mother', for example, makes sense only in the terms given by pedagogic, welfare, medical, legal and other discourses and practices. These observe, sanction and correct how we act; they attempt to define who and what we are. They are, however, crisscrossed by other discourses and practices – including those of popular entertainment, for example. This multiplicity means that the practices which position us may often be mutually contradictory. They are also sites of contestation and struggle. We never quite fit the 'positions' provided for us in these regulatory practices. That failure is, in Freudian psychoanalysis, both the point of pain and the point of struggle. It shows repeatedly that the imposition of fictional identities – or socialization – does not work.[25]

What I am proposing here is a model of how subjectification is produced: how we struggle to become subjects and how we resist provided subjectivities in relation to the regulative power of modern social apparatuses. This model rejects the old image of the masses trapped in false consciousness, waiting to be led out of ideology by radical intellectuals. Rather, I would argue, these two categories form a couple defined and produced in relation to each other. The modern bourgeois order depends upon a professional intellectual elite which 'knows' and regulates the proletariat.[26] One side-effect of the creation of this 'new middle class' has been that some of its radical members, having themselves achieved social mobility through the route of higher education, claim that it is *only* through rationality and intellectualization that the masses can see through the workings of ideology and so escape its snares.

The audience for popular entertainment, for example, is often presented as sick (voyeuristic, scopophilic) or as trapped within a given subjectivity (whether defined by the social categories of class, race and gender or by a universalized oedipal scenario). What is disavowed in such approaches is the complex relation of 'intellectuals' to 'the masses': 'our' project of analysing 'them' is itself one of the regulative practices which

produce *our* subjectivity as well as theirs. We are each Other's Other –
but not on equal terms. Our fantasy investment often seems to consist in
believing that we can 'make them see' or that we can see or speak *for*
them. If we do assume that, then we continue to dismiss fantasy and the
Imaginary as snares and delusions. We fail to acknowledge how the
insistent demand to see through ideology colludes in the process of
intellectualizing bodily and other pleasures.

It was in opposition to that approach that I tried to make sense of Mr
Cole's self-identification as a fighter. I argued that fighting relates not
only to masculinity but also to lived oppression, to the experience of
powerlessness and the fear of it. The implication is that we should stop
being obsessed by the illusory tropes of an oppressive ideology, and
should start to look at fantasy-spaces as places for hope and for escape
from oppression as well.

Asked why they read romantic fiction, the women Janice Radway
spoke to said that it helped them to escape from the drudgery of servicing
their families – and thus to cope with it. They read at quiet moments (in
bed, in the bath) when they could recall the tattered dreams of their
youth and long for someone to love them as they wanted to be loved.
Their reading was therefore double-edged: not only a way of coming to
terms with their daily lives, but also an act of resistance and hope. It is
this question of the hope and pleasure that women invest in romantic
fiction, which Radway brings out very clearly, that I want to dwell on.
But I depart from Radway's analysis, because she remains caught up with
the idea that these readers might move 'beyond' such romantic notions;
she also rejects psychoanalytic explanations for failing to engage with the
specificity of readers' lives.[27] That seems to underestimate both the
material *and* the psychic reality of these women's servitude and the pain
of their longing for something else.

The danger with such approaches to the study of the audience,
however radical in intent, is that their insistence on the transcendence of
ideology through the intellectualization of pleasure(s) can itself become
part of a broader regulatory project of intellectualization. This seems to
be implicit, for example, in the description of a course for women about
women and/in the cinema.[28] When the students were encouraged to
deconstruct the codes of representation in various types of film, some
found it difficult because it meant giving up, or supplanting, the pleasure
they had previously felt in watching movies. Similarly, in many media
studies courses in schools, children are asked to analyse popular television programmes. What concerns me is how these women, children,
whoever, are being asked to deal with their previous enjoyment of such
things – a pleasure shared with family, friends, and their general social
and cultural environment. It seems that they are being left little room for

any response other than feeling stupid, or despising those who are still enjoying these 'perverse' pleasures.

What this typically academic emphasis on rationality and intellectualization can overlook are the specific conditions of the formation of pleasures for particular groups at a given historical moment. Rather than seeing the pleasures of 'the masses' as perverse, perhaps we should acknowledge that it is the bourgeois 'will to truth' that is perverse in its desire for knowledge, certainty and mastery. This is the proper context in which to understand the *desire* to know the masses, the voyeurism of the (social) scientist. The crusade to save the masses from the ideology that dupes them can obscure the real social significance of their pleasures and, at the same time, blind us to the perversity of radical intellectual pleasures. The alternative is not a populist defence of Hollywood, but a reassessment of what is involved in watching films. This becomes part of the experience of oppression, pain and desire. Watching a Hollywood movie is not simply an escape from drudgery into dreaming: it is a place of desperate dreaming, of hope for transformation.

Popular pleasures produced in/under oppression can be contrasted with the more cerebral pleasures of discrimination or deconstruction. These ultimately derive from the scientific project of intellectualization, the Cogito, which culminates in the scientific management of populations, the power/knowledge of the modern social order. The intellectualization of pleasures, in other words, is linked not just to the desire to know but also to the project of controlling nature. This has had as its Other and opposite a fear of the powers of the unknown, the animal, the unlawful, the insane, the masses, women, blacks. These 'Others' became objects to be known and thus civilized and regulated. There exists among the bourgeoisie a terror of the pleasures of the flesh, of the body, of the animal passions seen to be burning darkly in sexuality and also in violent uprisings. No surprise then, that the regulation of children's consumption of the modern media focuses so obsessively on sex and violence.

In the end, then, the 'problem' of popular pleasures – the Coles' enjoyment of *Rocky II* – turns out to lie not (only) with 'the masses' but (also) with the fears and desires of the bourgeois intellectual. The desire to know and to master conceals the terror of a lack of control, a paranoia which is the opposite of omnipotent fantasy, a megalomania. These I have called perversions to point up the way in which they project their own terror of the masses on to the masses themselves. It is this projection that motivates the desire to rationalize the pleasures of the body, to transform them into pleasures of the mind. This body/mind dualism valorizes mental labour as genius or creativity and denigrates the servicing and manual work which make them possible – the labour of the masses and their terrifying physicality. It is in this context of the mental/

manual division that the physicality of *Rocky*, expressed so clearly in its violence, should be placed.

I have tried to establish the difference between the 'cold' aesthetic of high culture, with its cerebral and intellectualized appreciation, and the bodily and sensuous pleasures of 'low' cultures.[29] What is most important is to understand the different conditions in which these pleasures – and their associated pains and hopes – are produced. In the oppressive conditions of the bourgeois order 'animal passions' are regulated, the 'rising of the masses' is feared, the individual is defined in terms of brain or brawn, the only way out offered is through cleverness, guile, making it, working, trying. And so embourgeoisement is the only dream left in all those desires for, and dreams of, difference ...

Notes

This analysis would not have been possible without the work and insights of Helen Lucey and Diana Watson of the Girls and Mathematics Unit, University of London Institute of Education. Many of the arguments are developed in Chapter 5 of this book; in V. Walkerdine, *Surveillance, Subjectivity and Struggle*, Minneapolis, University of Minnesota Press 1986; and *The Mastery of Reason*, London, Methuen 1989; V. Walkerdine and H. Lucey, *Final Report of Grant No.C/00/23/033/1 to the Economic and Social Research Council*, 1985; and V. Walkerdine, H. Lucey and D. Watson, *The Regulation of Mothering* (working title), Cambridge, Polity Press, forthcoming. I would also like to thank Philip Corrigan, Dick Hebdige and David Morley for helpful comments and criticism.

1. Foucault has documented this in relation to a 'will to truth' in which the production of a knowledge has real effects in the surveillance and regulation of the Other. I add the dimension of *voyeurism* to this perverse will to truth because it allows us to explore the fears and fantasies present in this watching, classifying surveillance – the desire to *know* the Other and therefore to have power over, to control, to explain, to regulate it. This claim to certainty and truth becomes not normal, but profoundly perverse. It is linked both with disgust and with shame: shame at watching – desire to see how 'the other half lives' – and the vicarious excitement in that which is forbidden to the bourgeois researcher and in which s/he profoundly desires to engage but must only monitor, watch, describe and moralistically criticize and prevent. (Cf. S. Freud, *Standard Edition*, vol. 7, pp. 156–7).

2. In that sense I shall argue that the 'truths' which create the modern form of sociality are fictions and therefore themselves invented in fantasy. 'The real' therefore becomes a problematic category which I shall deal with only by reference to 'veridicality', on the one hand, and cultural forms and practices, on the other. That is, both scientific and cultural practices produce regimes of meaning, truth, representation in which there are particular relations of signification. What is important about these is the production of a *sign* – i.e. how we enter as 'a relation' and how in actual social practices and cultural forms we become 'positioned'. The concept of positioning relies upon the importance attached to signifier/signified relations. In addition, we can utilize the concept of fantasy to understand our insertion within other 'dramas'. In this respect, then, the mode of analysis is similar, and also potentially allows an examination of fantasies inscribed in *both* the imaginary and the symbolic.

3. Freeway is the name of an extremely small dog in the television series 'Hart to Hart'. Using it as the Alsatian's name is therefore something of a joke.

4. That pain of becoming bourgeois through work: a route opened to working-class

women, perhaps for the first time, in the post-war education expansion. See Chapter 17 of this book.

5. The dramatic butchery of the fights in the *Rocky* films would be impossible under the existing laws of amateur and professional boxing. Kathryn Kalinak makes a similar point about the impossibility of the escape route through dance presented in *Flashdance*; the heroine is simply much too old to take up a classical ballet career. See '*Flashdance*: The Dead End Kind', *Jump Cut*, no. 29, 1984, pp. 3–4.

6. See, for example, S. Neale, 'Masculinity as Spectacle', *Screen*, vol. 24, no. 6, 1983.

7. The term 'pencil-pusher' for a man with a clerical job was (at least in my family) a term of both abuse and envy. It was what everyone wanted, because it was easy, but it could not count as real work because it did not involve heavy manual labour.

8. This reading reflects my own identifications with *Rocky II*, but it is also evident in an account of reactions to the film among members of CSE Media Studies class, who were mostly male, white and working-class; see A. Brookfield, 'Reading *Rocky* Films: Versions of Masculinity', in *Working Papers for 16+ Media Studies*, Clwyd County Council 1985. Brookfield describes the working-class youths' identification with Rocky, but 'although the narrative framework was structured around a "success story", the group challenged some aspects of the representation of success. In discussions of aspects of social class within the film the boys tended to adopt an oppositional stance towards the "American Dream" ideology. In doing so they picked up as relevant to their lives an element present in the lyrics of the theme music to the film. These suggest that poverty brutalizes and makes it necessary to take to the streets and kill to survive' (p. 88). I would take issue with Brookfield's assumption that 'the [*Rocky*] films address a wide and differentiated audience, who will bring a variety of readings to them; these different readings are based on different assumptions about "masculinity"; in general students' readings of the films remained within a dominant framework' (p. 85). This implies precisely the notion that I have criticized – namely, that working-class masculinity is a sexist, stereotyped version which certain views 'bring to' the film. Rather, I would suggest that masculinity is always lived as class-specific, in relation to the body and the mental/manual division of labour. These are not, therefore, in any simple sense 'different assumptions about masculinity'.

9. The numbers refer to the counter on the tape recorder, and therefore provide a record of the passage of time during the recording. 'Untranscribed' refers to utterances which were inaudible and could therefore not be transcribed.

10. See Chapter 5.

11. D. Cherry and G. Pollock, 'Women as Sign: The Representation of Elizabeth Siddall in Pre-Raphaelite Literature', *Art History*, vol. 7, no. 2, 1984. This analysis owes much to the work of Diane Watson: *Women as Sign in Educational Discourse*, MSc Dissertation, University of London 1984.

12. J. Mitchell, *Women: The Longest Revolution*, London, Virago 1983, pp. 115–24.

13. Flower fairies: see Cicely Mary Baker, *A Flower Fairy Alphabet*, London, Blackie (date not given: the edition I read must have been produced in the 1950s and it is still available in paperback).

14. To take this analysis further, this fiction inscribed me in a fantasy-scenario in which the desire of the Other provided me with a fantasy of omnipotence – the power to do magic. This necessitated a bodily fragility; I was always sickly. Such a fantasy inscribes me, therefore, at various levels which cannot be equated with a fantasy/reality distinction. They are both adults' fantasies of their own suppressed desires directed *at* children (see J. Rose, *The Case of Peter Pan or The Impossibility of Children's Fiction*, London, Macmillan 1984) and the positions for the children to enter. Cicely Mary Baker's fictional child-fairies, the paper-pattern manufacturers of the bluebell costume, the neighbour who made it, my parents, the press photographer, the amateur snapshots, etc., become a place where I can be gazed at and therefore create for me an enormous power. They provide the stuff of fantasy, therefore, in its widest possible sense: unconscious fantasies, daydreams of *being* a fairy and the acting out and living through this in the family relations themselves, viz. 'Tinky'.

15. J. Lacan, 'God and the *jouissance* of Woman', in J. Mitchell and J. Rose, eds, *Femi-*

nine Sexuality, London, Macmillan 1982.

16. See J. Henriques, W. Hollway, C. Urwin, C. Venn and V. Walkerdine, *Changing the Subject: Psychology, Social Regulation and Subjectivity*, London, Methuen 1984.

17. C. Johnston, *Edinburgh Television Papers, 1979*. For elaboration on this issue, see D. Morley, 'Texts, Readers, Subjects', in S. Hall, D. Hobson, A. Lowe and P. Willis, eds, *Culture, Media, Language*, London, Hutchinson 1980.

18. For further discussions of families watching television, see D. Morley, *Family Television*, London, Comedia 1986; and A. Gray, 'Women and Video: Subject–Text–Context', in D. Phillips and M. Marshment, eds, *Women and Popular Culture*, London, Croom Helm.

19. L. Mulvey, 'Visual Pleasure and Narrative Cinema', *Screen*, vol. 16, no. 3, 1975; J. Radway, 'Women Read the Romance: The Interaction of Text and Context', *Feminist Studies*, vol. 9, no. 1, 1983.

20. C. Urwin (1985) 'Wonder People', BPS Developmental Psychology Conference, Belfast.

21. For examples of current work on family dynamics and television which use various therapeutic models to identify normal and pathological viewing, see Goodman, 'Television's role in family interaction', *Journal of Family Issues*, vol. 14, no. 2, 1983, pp. 405–24.

22. It is here that a struggle must be located. This takes us away from the implied determinism and fixity of 'interpellation' to the possibility of a struggle over meaning.

23. Rather than analysing fantasy and reality as dichotomous, I approach *positions* and *meanings* as fictional spaces in which fantasy is lived out. The actual operations of fantasy are complex: they are inscribed not only in the lived relations of the family, I am suggesting, but also in the relations between observer and observed, in transference and countertransference. Such relations are characterized by power.

24. C. Urwin, 'Power Relations and the Emergence of Language', in Henriques, Urwin, Venn and Walkerdine.

25. J. Rose, 'Femininity and Its Discontents', *Feminist Review*, no. 14, 1983, p. 9.

26. For a discussion of intellectuals, see P. Schlesinger, 'In Search of the Intellectuals: Some Comments on Recent Theory', *Media, Culture and Society*, no. 4, 1982.

27. Radway's rejection seems to rest on an equation between psychoanalysis and a purely formalist account of how texts 'position' subjects. Although there have been occasional attempts at just such a synthesis, at a theoretical level the equation is misleading. It seems to me that psychoanalysis might open up a way of engaging with the reality of women's fantasies, pleasures and desires as they read the novels – see, for example, Cora Kaplan's 'The Thorn Birds', in V. Burgin, J. Donald and V. Kaplan, eds, *Formations of Fantasy*, London, Methuen, 1985.

28. S. Clayton, 'Notes on Teaching Film', *Feminist Review*, no. 14, 1983.

29. P. Bourdieu, *Distinction: A Social Critique of the Judgement of Taste*, London, Routledge & Kegan Paul 1984, ch. 1.

20

Fantasy and regulation

(Taken from a longer piece, given as a talk at the ICA, 'The Mass Psychology

of Thatcherism', in the series 'Critical Psychology', 1989)

I am arguing that the so-called problem of 'The Working Class' has a psychic dimension which is very important in understanding the present political conjuncture. Whether The Working Class is seen as the 'bedrock of the revolution', having a positive sexuality outside bourgeois confines, or as an authoritarian class who are reactionary and put Thatcher into her third term of office, the issue is similar. All these positions attest not to the 'reality' of working-class life but to bourgeois fantasies that are incorporated into 'truths' through which The Working Class is created as an object, governed and regulated. Working-class life as I have lived it bears little relation to these fantasies, which circulate in strategies of government and on the Left and present a real problem for a radical politics of difference. In 1984 I wrote an article about growing up working-class in the suburbs of Derby (see Chapter 17 of this book). It was for me the most painful and important 'coming out': the engagement with the way in which, for many years, I had 'passed' for middle-class. My pain and then my anger at first knew no bounds.

I want to relate this to several issues which have come out in my research, to indicate more clearly the relationship between the regulation of 'The Working Class' and fantasy. The first incident comes from research I was conducting on girls' education (see Chapter 19, above). As part of this, I was making audio-recordings in the home of one six-year-old white working-class girl. I could almost imagine that I was at home again, a little working-class girl. I felt part of the scene but at the same time recognized that the family could not see this me; instead, all they could see was a middle-class researcher who had come to see what they were up to. This led me to think about surveillance and regulation more closely.

The family saw my visit as regulative, getting their daughter to say 'how now brown cow' and 'the rain in Spain falls mainly on the plain' – straight from elocution lessons. I argue in Chapter 19 that social science, in claiming 'to tell the truth' about The Working Class, claims to know them, but that knowledge is based on the necessity to know the population to be governed (in Foucault's sense) and is therefore surveillant. It creates The Working Class as its object. I argue further that such truth is not based on the 'real' of working-class life, but that The Working Class becomes one of the categories based on bourgeois fantasies: the Other, everything to be guarded against, to be kept in check – the feared rising of the masses, the desired and feared animal passions projected on to the proletariat. All these form the bases of truths, and the social scientist becomes a sort of paid voyeur. I am using this pathology because I want to point up something in the bourgeoisie (not Wilhelm Reich's repressed sexuality but some deep and difficult fears and fantasies). Voyeurism (scopophilia) has been suggested as the basis of mass cinematic viewing. I am suggesting it as the basis of mass social science, social science of the masses. What is to be known and what is to be kept in check?

Homi Bhabha (1984) argues that colonial government operates on the basis of fear, phobia and fetish. The colonized subject is both created and regulated by colonial discourses, but these tell us more about the fantasies of the colonizer than about the colonized. However, as he argues, the stories about those Others have to be endlessly retold as if to make them true: the yellow peril, the inscrutable Chinese, the animal sexuality of Blacks, the laziness of colonial peoples.

And what of The Working Class? What are the fantasies proved time and time again in empiricist social science? There are too many to name, but those of us who have grown up as any of those Others know exactly how we have become subjected. We are the salt of the earth, the bedrock of the revolution; we are working-class women with big hearts, big arms, big breasts; we are stupid, ignorant, deprived, depriving; we are re-pressed, authoritarian, and above all, we voted Thatcher into her third term of office. We are revolting, anti-democratic. We suppress our children and do not allow them autonomy. How many more of these truths will there be?

When Helen Lucey and I wrote Democracy in the Kitchen (1989) we were writing about a study of white working-class and middle-class mothers and daughters (Tizard and Hughes, 1984). We criticized the way in which The Working Class was viewed in this study and discussed our own feelings on first reading the transcripts of the recordings of the girls and women at home. When we first read one chapter of the write-up of this work, 'An afternoon with Donna and her mother', we were nearly sick. It seemed to us like the voyeurism I mentioned earlier. It felt as though we were gazing at animals in a zoo who, after all, were rather tame. Yet what was it about this ordinary afternoon which had to have a special place in the book? There were no descriptions of middle-class afternoons. We felt that it was because something had to be explained, a fearful object had to be rendered harmless, because it produced a deep fear in middle-class psyches, a fear of The Working Class. We turned to the transcript of that afternoon and we felt even sicker. Was it this, this terrifyingly ordinary afternoon, which was the cause of so much (unconscious) fear and so had to be held up for scrutiny? We felt that we were in deep trouble, for it reminded us of so many afternoons at home with our mothers. But here the similarity ended. The *description* of this, like all those other fantasies of the Left and Right, bore so little relation to our understanding that we began to think that they represented the fears, phobias and fetishes of middle-class researchers.

Researchers, often on the Left, frequently ask too *why*, why, how can they endure it, as they conduct one more study of the line, or penetrate the factory gates once more to rush out, reeling, to wonder how people can put up with it and why they don't rebel. How *can* they? How can they endure and how can they *be* like that? Fascinated horror. The Left wants to know they could live in conditions that they will never experience (and 'wouldn't they like to know', really, so much fetishization of the Other). But what – no rebellion and Thatcher in for her third term? The Working Class must then have variously 'never had it so good', 'no longer be a viable category' and 'have ended'. So many stories which wipe us out. Why? My explanation relates in part to those fantasies that don't seem to come true. The Working Class hasn't done its revolutionary job, bringing Thatcher instead of the revolution. There is huge disappointment that The Class has failed. The Left then behave like an angry child in a tantrum which wants to wipe us out rather than face its own disappointment, its own massive fantasies that we have failed as the love-object. They either eulogize us or hate us. Same difference.

And what of our fantasies? When Helen and I first read the transcripts of the middle-class mothers and daughters, we too were shocked. All recordings began with lunch, and what seemed to touch me more than anything was their choice of meals. It seemed as though the little girls were constantly being asked what they wanted to eat. There always seemed to be plenty to choose from. It contrasted greatly with our memories of meal times. At that moment every feminist sympathy with the oppression of all women disappeared. Helen felt contempt and I felt hate, and both with a deep intensity. All the class envy and hatred, hurt and humiliation welled up in those moments. We were again those small children, and the mixture of envy and longing was almost too painful to remember. What can the little girls inside us tell us now? First, that the problem was and is not, in any simple sense, the middle-class families, but the pain smouldering inside us. It was our fantasies of that Other Other, The Middle Class, as having everything we felt we lacked. And those fantasies, middle-class and working-class, are endlessly repeated in 'objective social science'.

How is it that the oppressor can fear the oppressed? How do Bhabha's categories of fear, phobia and fetish apply? Frantz Fanon (1968) tells us of a frightened white girl speaking to her mother about him, a black man: 'Look, Mama, look, a Negro, I'm frightened, frightened'. Audre Lorde (1984) tells too of the time when she was a child sitting on the New York subway. A white woman sitting next to her seemed to be repelled. At first the young Audre thought she had something on her clothes, and then realized that the woman was repelled by *her*: 'I will never forget it. Her eyes, the flared nostrils, the hate.' Conversely, Ronald Fraser (1984), who grew up in an English manor house, tells of the time when he answered the door, pleased to be doing the butler's job and let a beggar into the house. But his parents, far from being pleased, reproached him. This is an episode he remembers painfully as an adult in psychoanalysis. It was traumatic then to learn that there were guests and there were beggars. Samantha, a four-year-old white middle-class girl, also learns that a fearful working-class window cleaner earns money. She doesn't understand why he has to be paid for cleaning the windows of her home. Many middle-class women are afraid of dirty working-class men.

Difference, division, power, oppression. Fear of the Other. This fear could be seen as a central constituent of a politics of difference. What do Whites have to fear of Blacks, the middle and upper classes to fear of the working class? What, we may equally ask, do they have to lose? What unspeakable, forbidden desire has to be transformed into fear and hate? I am suggesting that such fantasies play a central part in our present political situation. Timothy Ashplant (forthcoming) tells of male middle-class Left intellectuals in the thirties who chose those Others, working-class women, black men, as objects of desire in order to avoid middle-class masculinity. That desire was therefore both to exoticize and to rebel. But what does it mean if middle-class radicalism has a component of exotic fetishization of the Other? Moreover, the exoticization of the Other is a common pursuit of the white, middle-class male. Dick Hebdige (1979) quotes Jack Kerouac in *On the Road*, the white college boy who envies the exoticism of black American culture: jazz, blues, drugs, danger. As he expresses it, white culture has 'not enough night'. But what he manages to forget is that the culture of the margins which he so envies is built out of oppression. He doesn't want that, only the exotic night. And he retells sexist and racist adventures. Yet it is this, this envy and longing for what is suppressed in the white culture, this fantasy of the Other, which is central. The oppressor envies the oppressed, but what he envies is an exotic fantasy, not the reality of living under oppression. That is just as neatly forgotten and suppressed.

REFERENCES

Ashplant, T. (forthcoming) *Dissident Identities: Masculinity, Class and Oppositional Politics among British Intellectuals 1918–39*.

Bhabha, H. (1984) 'The Other Question: The Stereotype and Colonial Discourse'. *Screen*, no. 24, 18–36.

Fanon, F. (1968) *Black Skins, White Masks*. London, Paladin.

Fraser, R. (1984) *In Search of a Past*. London, Verso.

Hebdige, D. (1979) *Subculture, The Meaning of Style*. London, Methuen.

Lorde, A. (1984) *Sister, Outsider*. New York, Crossing Press.

Tizard, B. and Hughes, M. (1984) *Young Children Learning*. London, Fontana.

Index